Cadillac Eldorado
PERFORMANCE PORTFOLIO
1967-1978

Compiled by R M Clarke

ISBN 1 85520 5378

BROOKLANDS BOOKS LTD.
P.O. BOX 146, COBHAM,
SURREY, KT11 1LG. UK
sales@brooklands-books.com

A-CADEPP

Printed in Hong Kong

ACKNOWLEDGEMENTS

Cadillac's Eldorados of the Sixties and Seventies have always been highly regarded models, and today they continue to excite enthusiast interest. So when stocks of our earlier Road Test book about them were exhausted, we decided to produce a bigger volume on the subject to replace it. As a result, this book adds to what was available before plus an extra 40% of material found in our archives.

All the copyright material in this volume is used with the kind permission of those magazine or book publishers who originally commissioned it. They are *Auto Topics, Autocar, Automotive, Cadillac, Car and Driver, Car Annual, Car Life, Motor Trend, Motorcade, Petersen's Complete Book of Engines, Popular Car, Preview Cars, Road Test, Special Interest Autos, World* and the *World Car Catalogue*. Our sincere gratitude goes to all of them.

R.M. Clarke

The 1967 Cadillac Eldorado marked a turning-point in the evolution of Cadillac's luxury coupé, for this was the first of the line to have front-wheel drive. The basic hardware had made its debut a year ealier on the Oldsmobile Toronado, but Cadillac added a 429 cubic-inch 340bhp V8 and a body which was crisply styled. Much to the surprise of many commentators, the new Eldorados also handled well on twisty roads.

These first-generation front-wheel drive models lasted for three seasons with only cosmetic changes, but in their fourth and final season came a new 500 c.i. V8 with 400bhp - the largest production passenger-car engine in the world at that time. With the second-generation cars for 1971 came a longer wheelbase, a new perimeter frame with coil-spring rear suspension, more rounded styling and heavy safety bumpers. Tightening safety and emissions regulations were the major influences on changes to this design over the next few years. By 1975, the 500 cubic-inch V8 was rated at only 190bhp (nett), and the convertible which had arrived with the 1971 models finally bowed out at the end of 1976. For 1977 and 1978, the Eldorados resisted the general downsizing trend at Cadillac, but for '79 a new and radically smaller model took over the name.

The Eldorados of this period are highly regarded among enthusiasts and collectors today, both for their engineering and for the fact that they represent the last of the really big Cadillacs. Anyone who has an interest in these cars will find the present Performance Portfolio compulsive reading.

James Taylor

CONTENTS

Page	Article	Source	Date	
4	Cadillac Eldorado	*Motor Trend*	Nov	1966
6	'67 Cadillacs	*Auto Topics*	Dec	1966
8	Eldorado	*Preview Cars*		1967
9	Eldorado Switches from Push to Pull　　Road Test	*Motor Trend*	Jan	1967
13	New Cadillac Eldorado - 7031cc and f.w.d.	*Autocar*	Oct 7	1966
14	Ford Thunderbird vs. Cadillac Eldorado　　Comparison Test	*Car and Driver*	Nov	1966
21	Assembling the Eldorado	*Automotive*	Jan	1967
24	Cadillac V8 - 429 Cubic Inches	*Complete Book of Engines*		1967
28	'67 Cars - Cadillacs	*Car Annual*		1967
31	Driving the '68 Luxury Specialty Cars	*Motor Trend*	Nov	1967
32	An Admirable Flagship - Fleetwood　　Road Test	*Car Life*	Apr	1967
38	Five Luxury Specialty Cars - Riviera GS vs. Thunderbird vs. Grand Prix vs. Eldorado vs. Toronado　　Comparison Test	*Motor Trend*	Aug	1967
44	New Cadillac and Oldsmobile	*Autocar*	Sept 14	1967
46	Cadillac for 1968	*Car Life*	Dec	1967
48	Eldorado Luxury-Plus from Cadillac	*Motorcade*	Dec	1967
50	The Most Wanted Car in the World　　Road Test	*Road Test*	Sept	1968
56	Too Rough a Ride for the Soft Life　　Owners Report	*Popular Car*	July	1969
58	Eldorado - Luxury Specialty	*World Automotive*		1969
60	Eldorados	*Cadillac*	1967 - 1976	
62	Cadillac & Eldorado	*Car Life*	Oct	1969
63	Cadillac - Fleetwood Eldorado	*World Car Catalogue*		1969
64	Cadillac Eldorado Still Wanted but Worth It?　　Road Test	*Road Test*	Apr	1970
70	King of the Hill - Lincoln Continental Mark III vs. Cadillac Eldorado　　Comparison Test	*Motor Trend*	July	1970
73	Cadillac Fleetwood Eldorado　　Road Test	*Car and Driver*	Apr	1970
78	The Standard of Excellence - Revised	*Motor Trend*	Oct	1970
80	GM Cadillac	*Motor Trend Buyers Guide*		1971
84	Casa De Eldorado - Wagon Special	*Road Test*	Mar	1971
86	King of the Hill Revisited - Lincoln Continental Mark III vs. Cadillac Eldorado　　Comparison Test	*Motor Trend*	July	1971
90	Top Luxury For Pennies - Fleetwood Coupe　　Road Test	*Road Test*	May	1972
96	King of the Hill - Lincoln Continental Mark IV vs. Cadillac Eldorado　　Comparison Test	*Motor Trend*	July	1972
104	The Eldorado Convertible	*Cadillac*		1972
105	Lincoln Continental Mark IV & Cadillac Eldorado	*Motor Trend*	Aug	1973
106	Cadillac	*Motor Trend Buyers Guide*		1973
108	Cadillac Eldorado: The King, Revisited	*Motor Trend*	Oct	1972
110	Cadillac Eldorado　　Brief Test	*Autocar*	Feb 1	1973
113	Cadillac Eldorado Coupe	*Cadillac*		1973
114	The King of the Hill - Lincoln Continental Mark IV vs. Cadillac Eldorado　　Comparison Test	*Motor Trend*	Aug	1973
118	King of the Hill - Lincoln Continental Mark IV vs. Cadillac Eldorado　　Comparison Test	*Motor Trend*	July	1974
121	The King's Ransom - Eldorado vs. Mark IV vs. Imperial vs. BMW vs. Jaguar vs. Mercedes-Benz　　Comparison Test	*Motor Trend*	July	1975
129	Cadillac Eldorado	*Car and Driver Buyers Guide*	1977 & 1978	
130	1967 Eldorado - It's What's up Front That Counts	*Special Interest Autos*	Feb	1982
138	Cadillac Eldorado 1953-1973	*Motor Trend*	Mar	1994

SPECIALTY

CADILLAC

Eldorado

Easily recognizable as a Cadillac, new Eldorado fwd shares egg-crate grille with other models in line. Sculptured styling around hood nose is practically knife-edged.

WHAT'S NEW: Completely new front-wheel-drive 6-passenger coupe... front disc brakes optional first time on Cadillac... 31 square inches of padding on steering wheel besides collapsing column... tires with higher load ratings and high-speed capability.

IN GIVING FWD its stamp of approval and bringing out the new Eldorado, Cadillac has in all likelihood furnished the imprimatur on such an arrangement that many had been waiting for. Nearly 50,000 Toronados the first year should be convincing enough, but judging by the rumors (completely unfounded) that heretofore have kept cropping up about fwd troubles in that car, some added convincing was necessary to set the record straight.

The new Eldorado, which is curiously billed by Cadillac as a replacement for the Eldorado convertible in the Fleetwood series, is shorter and lower than comparable models in the Calais and De Ville series. Its wheelbase is 9.5 inches shorter, and overall length is 3 inches less. Also, it's nearly an inch lower than the Coupe De Ville. But due to the advantages of fwd, it is of full 6-passenger capacity and has generous luggage space.

Is it just a Toronado with Cadillac styling? No more so than is one of the sedans an Olds luxury sedan with Cadillac styling (or vice versa). It is of the same genre as the Toronado and uses the same body shell. The front suspension and drive-line components, if not actually interchangeable, appear identical to the eye.

Cadillac has adapted its own engine for fwd with changes in the oil pan, exhaust manifolds, accessory layout and belt drives, and engine mounting system. Because the Eldorado's hood doesn't slope downward as much as the Toronado's, a new squashed intake manifold wasn't needed for clearance.

Dual exhausts lead from the engine to a single large muffler with a single outlet to resonator and tailpipe. The dual-shocked, single-leaf-sprung stamped rear axle looks the same as that on the Toronado, but spring rates are lower. The lower spring rate is compensated for by an automatic load-leveler, which is standard equipment. This eliminates sag with increasing load and provides an improved ride for a wide range of loading conditions.

The Eldorado has a fresh-air system that eliminates the need for vent panes as does the Toronado. Air enters the cockpit through the upper air-conditioning outlets, but instead of exhausting under the rear window, it flows under the rear seat and is ducted through the trunk to grilles on the inner sides of the rear fenders and on the door pillars. The fender grilles are visible from the outside, but the pillar grilles can be seen only when a door is open.

Safety equipment, accessories, and all optional equipment available on the other Cadillacs are also offered on the Eldorado. It also shares many things new to the whole line for 1967, such as a Mylar-backed, printed circuit instrument panel, bigger brake booster, slide-out fuse box, improved automatic headlight-dimmer, and braided rayon brake hoses.

Front disc brakes are optional on the Eldorado alone, however. These tuck neatly inside the wheel and are well ventilated by perforations in both the wheel and wheel cover, as are the standard finned, cast-iron drums.

As might be expected, the Eldorado feels and behaves very much like the Toronado under similar driving conditions. Rather than a more or less special tire like the Toronado's, the Eldorado uses the same fairly conventional 9.00 x 15 tire as the other Cadillacs. Because these start to squeal in protest sooner, they are not as conducive to sporty driving as the wide-tread Toronado tires. Their more conventional cord angles provide slightly softer riding at low speeds, however.

The large doors have springs to take some of the effort out of opening them when that side of the car is up an incline. Two handles per door are standard for the convenience of rear-seat passengers.

Probably the sportiest Cadillac made to date, the 1967 Eldorado also has all the traditional silence, comfort and luxury that buyers of this nameplate expect. /MT

CADILLAC

Eldorado

BODY STYLES	2-dr hardtop
WHEELBASE	120.0 ins
TRACK	63.5 ins front, 63.0 ins rear
OVERALL LENGTH	221.0 ins
OVERALL WIDTH	80.0 ins
OVERALL HEIGHT	53.3 ins
TURNING CIRCLE	41.4 ft curb-to-curb
ENGINES, std	V-8, 429 cu ins, 340 hp
ENGINES, optl	None
TRANSMISSIONS	3-spd Turbo Hydra-Matic automatic; none optl
BRAKES	drums std, front discs optl
SUSPENSION	Independent front, 1-piece rear axle; torsion bar front, single-leaf spring rear
CURB WEIGHT	4947 lbs
GAS CAPACITY	26 gals

NOSE OVERHANG BECOMES APPARENT ONLY IN LOW SILHOUETTE. MODERN LONG-NOSE/SHORT-TAIL MOTIF BLENDS WITH TRADITIONAL STYLE.

Headlamps stay put, while portion of grille hinges forward and downward to expose them. Alignment remains undisturbed.

Flat foot board, absence of driveshaft tunnel accrue from fwd. Small rear side pane recedes backwards into C-pillar.

BODY-COLORED METAL DIVIDES EACH TAIL LAMP, REFLECTS SOME LIGHT TO SIDE. GRILLE ATOP FENDER EXHAUSTS AIR FROM INSIDE CAR.

'67 Cadillacs

Front Wheel Drive Eldorado Steals The Limelight

Cadillac's 12 models for '67 are highlighted by the all-new Fleetwood Eldorado (foreground).

Forward leaning headlights and grille are evident on this Fleetwood Brougham. Cross-hatch grille retains traditional Cadillac look.

Coupe De Ville has a new roofline, with smaller quarter windows. Exterior color choices total 16, plus 5 Firemist colors are offered as options.

WHAT MAKES THE styling of a certain car successful? Not many people can say. But what ever it is, Cadillac has got it. Fresh styling, but still unmistakable Cadillac. The '67 lineup will have 12 models — the same as last year — plus the all-new Eldorado, which replaces the Eldorado convertible in the Fleetwood series.

Crisp, tailored lines dominate the styling theme of the new five-passenger Eldorado. A short rear deck, long hood and full wheel openings are reminiscent of other GM products, notably the Toronado. The Eldorado has the Toronado's front wheel drive mechanical design, and that is about the only similarity between them. The standard Cadillac engine is mated to a Toronado-type front wheel drive for the Eldorado.

The Eldorado suspension incorporates a torsion bar system in the front, while single-leaf springs, a drop-center axle and four shock absorbers are used at the rear. The transmission is located directly alongside the engine, and is connected to the differential which drives the front wheels and axles.

All the Cadillac models have the same V-8 engine, which has a displacement of 429 cu. in. Horsepower is rated at 340, with torque a whopping 480 lbs. at 3000 rpm. The valve train has been completely re-designed, and fuel economy is improved with the addition of a Quadrajet carburetor. Better cylinder bore finishing and new oil control piston rings give improved oil economy. The Eldorado engine differs from engines in other models in that it has a different oil pan, exhaust manifolds, accessory mountings, and different engine mounts.

Safety improvements are the same as used in the other GM cars, such as the collapsable steering column. The steering wheel also deflects upon severe impact, and has a padded surface piece in the center of it. Front disc brakes are optional only on the new Eldorado.

Styling of the standard models carries over from years previous with the slab side panelling and vertically stacked headlights. This theme styling is continued with the taillights housed in the vertical bumper outer sections. ∎

Outer sections of the Eldorado grille swing down to expose headlights. The small rear quarter windows slide back into the roof quarter.

new car peviews

eldorado

This is Cadillac's much-heralded entry in the booming "sports-luxury" market. It's a car along the same lines as the Thunderbird, Riviera, Toronado, etc. — but much more expensive, probably near $7000. As is well known now, the new car will feature front-wheel-drive, using most of the same front end components now being used by the Olds Toronado. The tooling for these parts was very costly, and GM wants to get more "mileage" out of it than just the Toronado. In fact it's not impossible that there will be a third or fourth GM line in 1968 that will share the same front end setup. Anyway this means that Cadillac's new El Dorado will be very similar mechanically to the Toronado. Front end layout is the same, it will use a modified Cadillac V-8 in the same position (rumors of a new V-12 engine for this car were unfounded), and it will use a shortened "stub" frame like the Toronado. Word is that coil springs may be used in the back, instead of single-leaf springs as on the Toronado.

The new car will also use the basic GM "E" body shell, now being shared by the Toronado and Buick Riviera. GM also wants to get more mileage out of this tooling. But you won't recognize this beautiful fastback body shell as they have applied it on the El Dorado. The rear quarter panels have been re-styled to get a distinct notchback look, with a sharper drop to the rear window, and a flatter rear deck. The rear deck is also longer than on the Toronado or Riviera, and there is more rear overhang. The car looks much longer and boxier (and it is). The front hood is quite long, but there isn't as much front overhang as on the Toronado. The side view of the car is actually quite distinctive because the rear deck line is slightly above the top of the rear fenders, and the rear side window is just a narrow rectangle about three inches wide. It slides *back* into the quarter panel instead of down. Really different. It reminds you a little of the prewar Lincoln Continental! The front grille is a massive waffle-iron motif, with a hump in the hood. Taillights are narrow slits in big chrome fender tips.

ELDORADO
BY ROBERT SCHILLING

SWITCHES FROM PUSH TO PULL
...AND IT'S HARD TO FIGHT SO MUCH LUXURY STANDARD EQUIPMENT

IT WAS INEVITABLE that we would bring to the Cadillac Eldorado road test some preconceived ideas about what the car would be like. We had driven other Cadillacs and were aware of the standard of luxury. We had already driven the Oldsmobile Toronado and knew what front-wheel-drive is like. We knew that the Eldorado and Toronado (along with the Buick Riviera) share Fisher Body Division's "E" shell. So the Eldorado would obviously be a plush Toronado with a Caddy grille and engine, right?

Wrong. It took us less than half an hour away from city traffic to realize that for all the similarities, the Eldorado has a character and personality *all* its own. Our previous concept of Cadillac luxury also went out the window — we were way short of the mark.

Some clue as to the public's changing taste emerges when you realize that the Eldorado, a 2-door hardtop, replaces the Eldorado convertible in the Fleetwood line. Once a symbol of youthful success and prestige, the ragtops have declined in popularity in recent years. Those buyers looking for the wind-in-the-hair sensation are now likely to buy a real sports car. Another segment of the market has been attracted to luxury personal cars. It is this second group that the Eldorado is aimed at, as well as the "conquest" market — those buyers who can be enticed into buying their first Cadillac. Cadillac Division's confidence in both their product and market is reflected in the addition of a second assembly line for the first time in the 64-year history of the make. This line will produce nothing but Eldorados, with the first year's production scheduled for 15,000 units — enough to fill the demand (which already appears strong) but still remain exclusive.

Driving an Eldorado is something of an Alice in Disneyland experience. It takes longer to get used to all the

ELDORADO'S CRISP, TAILORED LINES AROUSED ADMIRATION EVERYWHERE, SHOULD WEAR WELL WITHOUT REQUIRING MUCH ANNUAL FACE-LIFTING.

ELDORADO

automatic convenience accessories than to the car itself. One accessory our test car did not have which would have affected the driving was disc front brakes but more on this later. Standard equipment includes Hydra-Matic, variable-ratio power steering and an automatic load-leveling control. In addition, this car had the 6-way power seat, power windows, and power door and window locks. As was true of 88% of all Cadillacs ordered in 1966, this one had the automatic climate control air-conditioner/heater. An inside trunk control, automatic headlight control, speed control, AM-FM stereo radio with power antenna (that sounded better than the elaborate rig in our home), and a seat heater fill out the complement of automatic devices and controls the driver has to contend with. About the only extra the Eldorado doesn't have is a remote control for the driver to open the passenger's door.

Before taking the car to the track for performance testing we drove for about 600 miles under a variety of conditions. These ranged from deserts below sea level to mountains, and both expressways and rush-hour surface streets. In all of these circumstances at normal speeds the Eldorado, like any Cadillac, was an almost soporific machine but unlike its stablemates, it didn't *drive you*. That nebulous quality called "feel of the road" was definitely present. The only evidence of front-wheel-drive was the absence of a transmission/driveshaft tunnel on the floor. It was only in long tight bends when driven hard that the Eldorado had to be handled differently. Like most large American cars, the Eldorado has a front-end weight bias. Because of the fwd, this is even more pronounced, resulting in very noticeable understeer — what race drivers call "pushing the front end"— when driven hard into a turn. In a rear-drive car this can be corrected by feathering off the throttle, but on a fwd this only increases the understeer. The right way to do it is to slow down far enough in advance that you can enter the turn with the throttle open to pull the car through. If you get in over your head, the best thing to do is stay on the throttle and use more steering lock rather than feather. The front tires make a lot of noise, but the car will stick.

Such trick stuff becomes necessary only when driving with more verve than is usually needed or legal. For the most part, we were more inclined to relax and enjoy the Eldorado than with any other car we've tested. Whenever possible we found the pace of traffic, set the speed control, and just steered. You can poor-mouth the super-automation of the luxury cars as gadgetry, if you wish, but those gadgets grow on you and do serve a purpose. On a 250-mile round trip taken on a familiar route we were amazed at how much fresher than usual we were at the finish, despite starting out at the end of a working day, in typical 6 P.M. expressway traffic, and returning the same night.

A flaw in all this plush is the seating. The 6-way power seat and adjustable steering column offered every arrangement but that which seemed entirely right to three of our testers. The front seat itself is an interesting compromise between a bench and buckets. It is a bench, but with the opposite ends contoured like a pair of buckets. They give excellent back support, but are just a bit too firm. The center part of the bench between the contoured parts is somewhat raised and too hard to be used for any length of time. Real buckets with individual adjustment, which

Pumps, plumbing, vacuum reservoirs, etc., necessary for accessories, completely hide the engine and front-wheel-drive.

Variable-ratio power steering makes possible a smaller steering wheel. Overall diameter is the same as the 1958 horn ring.

Accessory controls fill door. Testers would pinch their fingers in door latch recess.

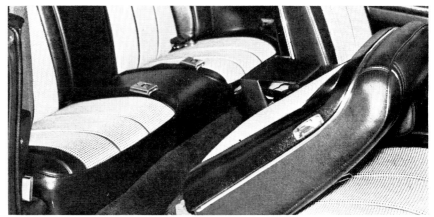
Despite the bucket seat look, the front is a bench. A separate handle allows rear-seat passengers to open door from their seat. Note the shoulder harness at far left.

are optional but rather expensive because they are genuine leather, seem to be a better approach and altogether in keeping with the new-to-Cadillac character of the car. Another flaw to some of us is the horn-ring-size steering wheel.

The Eldorado at 221 inches overall is 3 inches shorter than the Coupe de Ville, despite the impression of length caused by the long hood and front overhang. That hood, by the way, is no optical illusion — it's 7 inches longer than on other Cadillac models. We found that the car was longer than many of the optimistic parallel parking spaces painted on the pavement.

Shrewd work with sheetmetal has created a car that is instantly recognizable as a Cadillac with hardly an impression of the other cars that share the same body shell. Eschewing the curves of the Toronado, Eldorado features crisp, tailored, almost razor-sharp lines. Prominent identification mark is the coffin-shaped hump on the hood which was likened to the Cord by more than one onlooker and incidentally, the Eldorado was a real attention-getter. Styling of any car may be a matter of taste, but Cadillac has done a fine job with the tricky task of mating a classic, elegant look to contemporary verve. They've come quite a way in good taste since the garish fins of the late '50s.

The small back window with its vertical center crease was another matter. It may give a sense of privacy to the back seat, but this is not really a back-seat-passenger oriented car. We soon got used to bifurcated images seen through the creased glass, but the small size of the window made it difficult to see any part of the rear deck or fenders through it. This configuration required some very circumspect behavior when backing up. Not too surprisingly, gas station and car wash attendants were very careful to check if that creased window was plexiglass before wiping it. Despite the plastic appearance, it is made of glass.

The slotted vents on the inner sides of the rear fenders also caused much speculation. They are exhaust vents for the forced-air ventilation system. Two more are located in the rear side of the door frames outboard of the rubber seal, but are visible only when the door is open. We found this system very effective, even in the desert, when we turned off the automatic climate control for a while.

The performance tests were very revealing, and in some ways quite surprising. Briefly, the car went much quicker than we anticipated, but didn't stop quite as planned.

One thing we hadn't expected was much performance off the line. The 429-cubic-inch V-8 puts out a perhaps conservatively rated 340 hp, not too spectacular for a car with a curb weight in excess of 4700 pounds. Nevertheless, the Eldorado was more than willing to smoke the front tires every time and recorded a high 8.9 seconds in the 0-to-60-mph department. It will come as a blow to the stop light grand prix set to know that the best times, both e.t. and trap speed, were made starting in "Drive 2" with very low stall speed. Even this technique burned some rubber, but gained us nearly a second over the more spectacular starts. Performance was not in a class with a Hemi Charger or GTO, but the car was certainly no stone either.

The trip through the mountains had revealed no brake problems, but our stopping tests at the drag strip certainly did. The test from 30 mph concerned us less because of the distance than the fact that the car slid around 45 degrees before stopping. Test cars often get out

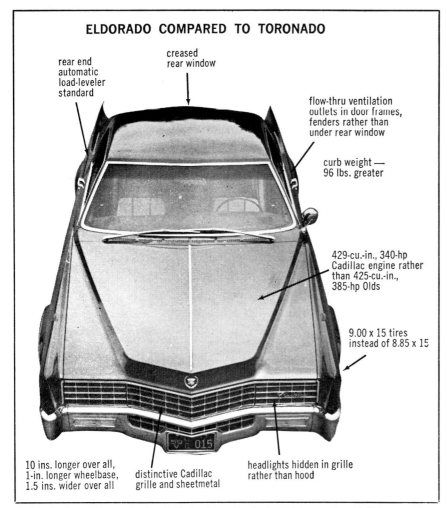

ELDORADO COMPARED TO TORONADO

- rear end automatic load-leveler standard
- creased rear window
- flow-thru ventilation outlets in door frames, fenders rather than under rear window
- curb weight — 96 lbs. greater
- 429-cu.-in., 340-hp Cadillac engine rather than 425-cu.-in., 385-hp Olds
- 9.00 x 15 tires instead of 8.85 x 15
- 10 ins. longer over all, 1-in. longer wheelbase, 1.5 ins. wider over all
- distinctive Cadillac grille and sheetmetal
- headlights hidden in grille rather than hood

Although they share a body shell, Saginaw front-wheel-drive unit and GM parentage, the Eldorado differs from the Toronado in every department — size, shape, engine, and prestige. Production is limited to 15,000 with hand-picked men on the assembly line.

eldorado at a glance...

Most luxurious personal car on the road... features front-wheel-drive and host of automatic conveniences, including many as standard rather than extra-cost options... excellent ride... 340-hp V-8 has plenty of power, but car needs disc-brake option for satisfactory stopping power.

how the car performed...

ACCELERATION (2 aboard)
- 0-30 mph .... 3.5 secs
- 0-45 mph .... 5.3 secs
- 0-60 mph .... 8.9 secs
- 0-75 mph .... 13.9 secs

TIME AND DISTANCE TO ATTAIN PASSING SPEEDS:
- 40-60 mph .... 4.4 secs., 322 ft.
- 50-70 mph .... 5.1 secs., 448.8 ft.

STANDING START QUARTER-MILE:
17.01 secs., 84.04 mph

SPEEDS IN GEARS @ SHIFT POINTS:
- 1st .... 46 mph @ 4500 rpm
- 2nd .... 75 mph @ 4500 rpm
- 3rd ....(not max) 72 mph @ 3000 rpm

SPEEDOMETER ERROR:
- Electric Speedometer 30 45 50 60 70
- Car Speedometer 31 47 53 64 75

MPH PER 1000 RPM: 24.0

STOPPING DISTANCES:
From 30 mph, 43 ft.; from 60 mph, 204 ft.

specifications...

ENGINE: Ohv V-8
- Bore and stroke (ins.): 4.00 x 4.13
- Displacement (cu. ins.): 429
- Horsepower: 340 @ 4600 rpm
- Max. torque (lbs.-ft.): 480 @ 3000 rpm
- Compression ratio: 10.5:1
- Carburetion: 1 4-bbl.

TRANSMISSION: 3-spd. auto
FINAL DRIVE RATIO: 3.21:1
SUSPENSION: Independent front by torsion bars. Rear beam axle by single-leaf springs per wheel and dual tubular shocks per wheel.
STEERING: Concentric gear with variable-ratio power boost, 16.3:1. Turning diameter: 44.5 ft curb-to-curb. Turns lock-to-lock: 2.6.
WHEELS: 15 x 6.00 stamped steel.
TIRES: Goodyear 9.00 x 15 2-ply.
BRAKES: Dual-system hydraulic with power boost — 12-in.-dia. drums front and rear.
FUEL CAPACITY: 24 gals.
MILEAGE RANGE: 11.9 — 12.6 mpg
BODY & FRAME: Boxed perimeter.
DIMENSIONS: Wheelbase: 120 ins. Track: 63.5 ins. front, 63 ins. rear. Overall length 221 ins., width 80 ins., height 53.3 ins. Usable trunk capacity: 13.7 cu. ft.
CURB WEIGHT: 4647 lbs.

prices and accessories...

MANUFACTURER'S SUGGESTED RETAIL: (excludes stat and local taxes, license, options, accessories, and transportation) 2-door hardtop $6327.

OPTIONS & ACCESSORIES:
- Power rear vent windows (door windows std.) .... $ 63.15
- 6-way power seat (4-way std.) 83.15
- Radio AM/FM stereo 287.90
- Climate Control (heater/air cond.) 515.75
- Adjustable steering wheel 89.50
- Automatic headlight control 50.00
- Cruise Control 94.75

ELDORADO

of shape when we miss the ideal feathering pressure at 60 mph, but rarely at 30. We were more judicious on subsequent 30-mph stops, and it pulled up straight, but never in less distance.

With no desire to lose anything that big or that expensive at 60 mph, we looked for the best stop we could manage in a straight line. The stopping distance of 204 feet was the same as that required to stop a Chrysler Town & Country station wagon carrying an 840-pound payload (MT, Sept. '66). In more graphic terms, it was almost two car lengths more than we would have expected. The answer seems to be that the Eldorado really needs the disc front brake option (our test car had drums), which looks like a bargain at $105.25.

It is axiomatic that if you can afford a Cadillac, you shouldn't have to worry about gas mileage. On the other hand, many of the people who can afford such cars have now reached that enviable position because they do worry about such things. Our best mileage was on the high-speed, flat straights of the desert at 12.6 mpg. In the mountains the figure dropped slightly to 11.9, about the same as we got in the city. During our performance test when the car was driven very hard the entire time, mileage dropped to just 10 mpg, still not a bad figure for such a big car, even under the best of circumstances.

This isn't the first time a major engineering concept has been introduced by Oldsmobile the year before its adoption by Cadillac. With public acceptance of the then unique Toronado established by 50,000 sales in 1966, Eldorado seems unlikely to have trouble selling the forecasted 15,000, even with a much bigger price tag. Introduction week enthusiasm in the showrooms bears this out, too. Maybe it just takes pull. /MT

NEW CADILLAC ELDORADO—7,031 c.c. and f.w.d.

LAST week Cadillac announced a completely new model as the star of their 1967 range of exclusive cars. It is based on the bold concept of the Oldsmobile Toronado with front-wheel drive and a 7-litre engine, but features the traditional luxury Cadillac equipment and a sharply sculpted body in two-door coupé form. All the General Motors safety features for 1967 are included in the specification.

The engine is the same 7,031 c.c. over-square unit that powers the other models in the range, but it has been improved by a new valve train and Quadrajet carburettor. Oil consumption is controlled better by smoother bore finish in production and new oil rings for the pistons. Maximum gross power output is 340 b.h.p. at 4,600 r.p.m.

Compared with the Toronado, the new Eldorado is 1in. longer in the wheelbase (10ft.) and 10in. longer overall (18ft. 5in.). Even so, these figures show the new car to be 9·5in. shorter in the wheelbase than the other two-door Cadillacs and 2ft. 6in. shorter than the limousine models.

Despite this abbreviation of the dimensions, the Eldorado is still a full five-seater and because the front-wheel-drive leaves the floor flat, front and rear, there is more legroom. The bonnet of the new model is exceptionally long, with a huge front overhang incorporating the familiar Cadillac double-fronted notches.

Front quarterlights have been eliminated, as on the Toronado, because there is positive air extraction around the rear window and facia vents for cool air delivery. The small rear panes behind each door window slide back into the roof panel. Headlamps are concealed behind the outer extremities of the "egg-box" radiator grille, with vacuum-operated covers which swing back when the switch is pulled.

Special safety features in the Cadillac, additional to the GM items such as collapsible steering column, four-way hazard flasher and padded facia, are a triple braking system with new rayon braid hoses and (as on several other American cars) the option of discs for the front. The diameter of the servo has been increased from 8 to 9·5in. dia. Tyres have been improved with stronger carcases to withstand sustained high speed.

The construction of the body follows the lines of the Toronado, having a separate sub frame to carry the engine and integral transmission unit, with pick-up points under the front seats and at the front eyes of the rear half-elliptic leaf springs. Torsion bars are used at the front and 3-speed Turbo Hydra-Matic transmission is standard. ∎

Above: Just as individualistic in its styling as other Cadillacs, the new Eldorado has a much more sporting line and features front-wheel drive for the first time. Below: The coupé roof hides five full seats and the sharp edges to the rear wings are really tail lamps which show to the sides as well as behind

CAR and DRIVER ROAD TEST

FORD THUNDERBIRD CADILLAC ELDORADO

Thunderbird

Here it is, country-clubbers, the fourth edition of the Thunderbird, America's first mass-class, *va-va-voom*, fantasy-sports "personal" car. And here's the Eldorado too, Cadillac's razor-edged hardtop, representing the latest entry in this burgeoning field of cars aimed at the faceless splitdwellers of America's better subdivisions.

It seems appropriate to compare the Thunderbird and the Cadillac for several reasons. In the first place, the T-Bird is the vehicle that started it all, while the Eldorado is the most recent contender. Secondly, the two cars are all-new for 1967, though both utilize well-established components from their respective parent corporations. The Thunderbird's undercarriage is laden with bits and pieces from the successful and sharply-designed Ford Galaxie and LTD series, and the Eldorado is a mechanical twin sister of the much-ballyhooed, somewhat disappointing Oldsmobile Toronado.

It's a curious fact that both the Thunderbird and the Eldorado/Toronado are Ford concepts. The T-Bird obviously is, but it's an open secret that the front-wheel-drive layout GM uses in the Eldorado/Toronado is covered by a Ford patent. Ford experimented at length with a fwd Thunderbird in the late Fifties, but abandoned the idea in 1960 because of the system's high unsprung weight and staggering costs. Ford insiders imply that GM has had nothing but headaches with unconventional drive trains (front-engine front-drive, and rear-engine rear-drive), while receiving few benefits.

Before we begin to probe the in-

Neither the Thunderbird nor the
Eldorado caused us any fits of rapture.
To be sure, both had their appealing aspects,
but in total, they left us with
an impression of bulk and clumsiness.
This is an unfortunate departure from
the original concept of the "personal" car

Eldorado

sides of these two automobiles, we might as well say that neither caused us any fits of rapture. To be sure, both had their appealing aspects, but as total automobiles they left us with an impression of bulk and clumsiness. This is unfortunate, because it means a further departure from the originally refreshing concept of luxury "personal" transportation. The first four-place Thunderbird was not a memorable car, but the second entrant in this field, the Buick Riviera, was one of the most interesting and stimulating vehicles produced by Detroit since World War II. Alas, The Motor City's doctrine of evolution dictates that all good things must increase in size, and now the poor Riviera has grown long and wide and lost much of its original litheness. This is the sad case of all "personal" cars, and today the basic concept of a luxurious, close-coupled, four-place automobile has all but been obscured in an overlay of bulging sheet metal. The T-Bird, in its brand new four-door version, is 209 inches long and weighs a chubby 4750 lbs. (the two-door is two inches shorter and a hundred pounds lighter). The Eldorado is heftier, being 221 inches overall and tipping the scales at 4950 lbs. Hardly what you would call agile, sporting vehicles.

Both cars are aimed at the wealthy exurbanite who fancies himself something of an automotive connoisseur, but in reality doesn't know a valve spring from a door latch. By pitching him with the idea that these cars are specially designed for high-speed highway travel, Ford and General Motors are able to woo

The Thunderbird and the Eldorado are mass-class status symbols. In many ways good automobiles, they are not uniquely different—except in a styling sense—from a dozen high-priced luxury vehicles being marketed in the United States

Eldorado

Thunderbird

the buyer into thinking he's being just a bit more daring and discriminating by purchasing something significantly hairier than his neighbors' deVilles and Continentals.

Both the Thunderbird and the Eldorado are mass-class status symbols—let's not delude ourselves that they are intended to be anything more or less. They are in many ways good automobiles, but they are not *uniquely* different—except in a styling sense—from a dozen high-priced luxury vehicles presently being marketed in the United States.

Because the Eldorado's chassis and drive-line are basically the Toronado's, the four-door Thunderbird becomes the more interesting car of the two by default. Not that it contains any sparkling engineering feats, or breakthroughs in the art of body building, but it is the first four-door "personal" car and for that it must earn a few points. The idea of adding two more doors to the T-Bird is being treated like the invention of the cotton gin by Ford, but the change is hardly worth the hoopla. The result is a sharply styled, slightly smaller Galaxie with all the trimmings (trimmings, we must allow, that seem to have been lifted intact from Chrysler's postwar K310, a Ghia-bodied dream car). Ford people will protest this analogy, citing the different physical dimensions of their sister vehicles, but the fact remains that the T-Bird and the Galaxie are *conceptually* similar and in fact share the same engines, the same three-speed automatic transmission and the same all-coil suspension systems.

Our test T-Bird was a sinister-looking black Landau with the ever-faithful Ford 390 engine (standard) and a representative collection of extras like air conditioning, stereo tape unit, et cetera. Upon climbing into the lush, black vinyl interior, we were pleased to see that Ford has finally cooled it with the airplane-pilot syndrome that has turned previous Thunderbirds into bogus jet-liners. The Twenty-First Century instruments are gone, replaced by a set of four straightforward—if mildly illegible—dials across the dash panel. The optional warning lights are still in their old hangout on the moulding under the roof but they are more subdued.

The front bucket seats are plenty comfortable but lack any suggestion of lateral support. Because the body is mounted very low on the frame rails (the car has been switched from a unit body to a perimeter frame for 1967), there is no room for a compartment in the console between the front seats, and interior storage space is limited to a meager glove box. A dual set of stereo speakers are ingeniously mounted in the front doors.

The doors also contain handles that might serve as grab rails for panicked passengers in an emergency, but Ford is quick to point out that the latches won't work if the doors are locked. Actually, the Thunderbird is amply equipped with safety gear, including neat shoulder harnesses for the front seats that are stowed conveniently by Velcro fasteners above the doors. They are quick and simple to latch into place and are the first harnesses that can

Ford and General Motors are able to woo the buyer into thinking he's being just a bit more daring and discriminating by purchasing what he thinks is a significantly hairier machine than his neighbors' deVilles and Continentals

Eldorado

Eldorado   *Thunderbird*

truly be described as suitable for the impatient, ham-fisted public. Ford has obviously responded to the safety furor and the T-Bird has several components that should make Senator Ribicoff dance with joy. The sun visors are recessed into the headliner, precluding any chance for them to cause head injuries during a crash. The grab bars on the doors are made of pliable rubber, as are a pair of tiny dorsal fins mounted on the front fenders—made soft presumably to reduce the possibility of eviscerating hapless pedestrians.

Though the safety gang seldom concerns itself with such things, the Thunderbird's visibility appears to be a rather important drawback to its overall capability for preventing accidents. Built with a high beltline and low roof, the windows, front, side and rear, are small enough to make some passengers feel a touch of the old claustrophobia. Forward vision is reduced by a padded cowling that looms above the instrument panel, and a hood bulge that accommodates the engine air cleaner. Additional blockage comes from the large rear-view mirror that has been epoxy-mounted dead center and quite low in the glass, making the forward-viewing arc as narrow as we have found on any recent test car. Visibility to the side and rear is also inadequate, due simply to the skimpy glass area.

Once underway, the Thunderbird is just another big domestic car, *Specifications overleaf;*
CONTINUED ON PAGE 20

FORD THUNDERBIRD

Manufacturer: Ford Motor Company, 20000 Rotunda Drive, Dearborn, Michigan.
Vehicle type: Front-engine, rear-wheel-drive, 4-passenger luxury/personal sedan, all-steel body with separate chassis.
Number of dealers in U.S.: 6200
Price as tested: $N.A. (Prices for the 1967 models had not been released by the manufacturers at press time. Our unofficial estimate would be ca. $5200.00, as our test car was equipped.)
Options on test car: Air conditioning, automatic speed control, power seats

ENGINE
Type: Water-cooled V-8, cast iron block and heads, 5 main bearings
Bore and stroke.....4.05 x 3.78 in, 103 x 96.2 mm
Displacement..............390 cu in, 6340 cc
Compression ratio...............10.5-to-one
Carburetion..................1 x 4-bbl Autolite
Valve-gear. Pushrod-operated overhead valves, hydraulic lifters
Power (SAE)............315 bhp @ 4600 rpm
Torque (SAE)..........427 lbs/ft @ 2800 rpm
Specific power output....0.80 bhp/cu in, 49.5 bhp/liter
Maximum recommended engine speed..............4600 rpm

DRIVE TRAIN
Transmission..3-speed automatic plus torque converter
Gearshift position..........Console-mounted (PRND₁D₂L)

Gear	Ratio	Mph/1000 rpm	Max. test speed
I	2.46	10.8	45 mph (4200 rpm)
II	1.46	18.3	82 mph (4500 rpm)
III	1.00	27.7	111 mph (4000 rpm)
R	2.18	−12.2	N.A.

Max. torque converter ratio........2.10 to one
Final drive ratio...................3.00 to one

DIMENSIONS AND CAPACITIES
Wheelbase..........................115.0 in
Track...............F: 62.0 in, R: 62.0 in
Length............................206.9 in
Width..............................77.2 in
Height.............................52.8 in
Ground clearance....................5.6 in
Curb weight.......................4755 lbs
Test weight.......................5239 lbs
Weight distribution, F/R........55.0/45.0%
Lbs/bhp (test weight)..............16.6
Battery capacity........12 volts, 70 amp/hr
Alternator capacity.............660 watts
Fuel capacity....................24.1 gal
Oil capacity......................5.0 qts
Water capacity...................20.5 qts

SUSPENSION
F: Ind., upper wishbone with lower transverse link, drag strut, coil springs, anti-sway bar
R: Rigid axle, two trailing arms, track bar, coil springs

STEERING
Type.....................Recirculating ball
Turns lock-to-lock........................3.6
Turning circle............................42 ft

BRAKES
F: Kelsey-Hayes 11.87-in. vented discs
R: 11.0 x 2.25-in. drums
Swept area.....................335.6 sq in

WHEELS AND TIRES
Wheel size and type...........5.5J x 15-in, pressed steel disc, 5-bolt
Tire make, size and type...Firestone 8.15-15
Test inflation pressures..F: 24 psi, R: 24 psi
Design load capacity..1370 lbs per tire @ 24 psi

PERFORMANCE
                                    Seconds
Zero to 30 mph 4.6
Zero to 40 mph 6.6
Zero to 50 mph 9.3
Zero to 60 mph 12.0
Zero to 70 mph 15.1
Zero to 80 mph 19.2
Zero to 90 mph 23.9
Zero to 100 mph 29.9
Standing ¼-mile..........17.8 sec @ 78 mph
80–0 mph.................330 ft (.65 G)
Fuel mileage 12–15 mpg on premium fuel
Cruising range................288–361 mi

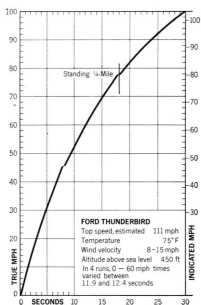

FORD THUNDERBIRD
Top speed; estimated   111 mph
Temperature   75°F
Wind velocity   8–15 mph
Altitude above sea level   450 ft
In 4 runs, 0 − 60 mph times varied between 11.9 and 12.4 seconds

CHECK LIST

ENGINE
Starting.........................Very Good
Response.............................Good
Vibration.........................Excellent
Noise............................Very Good

DRIVE TRAIN
Shift linkage..........................Good
Shift smoothness................Very Good
Transmission noise..............Excellent

STEERING
Effort...........................Excellent
Response.............................Fair
Road feel............................Fair
Kickback........................Very Good

SUSPENSION
Ride comfort.........................Good
Roll resistance......................Fair
Pitch control........................Good
Harshness control...............Very Good

HANDLING
Directional control..................Good
Predictability.......................Good
Evasive maneuverability..............Fair
Resistance to sidewinds........Very Good

BRAKES
Pedal pressure......................Good
Response........................Very Good
Fade resistance......................Good
Directional control..................Good

CONTROLS
Wheel position..................Very Good
Pedal position..................Very Good
Gearshift position...................Good
Relationship.........................Fair
Small controls.......................Poor

INTERIOR
Ease of entry/exit...................Good
Noise level (cruising)..........Very Good
Front seating comfort...............Good
Front leg room..................Very Good
Front head room......................Fair
Front hip/shoulder room.............Good
Rear seating comfort................Good
Rear leg room........................Good
Rear head room.......................Fair
Rear hip/shoulder room...............Fair
Instrument comprehensiveness........Fair
Instrument legibility................Fair

VISION
Forward..............................Fair
Front quarter........................Poor
Side.................................Good
Rear quarter.........................Poor
Rear.................................Fair

WEATHER PROTECTION
Heater/defroster................Very Good
Ventilation..........................Good
Air conditioner.................Very Good
Weather sealing.................Very Good

CONSTRUCTION QUALITY
Sheet metal.....................Very Good
Paint...........................Excellent
Chrome..........................Excellent
Upholstery...........................Good
Padding.........................Very Good
Hardware........................Very Good

GENERAL
Headlight illumination..........Excellent
Parking and signal lights............Good
Wiper effectiveness..................Fair
Service accessibility................Fair
Trunk space..........................Fair
Interior storage space...............Poor
Bumper protection....................Good

CADILLAC ELDORADO

Manufacturer: Cadillac Motor Division
General Motors Corporation
2860 Clark Ave.
Detroit, Michigan

Vehicle type: Front-engine, front-wheel-drive, 5-passenger luxury personal sedan, all-steel integral body/chassis, with stub frames

Number of dealers in U.S.: 1700

Price as tested: $ N.A. (Prices for the 1967 models had not been released by the manufacturers at press time. Our unofficial estimate would be ca. $8250.00, as our test car was equipped)

Options on test car: Climate Control air conditioning, cruise control, automatic head-light dimmer, twilight sentinel, headrests, reclining seats, AM radio, electric seat heater, rear window defogger

ENGINE
Type: Water-cooled V-8, cast iron block and heads, 5 main bearings
Bore x stroke....4.13 x 4.00 in, 104.8 x 101.5 mm
Displacement.............429 cu in, 6975 cc
Compression ratio................10.5-to-one
Carburetion...............1 x 4-bbl Carter
Valve gear. Pushrod-operated overhead valves, hydraulic lifters
Power (SAE)..........340 bhp @ 4600 rpm
Torque (SAE)........480 lbs/ft @ 3000 rpm
Specific power output......0.79 bhp/cu in, 48 bhp/liter
Maximum recommended engine speed..5200 rpm

DRIVE TRAIN
Transmission:...........3-speed automatic, plus torque converter
Gearshift position...........Steering column (PRND₂D₂L)

Gear	Ratio	Mph/1000 rpm	Max. test speed
I	2.48	10.5	41 mph (3900 rpm)
II	1.48	17.5	68 mph (3900 rpm)
III	1.00	26.0	109 mph (4200 rpm)
R	2.09	-12.5	N.A.

Max. torque converter ratio........2.20 to one
Final drive ratio.................3.21 to one

DIMENSIONS AND CAPACITIES
Wheelbase......................120.0 in
Track..................F:63.5 in, R:63.0 in
Length.........................221.0 in
Width...........................80.0 in
Height..........................53.3 in
Ground clearance.................5.4 in
Curb weight....................4950 lbs
Test weight....................5200 lbs
Weight distribution, F/R.........58.0/42.0%
Lbs/bhp (test weight)..............15.3
Battery capacity........12 volts, 71 amp/hr
Alternator capacity..............852 watts
Fuel capacity....................24.0 gal
Oil capacity......................4.0 qts
Water capacity..................18.6 qts

SUSPENSION
F: Ind., unequal-length wishbones, coil springs, anti-sway bar
R: Rigid axle, single-leaf springs, traction dampers, air-leveling

STEERING
Type......................Recirculating ball
Turns lock-to-lock..................2.75
Turning circle.....................41 ft

BRAKES
F: 12.0 x 2.75-in cast iron drums
R: 12.0 x 2.0-in cast iron drums
Swept area..................179.5 sq in

WHEELS AND TIRES
Wheel size and type........6.0JK x 15-in, pressed steel disc. 5 bolt
Tire make, size and type...U.S. Royal Laredo, 9.00-15
Test inflation pressures...F: 24 psi, R: 22 psi
Design load capacity. 1620 lbs per tire @ 24 psi

PERFORMANCE
	Seconds
Zero to 30 mph	4.4
Zero to 40	6.3
Zero to 50	8.9
Zero to 60	11.7
Zero to 70	15.3
Zero to 80	18.2
Zero to 90	24.0
Zero to 100	30.4

Standing ¼-mile......17.9 sec @ 76 mph
80-0 mph..................386 ft (.55 G)
Fuel mileage.....10-14 mpg on premium fuel
Cruising range..................240-336 mi

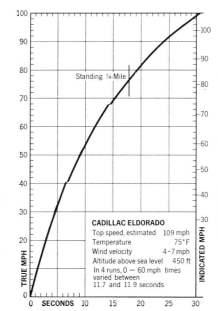

CADILLAC ELDORADO
Top speed, estimated 109 mph
Temperature 75°F
Wind velocity 4-7 mph
Altitude above sea level 450 ft
In 4 runs, 0 — 60 mph times varied between 11.7 and 11.9 seconds

CHECK LIST

ENGINE
Starting.........................Excellent
Response........................Very Good
Vibration........................Excellent
Noise............................Excellent

DRIVE TRAIN
Shift linkage........................Good
Shift smoothness..................Very Good
Transmission noise................Excellent

STEERING
Effort...........................Excellent
Response.........................Excellent
Road feel.......................Very Good
Kickback.........................Excellent

SUSPENSION
Ride comfort....................Very Good
Roll resistance......................Good
Pitch control........................Fair
Harshness control...............Very Good

HANDLING
Directional control..............Very Good
Predictability...................Very Good
Evasive maneuverability..............Poor
Resistance to sidewinds..............Good

BRAKES
Pedal pressure.......................Good
Response............................Fair
Fade resistance......................Fair
Directional control..................Good

CONTROLS
Wheel position...................Excellent
Pedal position..................Very Good
Gearshift position...................Good
Relationship........................Good
Small controls......................Good

INTERIOR
Ease of entry/exit..................Good
Noise level (cruising)...........Excellent
Front seating comfort............Excellent
Front leg room..................Very Good
Front head room.................Very Good
Front hip/shoulder room.............Good
Rear seating comfort...............Good
Rear leg room.......................Fair
Rear head room......................Fair
Rear hip/shoulder room..............Good
Instrument comprehensiveness........Fair
Instrument legibility...........Very Good

VISION
Forward.........................Very Good
Front quarter....................Excellent
Side............................Excellent
Rear quarter........................Poor
Rear................................Fair

WEATHER PROTECTION
Heater/defroster.................Excellent
Ventilation......................Excellent
Air conditioner..................Excellent
Weather sealing..................Excellent

CONSTRUCTION QUALITY
Sheet metal......................Excellent
Paint............................Excellent
Chrome...........................Excellent
Upholstery.......................Excellent
Padding..........................Excellent
Hardware.........................Excellent

GENERAL
Headlight illumination..........Very Good
Parking and signal lights...........Fair
Wiper effectiveness.............Very Good
Service accessibility...............Good
Trunk space.....................Very Good
Interior storage space..............Fair
Bumper protection...................Good

FORD THUNDERBIRD/CADILLAC ELDORADO

CONTINUED FROM PAGE 17

with a wonderful penchant for silent 70-mph cruising speeds and handling with a heavy dose of understeer. With its recommended tire pressures, the tires distort palpably, adding to the sensation that the car answers sluggishly to her helm. More tire pressure—enough to make the ride harsh for the average Thunderbird customer—helped with our test car, but not enough. We suspect that a set of wide-base wheels, low profile tires and stiff shock absorbers would markedly improve handling.

We were relatively pleased with the car's stopping potential, thanks to the standard front disc brakes and 11-inch rear brakes. Though we encountered some fade during 80-mph panic stops, the car maintained acceptable directional stability under heavy braking and came to a halt within reasonable limits. A proportioning valve that limits rear braking effort prevented us from locking the system and doubtlessly added to stopping efficiency. On the whole, the Thunderbird's brakes are as good as any American car of this bulk, but fall short of the optimum, as we have seen demonstrated on even heavier cars like the Rolls-Royce and the Mercedes-Benz 600.

While the T-Bird's brakes can be termed acceptable, the standard brakes on Cadillac's spiffy new Eldorado are a treacherous, unsafe Achilles heel on an otherwise pleasant luxury vehicle. Even though the Eldorado is nearly identical to the Toronado in technical detail, we had expected that some corrective measures would have been taken after all the car magazines and a few of the customers had griped about the Oldsmobile's poor stopping power. But the Cadillac engineering department has such a fetish for smoothness and silence that it appears willing to subordinate all other automotive functions to placing the passengers in a silky, acoustically dead environment.

Unfortunately, this preoccupation with "ride" and interior noise levels has distracted Cadillac's engineers from other pertinent matters—like how to get a vehicle weighing 2½ tons stopped from 80 mph. Our test car carried drum brakes all around and managed to smoke and slew to a halt—sideways in the road—in a pitiful 386 feet. The Cadillac people attempted to rationalize the difficulties of developing workable drum brakes for a vehicle of this size, which forced one observer to ask where they found the moral justification for marketing a car that they *knew* was too heavy for its brakes. The question prompted a certain amount of hand-wringing and eye-rolling, whereupon they produced a heretofore unseen Eldorado equipped with optional disc brakes. This car was much better—stopping in 312 feet with vastly improved directional stability—and was intended, according to Cadillac spokesmen, for the "performance-minded customer." This evidently means that the poor dolt who is not interested in "performance" is also apparently not interested in being able to stop effectively, and would prefer a silent, smooth crash into some unyielding object rather than pay extra for a "sporty" option like adequate brakes. This position is as obtuse as any that we have encountered, and the absence of disc brakes on *all* Eldorados is simply bad news, especially when the extra $100 added to the base price is relatively unimportant on an $8000 car.

Aside from the lackluster brakes, the Eldorado is an effective evolution of the front-wheel-drive Toronado concept. The basic body and driveline components are the same as its predecessor, though nine inches have been added to the stern section in order to make more trunk space available. The car also has one inch more wheelbase (120 in.), making it a total of 10 inches longer than the Toronado.

In order to obtain a softer ride the Eldorado utilizes the same air-leveling system that is employed on the regular Fleetwood line. Otherwise the suspension is the same as that of the Toronado. The Eldorado does not use radial tires (which can be purchased on the Toronado). It is delivered with 9.00-15 rubber that promotes road silence and smoothness but does little for the car's handling.

Cadillac's lightweight, low-revving 429 cubic inch engine is the only powerplant available in the entire line, including the Eldorado, and it is completely satisfactory. It is quiet and trouble-free and pumps out gobs of torque and enough horsepower to tow a 4950-lb. mammoth around with surprising alacrity.

The interior compartment, which is intended for five passengers (not six, as claimed by the Toronado makers), is as sumptuous as any automobile's. As we have said, passenger comfort is the big bag at Cadillac and every component from the uncanny Climate Control air conditioning to the optional all-leather upholstery is designed without compromise. The Eldorado interior is tasteful and efficient beyond reproach and we can only wish that half as much creative energy had been exerted on braking ability.

Details like the Saginaw variable-ratio power steering and the fiendishly complicated but effective interior ventilation system are what help justify the high price of the Eldorado, but the clincher comes with an examination of the general workmanship of the automobile. We found our test car to be impeccably assembled, with the kind of panel-fit and paint work that stands up against the best that Stuttgart-Untertürkheim and Crewe can produce. If there is any single outstanding feature of the Eldorado, it is this attention to detail that probably surpasses that given to any other American automobile, with the possible exception of Cadillac's own Fleetwood sedans.

Handling is about what you would expect for a front-wheel drive car with 58 per cent of its weight on the front wheels. Yes, folks, it understeers, though it must be said that it does it predictably and without any trick transitions to oversteer before the limit of adhesion is reached. Unlike Oldsmobile's approach to the Toronado, Cadillac intends to de-emphasize the fact that the Eldorado is powered through the front wheels and will underplay any references to the drive train in its sales literature. This is rather in keeping with the "play safe" philosophy of the entire car, which carefully avoids anything that might be misconstrued as unique or revolutionary.

We had hoped that Cadillac would use its considerable engineering talent to create a truly unique "personal" car when the Eldorado project was first rumored. Thinking about them starting with a clean sheet of paper, we fantasized about a completely original American luxury grand touring vehicle being produced by America's most prestigious automaker and were rather let down when we found nothing more than a warmed-over Toronado.

The Thunderbird and Eldorado are not unpleasant automobiles. They are civilized machines, keyed to a market that should expand significantly within the next decade, provided the economy doesn't take any nasty nosedives. They are basically unoriginal cars aimed at a segment of the market where imagination and non-conformity are taboo, and in this sense Ford and Cadillac have exhibited their traditional commercial acumen. New or old, bright or dull, safe or unsafe, they're bound to be a big hit with the Metrecal-for-lunch bunch. **c/D**

The chassis for the Eldorado is assembled while suspended on the overhead conveyor.

ASSEMBLING THE ELDORADO

By Joseph Geschelin Detroit Editor

ACCORDING TO PRELIMINARY reports, the projected output of Cadillac Eldorado front-drive cars could be sold on orders pending even before the dealers are stocked. Judging by this, Eldorado is off to a flying start.

Since this car differs in major respects from the regular Cadillac line not only in design but in assembly procedures, it has been divorced from the regular assembly line. Instead, Eldorado has become a small, self-contained operation with its own chassis assembly line, final assembly, and final inspection. In addition, the operation contains its own compact paint shop fully equipped for the finishing of sheet metal components such as hoods, fenders, and other items.

To accomplish this in a plant already strained to capacity, it was necessary to do some advance planning of major proportions. What was done, essentially, was to employ the area formerly occupied by the Cadillac foundry which had served the engine plant for a great many years, restore it to match the rest of the manufacturing departments, and to move in the Eldorado facilities.

The net result, as exemplified by the selected group of illustrations, shows the effects of this skillful advance planning particularly in the manner of tailoring the various operations and lines to suit the available configuration of space.

Despite the radical design of the car, assembly procedures are quite

ASSEMBLING THE ELDORADO

ABOVE—Off the end of the chassis assembly line is this sub-assembly station for preparing the rear suspension buggy.

ABOVE LEFT — General view of the overhead conveyor employed for producing sheet metal sub-assemblies. Note that the fixture is long enough to accommodate the large hood.

LEFT — Applying color coats in the Centri-Spray booth. Ventilation is by down draft.

BELOW — Final wet deck operation prior to reflow drying in the Fostoria tunnel.

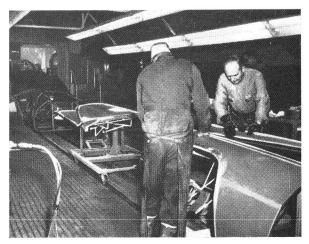

The Eldorado body is dropped over the chassis at a point just after the chassis has been lowered onto its wheels on the final assembly line.

simple and conventional, although the assembly operators have been specially trained to handle the job most efficiently.

Car assembly begins with chassis assembly which employs an overhead suspended conveyor line. This line is comparatively short in length, mainly due to the fact that the chassis frame is much shorter than a standard frame, terminating as it does at the mounting of the front eye of the single-leaf rear spring.

The powerplant assembly, on the other hand, is built and dressed in a mix on the regular engine assembly and dress-up lines. It is removed from the power-and-free conveyor system in the dress-up area and transported to the chassis assembly line where it is installed in the usual manner.

Near the end of the suspended assembly line is a sub-assembly station at which the trailing rear axle and single-leaf spring are assembled; and the pair of wheels attached to produce a rolling buggy. This is then wheeled under the chassis and loosely attached. At the same time the front wheels are installed. By this time the chassis assembly has been pretty well completed, including attachment of the transversely mounted muffler.

The chassis conveyor line then curves 90-deg to meet the final assembly line. Here the chassis rolls on its own wheels on a conventional power-driven floor conveyor with underfloor pits to facilitate underbody operations.

Next major stage is the body drop. It may be noted that the body structure incorporates its own integral rear frame extension of massive design to provide support for the rear suspension. Before the body is dropped on the line, it is fitted with the four rear shock absorbers, rear spring hangers, and shackles. Thus, the attachment of the rear buggy becomes a simple air-wrench operation.

Meanwhile, the various sheet metal components are attached in matched sets on a single overhead conveyor line as they come from the paint shop. This conveyor serves to complete the sub-assembly operations required for components such as hoods and fenders. It also serves to produce the front end sub-assembly consisting of the radiator, grille, and other components. These sub-assemblies then continue enroute to feed the final assembly line.

As mentioned earlier, one area of the department is devoted exclusively to the self-contained facilities for painting sheet metal. Compact in size, it features entirely new equipment for phosphating, application of prime and finish coats, wet sand decks, drying ovens, etc. Centri-Spray, down-draft spray booths are employed for the purpose.

We have illustrated the final stage of the paint shop operation. Here is seen the final wet sand deck for the finish color coat. The parts move on the conveyor through a short Centri-Spray booth to take care of occasional repairs, then directly into the Fostoria infra-red tunnel for reflow drying. Time and temperature are balanced here to produce the finish coating. The tunnel runs some 115 ft in length and is automatically controlled to maintain temperature at a constant level of 350 F. ∎

CADILLAC V8 *429 cubic inches*

The 1967 version of the Cadillac engine, which is used to power all models of this luxury car, remains virtually unchanged from the previous year. Horsepower and torque ratings remain the same. Although the horsepower rating in terms of horsepower per cubic inch of displacement falls somewhat short of many other engines, its high torque and total horsepower output serves to provide highly satisfactory performance in the heaviest cars in the line. Despite its large size, the Cadillac engine features a very high horsepower-to-weight ratio. The relatively light weight is due in part to a cored-out crankshaft and a die-cast aluminum combination of accessory drive and chain cover. The engine is given extraordinary care in the various manufacturing, assembly, and inspection processes. Many of these processes are conducted in air-conditioned areas to insure precise measurements. Relatively low production rates and considerable leeway in cost allowances make a high degree of quality control possible in the production of this fine and reliable engine, worthy of Cadillac's trademark, "Standard of the World."

Type: Ohv V8
Displacement (cu. in.): 429.
Horsepower @ rpm: 340 @ 4600.
Horsepower per cubic inch: 0.79.
Torque (lbs. ft.) @ rpm: 480 @ 3000.
Bore & Stroke: 4.13 x 4.00.
Compression ratio: 10.5.
Carburetion: 1 4-bbl.
Approximate weight: 600 lbs.
Weight-to-hp ratio: 1.77.

ENGINEERING EVOLUTION: While basic design criteria and tooling for the current Cadillac engine were laid down in 1948, the engine bears little resemblance to the engine of that year because of a radical updating in almost every feature. The 1966 version was bored and stroked to its present displacement at the end of the 1963 model year when the displacement was 390 cubic inches.

GENERAL: The Cadillac engine is a 90-degree V8 design with pushrod-operated overhead valves. Its 429-cubic-inch displacement is derived from a 4.13 cylinder bore and 4.00 stroke. The 340-brake horsepower peak is reached at 4600 rpm and its maximum torque of 480 lbs. ft. is generated at 3000 rpm. Carburetion is provided by a single four-barrel carburetor. Compression ratio is 10.5:1. Both the cylinder block and cylinder heads are cast iron. The die-cast aluminum front cover encloses the timing chain and provides a mounting for the oil pump, oil filter, oil filler tube, and water pump. Total weight of the engine including all accessories is only about 600 pounds.

PISTONS, RINGS, PINS, RODS: The only 1967 design changes in the Cadillac involves slight modifications of the pistons and lower ring to improve oil control and some slight modifications of the valve train. These aluminum alloy pistons have a double T slot, are cam ground and Stannate-coated to resist scuffing when the engine is new. The piston pins are fabricated from SAE 1045 steel, have a husky nominal diameter, just a whisker under one inch, and are a press fit in the connecting rods. While the pins have a floating fit in the pistons within very close tolerances, adequate provision has been made for their lubrication. Broached grooves in the piston pin bores direct oil from the cylinder walls to the bores. These pin bores in the pistons are offset .062 inch toward the major thrust side of the cylinders to contribute to engine operational smoothness. The short and stocky connecting rods are fabricated from SAE 1041 steel and weigh a relatively light 19.36 ounces. At the lower end, the rod bearings are contained in a substantial base just over three-quarters of an inch wide.

CRANKSHAFT: The crankshaft is cast from pearlitic malleable iron and hollow cored for lightness without sacrifice of stiffness. A design concept was adopted in earlier models of the engine which prescribed counterweights only three inches in diameter and so disposed to avoid any bending of the shaft. Because of the engine's short stroke and small-diameter crankshaft counterweights, only a small sump and crankcase were required and thus the crank assumed a short and stiff configuration. Both of these factors contributed to reducing the overall weight of the engine. The main crankshaft bearing journals have a nominal three-inch diameter. Crankpin journals on the shaft have a nominal 2.25-inch diameter. The rod bearings are M-400 aluminum and the main bearings a combination of M-400 aluminum and M-100 babbitt. Thrust is taken on the center main bearing. A rubber absorption-type harmonic vibration damper is pressed on the snout of the crankshaft.

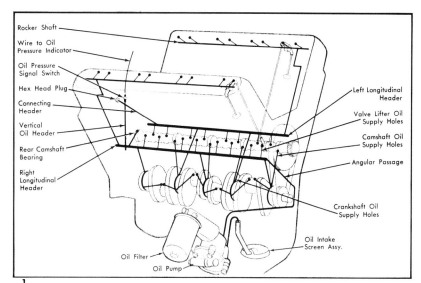

1

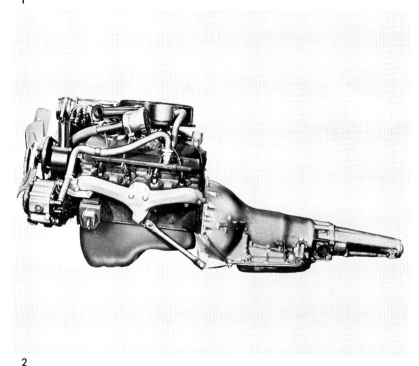

2

3

1. This shows the oiling system and oil flow in the Cadillac engine.

2. Despite the large size of the Cadillac engine, it has a very high horsepower-to-weight ratio. Engine shown is complete with power steering pump and air conditioning compressor.

3. Cutaway reveals cored-out crankshaft which eliminates a considerable amount of weight for engine assembly. Engine is given extraordinary care in various manufacturing and assembly processes. Controlled assembly conditions account for much more precise tolerances.

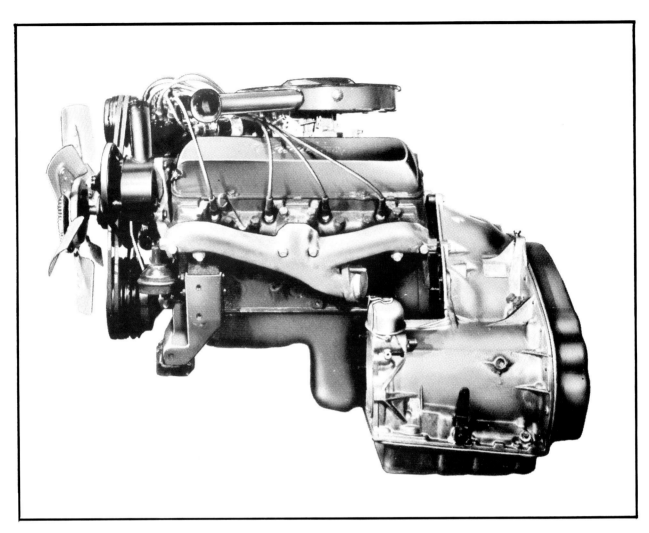

Above: Cadillac engine equipped with transmission and accessories for Eldorado front drive car. Eldorado uses the same engine as rear drive Cadillacs. The only difference is in the external parts, such as the oil pan, exhaust manifold, motor mounts, etc.

CAMSHAFT: The camshaft is cast from a General Motors-specified formulation of cast iron. Carried in five steel-backed babbitt bearings, it is driven by a silent chain. The crankshaft sprocket material is sintered iron and the camshaft sprocket is die-cast aluminum with nylon teeth. Camshaft lobe configurations provide a 290-degree duration on the intake valves, 332-degree duration on the exhaust valves and a 97-degree overlap. The lift is .427 on the intakes and .466 on the exhausts. While this cam action cannot be considered "mild," it apparently does nothing to detract from the smoothness of the engine throughout its entire rpm range.

VALVES: The intake valves are SAE 1041 steel with aluminized heads and the exhaust valves are SAE 21-4N steel. Head diameter of the intakes is 1.875 inch and the exhausts measure 1.50-inch. Single valve springs are used and exert a 60 to 65-pound pressure in the closed position. The spring pressure when the valves are open is in the range of 155 to 165 pounds. Hydraulic valve lifters operate in guide holes drilled in the cylinder block. To insure the quietest possible operation, the valve lifter plungers and lifter bodies are selectively fitted in matched pairs.

FUEL SYSTEM: Fuel is delivered from the vehicle tank to the engine by a mechanical pump. Two fuel filters are used, one located in the tank and the other at the front end of the engine. The engine in cars without air-conditioning may be delivered with either a Carter 3093-S or a Rochester 7025030 four-barrel carburetor. Factory air-conditioned cars are equipped with either a Carter AFB 3904-S or Rochester 7025031. All of these carburetors share a 1.4375 primary barrel diameter and a 1.6875 barrel diameter in the secondaries.

LUBRICATION SYSTEM: The lubrication system incorporates the usual full-flow oil filter. Oil is delivered by a spur-gear pump which develops a normal 30 to 35-pound pressure at a vehicle speed of 30 mph. Oil from this pump flows through two longitudinal headers drilled into the right and left sides of the cylinder block. Branch passages from these headers feed the crankshaft, cam, and rocker arm shafts. Oil directed to the rocker arm shafts builds up pressure within the shaft passages. There are two holes in the rocker shaft for each rocker arm. One set of holes are at the bottom of the shaft, intersecting grooves under the loaded area of each rocker arm. The other set of holes are slightly offset with an angular passage in the rocker arms. This angular offset acts as a metering device to supply the upper end of rocker arms with the correct amount of oil. The timing chain receives its oil by a metered centrifugal flow provision and the cylinder walls are lubricated by an intermediate jet.

Above: This shows the thermostatically controlled fan, and the many accessories driven by the front pulley. Clockwise, from left, are the alternator, air conditioner, power steering pump, and exhaust emission control pump.

Right: Rear view of the Cadillac engine equipped with Eldorado front drive transmission. Behind that large cover are two sprockets and a chain drive.

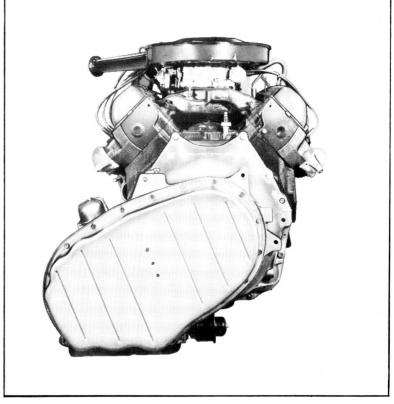

'67 cars
CADILLAC

a bold, new personal car sets a new "standard of the world"

A radical new Eldorado leads Cadillac's parade of '67 models. Featuring front-wheel drive, the Eldorado is a personal, 4-5-passenger luxury car in the same mood as the Thunderbird, Riviera and Toronado. Its final drive system, in fact, is patterned after that of the Toronado.

All '67 Cadillacs, Eldorado included, are powered by the same 340-horsepower, 429-cubic-inch engine. Turbo Hydra-Matic transmission is standard throughout the line.

The Eldorado has a wheelbase of 120 inches and is 221 inches overall. The lowest-priced Calais series and middle-of-the line De Ville share a wheelbase of 129.5 inches and a length of 224 inches.

Rear of Cadillac is highlighted by new bumper, taillight treatment. Lines are more tapered, angular.

Evolution and refinement are perennial hallmarks of new Cadillac designs. De Ville 2-door hardtop, above, typifies this year's expression of that styling philosophy.

Grille slopes forward in rakish new contour, fender line regains kickup, vestigial fin. Yet, as De Ville convertible at right shows, new model is clearly identifiable as a Cadillac.

The Fleetwood Brougham and Sixty Special sedan are both built on a wheelbase of 133 inches with an overall measurement of 227.5 inches. Finally, those in the market for a limousine will find the Cadillac Seventy Five on a 149.8-inch wheelbase. This huge model stretches 244.5 inches from bumper to bumper.

Bolder grille and fender lines, inspired by the all-new Eldorado, are found on all Cadillacs this year.

Eldorado, left, is built as 2-door hardtop only, features front-wheel drive system similar to that introduced last year on Olds Toronado.

Eldorado and Fleetwood Brougham, luxury leader of '67 Cadillac line, are contrasted in photo above. New front-wheel drive car has lights hidden behind sections of egg crate grille.

Front-wheel drive system of Eldorado has same basic arrangement of components as Olds Toronado introduced last year. Engine, however, is Cadillac unit displacing 429 cubic inches. Rated output is 340 horsepower at 4600 rpm.

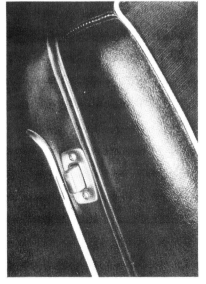

Safety latch on side of front seat back on 2-door models must be released before seat folds, prevents flopping.

In new Eldorado, door, window and mirror controls are gathered in neat cluster in driver's door. Car also features special flow-through ventilation, eliminating need for vent wings in doors. Eldorado is Cadillac's long-awaited personal car.

DRIVING THE '68 LUXURY SPECIALTY CARS

ELDORADO

The additional punch of the new 472-cu.-in. engine makes itself felt immediately when you touch the accelerator pedal. There's now enough torque available to spin the front wheels on the best of surfaces. But where the extra power is intended to be used — passing or accelerating into streams of fast-moving traffic — is where it will be most appreciated. Eldorado drivers who have wished for more when downshifting with the throttle can now find it there.

Although spring rates have been lowered (softened), it's almost unnoticeable on good surfaces. Poor ones produce less jolts than before.

RIVIERA

After taking a 1968 Riviera over some proving ground roads — especially designed to bring out the worst in a suspension — we came away convinced that the seemingly inconsequential changes made in the rear suspension really do make a difference. Rivieras have always been well-insulated, quiet cars, but the new one is practically immune to road noise.

If the emission-control-equipped engine in the car we drove was representative of what customers will be getting, some of the fears we had based on experience with other systems proved premature. General driveability and power were not noticeably affected by the presence of the smog modifications.

THUNDERBIRD

There's no major change in the '68 Thunderbird to set it drastically apart from '67 models. Ride and handling traits are the same as before. It is still an ideal car for pleasant journeying.

We drove several miles before noticing the biggest change for '68. We knew something was different, and finally noticed our 4-door had no center console or bucket seats. These are optional, but in standard form all T-birds are built for 6-passenger capacity with a full bench front seat.

We hardly noticed the new optional powerplant until raising the hood. It's a 429-cu.-in. V-8, rated at 360 hp, and was designed primarily to limit exhaust emissions. It is based on the thin-wall cast 289-cu.-in. Ford V-8. Being light, it doesn't burden the heavy T-bird front, while providing more than adequate power for the car.

CAR LIFE ROAD TEST

CADILLAC ELDORADO

An Admirable Flagship
For the Captain of Industry

IN CREATING its front-wheel-drive Eldorado, Cadillac Motor Car Division may well have generated yet another product category for today's much-segmented automotive market. Eldorado, though it borrows heavily from other GM products, seems already beyond the scope of today's luxury/specialty car concept; rather, it appears to be the sort of visually distinctive, tastefully luxurious, enormously expensive individualistic conveyance which characterized the Classic Era of automobile design.

Compare the Eldorado reviewed here with the classic Lincoln Continental (Pages 35–45). Overall aspects are remarkably similar. Both embody the long-hood, short-deck proportioning characteristic of the Classic Era cars. Both are ostensibly multi-passenger vehicles, though accommodation really best suits only the driver and a front-seat companion. Both utilize high performance (at least relatively) mechanical specification, although neither is actually an HP car. Both are, for their day, distinctively styled and expensively made.

However close a physical comparison may come, it remains for the senses to distinguish the ultimate relationship. Sight and touch say Eldorado is a classic car—a classic made in a modern manner of modern materials. Its appearance, tasteful and expensive, mirrors its owner/driver's good fortune and keen perception, and implies his social or financial status. By being both brisk and solidly constructed, the Eldorado imparts the same sort of feeling as a carefully machined block of platinum.

The Eldorado won't appeal to all owners of previous Cadillacs, for several reasons. The first is that it is visibly different—a stand-out—and thus distressing to those who require an expensive, yet homogenous conveyance. The second is that it doesn't offer the interior space, the luxuriously generous passenger accommodation of a standard Cadillac. A third reason is that the Eldorado simply may be too "sporting" in nature and radical in concept for the traditional Cadillac client.

However, *CL* believes Eldorado will encourage new customers, many of whom have spurned Cadillac for these reasons already cited.

Time was when Eldorado meant nothing more than a rococo convertible, overly adorned and tastelessly festooned with chromium knicknacks to set it apart from De Villes. In its 1967 form, it is a completely new model, similar to, but distinctly separate from, Calais and Fleetwood sedans and hardtops. Similarity ends at mere resemblance. No exterior panels are interchangeable. Certain mechanical components, such as engine, power steering, and various accessories, are interchangeable, though their specific arrangement is not at all similar. In actuality, the Eldorado relates more closely to Oldsmobile Toronado than any other vehicle.

IN THIS DAY and age, a front-drive system can be both luxury and necessity. In the case of Cadillac, Oldsmobile and certain European products, it becomes a luxury because its application accrues few benefits over those of an equally as expensive rear-drive system. In the case of much-smaller English and French cars, in which space and cost are factors controlled with fanatical care, front drive becomes a distinct advantage and is widely used. However, front-wheel drive can be a salable entity, in the name of mechanical extravagance, when the competing automobiles offer only the same old conventional rear-drive layout. With Toronado and Eldorado, front-wheel drive elevates them from the ruck.

Front drive, in the Cadillac/Oldsmobile-developed idiom, is so slick and smooth that a driver is hard-pressed to distinguish which set of wheels really propels the car. Only the occasional, discordant screech of full-throttle tire slippage, or the massive understeer of brisk cornering, give away the front drivers. Saginaw's marvelous hydraulic power assistant effectively masks any other untoward steering activity that might irritate an owner. Yet, the owner *knows* it is there, and he knows that not every car has, or can have, front drive.

Cadillac, as does Oldsmobile, utilizes the General Motors-developed Turbo Hydra-Matic transmission as the major adaptive unit for front drive. By separating the planetary gearbox section of the transmission from its torque converter drive unit, and swinging the gearbox 180° so it lies beside the converter, the two can be reconnected by a 2-in. drive chain in a transfer case. A spiral bevel ring and pinion, which has a planetary differential section, bolts to the front of the transmission and drives the wheels through short shafts and constant velocity universal joints. This system is so soundly de-

SHARPLY EDGED taillights have their own protection, yet are surprisingly visible.

ELDORADO

signed and carefully constructed it earned for Oldsmobile, *CAR LIFE*'s "Award for Engineering Excellence."

Key to this drive train's smoothness are chain and sprocket components. Manufactured by the Morse Chain Co., which developed it in conjunction with Oldsmobile Division, the chain is of the inverted tooth "silent" type. Tooth shapes depart slightly from true involutes, in the interest of lashless, quiet operation. The "Hy-Vo," for high velocity, chain is 46.5 in. long, has a pitch of 0.375 in. and 124 links. Sprockets have bonded-in rubber cushioning devices to further drive line smoothness. Interestingly, this drive chain has no tensioning mechanism. New chains are run in on special fixtures to pre-stretch them; then, before assembly, the chains are carefully measured for length and matched to appropriate sprockets.

The resulting drive train is so tautly connected that power-on, power-off throttle actions do not create the odd-steering characteristics *CL* has discovered with virtually every other front-drive car it has tested. Even with its big 429-cu. in./340-bhp engine supplying the power, the Eldorado offers little clue to which wheels are the driven ones.

Engine adaptation to the fwd layout required a reshaped oil pan, some revised exhaust manifolds and accessory mounts, and revised engine bearers. These were made to create space for the fwd differential, and the drive shaft that runs under the sump.

Cadillac's only engine offering, for Eldorado as well as all other models, is the standard 429-cu. in. V-8. With 480 lb.-ft. of torque, it moves even the 5200-lb. Eldorado with an ease bordering upon alacrity. Though this might be considered a "smallish" engine in comparison to its contemporaries' displacements, such as the 462 cu. in. used in Lincolns and the 440 cu. in. in Chryslers, comparative outputs are quite similar.

Of thoroughly modern, short and rigid block design, this Cadillac V-8 was introduced with the 1963 models. However, it already has undergone one displacement enlargement from its original 390 cu. in. With cylinder bores of 4.13 in. on 4.59-in. centers, it would appear there is little room for expansion (the 462 Lincoln has 4.38-in. bores on 4.90-in. centers), particularly with a 4-in. stroke already in use. Should Cadillac require additional displacement to compete in the apparent cubic inch race, it might put into production some of the experimental V-12s it has developed in the past few years.

Current power production is well utilized with the 3.21:1 differential gearing, particularly in conjunction with the torque converter automatic. The axle ratio yields 25.9 mph per 1000 rpm of the engine, which puts the torque peak at 78 mph and the horsepower peak at something around 120. The torque curve is really broad and flat, so throughout the car's high gear speed range, it produces very strong power delivery. Cruising is effortless and silent at any speed selected.

THE TORQUE converter stator blades change pitch upon command from the throttle pedal to provide more, or less, torque multiplication at lower engine speeds. This improves passing potential, as well as initial acceleration, and is another reason why the Eldorado, despite its 4790-lb. curb weight, induces impressions of a powerful, lively car. Gear changes in the 3-speed planetary gearbox are so smooth on part-throttle acceleration as to be virtually imperceptible. Under full-throttle demand, the engine turns to 4500 rpm before gear changes occur, though even then the shift is smooth but firm.

In *CL*'s performance measuring, both manually selected and automatic shift points were tried; the automatic worked best every time. Incidentally, the combination of gearing, torque converter multiplication and engine power was potent enough to spin the front-drive tires, though these fat

CLASSIC PROPORTIONS give Eldorado a long hood and front fenders. Inserts in leading edges have only a cosmetic function.

UNDERHOOD VIEW is astounding for its vision of intertwined systems. Front drive, air conditioning, speed control add to complexity.

9.00-15s were being pressed onto the dry pavement by nearly 3200 lb. of the car's total test weight.

As suggested by its muscular litheness, the Eldorado is quite a good performer, both on the open highway and away from stoplights. Data panel figures show reasonably quick 0–60 acceleration, while the 30–70 mph passing figure reflects a definite agility through mid-range speeds. Tapley measurements indicate Eldorado won't be embarrassed at hillclimbing, particularly if one of the lower gears is selected. However, the non-measurable factors make the greatest impression for Eldorado—its great comfort at fast highway pacing, and its alacrity at in-town maneuvering.

Both the comfort and alacrity are aided by firm suspension and fast steering. Eldorado, because of its inordinate front end weight, has far stiffer than normal front springing. The front ride rate is 140 lb./in. where a normal Cadillac Calais, for example, has just 86 lb./in. The rear ride rate is 105, compared to 110 lb./in. Additionally, Eldorado has a 1.062-in. diameter anti-roll stabilizer, where Calais has an 0.815-in. bar. This combines to give Eldorado a stout roll resistance, thus permitting it to corner flatter and more surely than any previous Cadillac. An automatic leveling system also contributes to comfort and stability by maintaining rear-end elevation at its prescribed height despite variations of up to 500 lb. in the luggage compartment. Only once did the suspension systems show a flaw; a "freeway hop" front wheel oscillation was encountered as

CESSNA 310K... Cadillac of the air

Cessna 310K courtesy of Torbet Aviation, Orange Co. Airport, Santa Ana, Calif.

FOR MANY of the same reasons cited for Eldorado, the Cessna 310K rates classicism within the aviation field. Its design is functionally esthetic, its performance outstanding and its price, at $61,950, enormous. And, it enjoys repute and respect akin to that accorded Cadillac.

A pair of wing-mounted 470-cu. in. engines give the 310K sparkling performance. These fuel-injected, 6-cyl. Continentals develop 260 bhp at 2650 rpm and drive 81-in. constant-speed propellers. The 520-bhp total lifts even a fully loaded 310K (6 passengers, 5200 lb. gross) off the ground within 1500 ft. of its starting point and sends it clawing skyward at 1540 ft./min. Throttled back for cruising at 75% power, the 310K skims along at 222 mph, and can travel 1000 miles.

Such niceties as electrically operated, fully retractable landing gear, stabilizing wingtip fuel tanks of 102 gal. total capacity and thrust-augmenting exhaust systems help the 310K achieve its outstanding performance.

The 310 series' 12-year production history is indicative of the longevity of good design. Model-year improvements to the basic structure have refined overall performance and encouraged sales. —*The Editors*

WELL-DESIGNED instrument panel combines function with use, is deeply recessed for safety. Upholstery, padding, carpets are all finished in attractive black.

the Eldorado was driven at 65 mph on an inbound stretch of the Los Angeles Harbor Freeway.

An exclusive Cadillac feature, Saginaw Steering Gear Division's "variable ratio" power steering was instrumental in Eldorado's sports car handling quickness. In essence, the steering gear ratio varies from its nominal, overall, 16.3:1 reduction in the straight-ahead position, to something like 14:1 at full lock. This provides "slow" steering in the middle, where gross movements are not required, and "fast" steering at the edges, where quick response is most desirable. With only 2.7 steering wheel turns required to move the road wheels from full left lock to full right lock, Eldorado can be steered around corners, through sharp or sweeping bends, and into tight parking spaces with surprising facility.

The test Eldorado was fitted with Cadillac's newly optional power-assisted disc brakes and these proved a slight disappointment. Where *CL* testers had recorded decelerations of 23 and 21 ft./sec./sec. with the drum-braked Calais (Aug. '66), the disc-braked Eldorado's best was only 19 and 20 ft./sec./sec. Despite the mediocrity of these rates, the braking effort had superior modulation and the stops were both deft and predictable, without that annoying tendency toward rear wheel lock-up and tire skidding exhibited by the overly-sensitive drum system. Low-speed stops were particularly smooth and efficient.

OPTIMUM PASSENGER comfort long has been an overwhelmingly strong consideration for Cadillac interior design. The Eldorado's front bench has shaped "buckets" for individual seating and a pull-down armrest. With a 6-way power option on the front seat, and the tilting/telescoping steering wheel column, comfortable driving positions for almost anyone could be found, though *CL*'s tallest tester, at 6 ft. 3 in., had crewcut brushing headliner in even the lowest, farthest rearward position

1967 CADILLAC
FLEETWOOD ELDORADO

DIMENSIONS
Wheelbase, in.	120.0
Track, f/r, in.	63.5/63.0
Overall length, in.	221.0
width	79.9
height	53.8
Front seat hip room, in.	62.2
shoulder room	59.6
head room	37.9
pedal-seatback, max.	42.5
Rear seat hip room, in.	54.2
shoulder room	55.7
leg room	36.2
head room	37.7
Door opening width, in.	46.5
Floor to ground height, in.	13.0
Ground clearance, in.	7.3

PRICES
List, FOB factory............$6277
Equipped as tested............8061
Options included: AM-FM stereo radio, padded roof, seat belts, wsw tires, tinted glass, 6-way power seat, climate control, headlamp control, tilt/telescope steering wheel, power door locks and rear vents, front disc brakes, emission controls.

CAPACITIES
No. of passengers	6
Luggage space, cu. ft.	13.5
Fuel tank, gal.	24.0
Crankcase, qt.	5.0
Trans./diff., pt.	24.0/n.a.
Radiator coolant, qt.	18.2

CHASSIS/SUSPENSION
Frame type: Boxed perimeter/integral.
Front suspension: Independent by s.l.a., ball joints, torsion bar springs, telescopic shock absorbers, link-type stabilizer.
 ride rate at wheel, lb./in. ... 140
 antiroll bar dia., in. ... 1.062
Rear suspension: Single-leaf springs, beam axle, horizontal and vertical shock absorbers.
 ride rate at wheel, lb./in. ... 105
Steering system: Power assisted varying ratio rack/piston with concentric valve; parallelogram linkage.
 gear ratio ... 16.0
 overall ratio ... 16.3
 turns, lock to lock ... 2.7
 turning circle, ft. curb-curb ... 41.3
Curb weight, lb ... 4790
Test weight ... 5200
Weight distribution, % f/r ... 60.9/39.1

BRAKES
Type: 2-circuit hydraulic; 4-piston caliper and radially vented discs, front; duo-servo shoes in finned drums, rear.
Front rotor, dia. x width, in. ... 11.00 x 1.25
Rear drum, dia. x width ... 11.0 x 2.0
 total swept area, sq. in. ... 360
Power assist ... integral, vacuum
line psi @ 100 lb. pedal ... 1100

WHEELS/TIRES
Wheel size ... 15 x 6JK
 optional size available ... none
 bolt no./circle dia., in. ... 5/5.00
Tires: Goodyear Power Cushion
 size ... 9.00-15
 recommended inflation, psi. ... 24/22
 capacity rating, total lb. ... 5680

ENGINE
Type, no. cyl. ... ohv, 90° V-8
Bore x stroke, in. ... 4.13 x 4.00
Displacement, cu. in. ... 428.466
Compression ratio ... 10.5
Rated bhp @ rpm ... 340 @ 4600
 equivalent mph ... 120
Rated torque @ rpm ... 480 @ 3000
 equivalent mph ... 78
Carburetion ... Rochester, 1x4
 barrel dia., pri./sec. ... 1.375/2.250
Valve operation: Hydraulic lifters, pushrods, overhead rockers.
 valve dia., int./exh. ... 1.875/1.50
 lift, int./exh. ... 0.44/0.44
 timing, deg. ... 39-109, 86-62
 duration, int./exh. ... 328/328
 opening overlap ... 101
Exhaust system: Dual with single outlet.
 pipe dia., exh./tail ... 2.00/2.24
Lubrication pump type ... spur gear
 normal press.@ rpm ... 30-35 @ 1600
Electrical supply ... alternator
 ampere rating ... 55 @ 12 V
Battery, plates/amp. rating ... 13/73

DRIVE TRAIN
Transmission type: Torque converter chain-driven planetary gearbox.
Gear ratio 3rd (1.00) overall ... 3.21
 2nd (1.48) ... 4.75
 1st (2.48) ... 7.95
 1st x t.c. stall (2.00) ... 15.9
Shift lever location ... column
Differential type: Planetary, front wheel drive.
 axle ratio ... 3.21

available. For the more average-sized, however, the front seat accommodations are particularly comfortable. Rear seat passengers won't be as happy, mainly because knee room is somewhat restricted, and because of the low seat height used to insure adequate head room. These slightly cramped rear quarters can be viewed as a sacrifice to the handsome proportioning and neo-classic appearance of the overall automobile.

Cadillac interiors—and Eldorado shares appointments and components with others in the Fleetwood series—have come to be particularly tasteful, well designed and well made in the past half-dozen years. Typical of this design excellence is the instrument panel and its protective glass cover. The speedometer is a huge, immensely readable instrument with white lettering on matte black background, flanked to its left by a vertical stack of warning lights clearly labeled as to which malfunction they are to signal. Fuel supply and coolant temperature also are reported by quantitative gauges. A clock is at the right. Protecting all this is a remarkable covering, concave and obviously made of non-reflecting glass. There was absolutely no instrument panel glare, day or night. Small items? Yes, but close attention to such detailing over the years has become a Cadillac hallmark.

TRUNK SPACE is all carpeted and flat, and is sufficient for a half-dozen golfbags or large suitcases. Filler/latch projection raises lift-over height significantly.

Eldorado carries a base price of $6277 and one as well equipped as the *CL* test car lists at $8061 (plus taxes, licensing fees and shipping costs). Though not everyone can afford such a car, there seems to be a sufficient number of customers who can: Production is currently 1900 cars per month and dealers report back-orders stacked 3 months deep. Eldorado is giving Cadillac its greatest-ever sales, despite a generally soft and receding automobile market. Obviously, Antoine de la Mothe Cadillac, the French explorer and founder of Detroit, has at last found *El Dorado,* the legendary land of gold. ∎

CAR LIFE ROAD TEST

CALCULATED DATA
Lb./bhp (test weight)	15.3
Cu. ft./ton mile	110
Mph/1000 rpm (high gear)	25.9
Engine revs/mile (60 mph)	2310
Piston travel, ft./mile	1540
Car Life wear index	35.6
Frontal area, sq. ft.	23.5
Box volume, cu. ft.	541

SPEEDOMETER ERROR
30 mph, actual	29.9
40 mph	39.5
50 mph	49.0
60 mph	58.4
70 mph	68.2
80 mph	77.6
90 mph	88.2

MAINTENANCE INTERVALS
Oil change, engine, mo.	2
trans./diff.	24,000/none
Oil filter change	6000
Air cleaner service, mo.	6
Chassis lubrication	6000
Wheelbearing re-packing	as req.
Universal joint service	none
Coolant change, mo.	24

TUNE-UP DATA
Spark plugs	AC 44
gap, in.	0.035
Spark setting, deg./idle rpm	5/480
cent.max.adv.,deg./rpm	16/4000
vac. max. adv., deg./in. Hg.	25.5/18.25
Breaker gap, in.	0.016
cam dwell angle	28-32
arm tension, oz.	19-23
Tappet clearance, int./exh.	0/0
Fuel pump pressure, psi.	5.25-6.50
Rad. cap relief press., psi.	13.5-16.5

PERFORMANCE
Top speed (4600), mph	120
Shifts (rpm) @ mph, automatic	
3rd to 4th ( )	
2nd to 3rd (4400)	79
1st to 2nd (4400)	46

ACCELERATION
0-30 mph, sec.	3.2
0-40 mph	4.8
0-50 mph	6.7
0-60 mph	9.2
0-70 mph	12.3
0-80 mph	16.7
0-90 mph	23.5
0-100 mph	32.2
Standing ¼-mile, sec.	17.2
speed at end, mph	81
Passing, 30-70 mph, sec.	9.1

BRAKING
(Maximum deceleration rate achieved from 80 mph)
1st stop, ft./sec./sec.	19
fade evident?	no
2nd stop, ft./sec./sec.	20
fade evident?	no

FUEL CONSUMPTION
Test conditions, mpg	10.5
Normal cond., mpg	10-13
Cruising range, miles	240-312

GRADABILITY
4th, % grade @ mph	
3rd	10 @ 78
2nd	20 @ 50
1st	27 @ 34

DRAG FACTOR
Total drag @ 60 mph, lb.	195

ACCELERATION & COASTING (graph: MPH vs ELAPSED TIME IN SECONDS, showing 1st, 2nd, 3rd gear curves and SS ¼ coasting line)

STORY BY JOHN ETHRIDGE   COLOR BY BOB D'OLIVO

LUXURY SPECIALTY CARS

☐ Before the advent of the Luxury Specialty car (T-bird was first), the buyer who wanted something with more spice than the stolid domestic cars could offer, even in their most jazzed-up forms, had to go to something from overseas. These classy imports had strong esthetic appeal and stood out like Brigitte Bardot in a line of Twiggys at a bikini show. ☐ But all was not wine and roses with these machines because their creators hadn't taken conditions in this country into account. It was always with great trepidation that the luxury import owner left his pride and joy stand on an urban street or parking lot, because likely as not some nice old lady, parking with all the tenderness and care of a destroyer ramming a U-boat, would de-flower it before his errand was accomplished. ☐ Besides having to replace and straighten flimsy bumpers and sheetmetal, frequent trips to the repair shop were necessary because these cars were very finicky compared to most of the domestics. And all too often garage owners, assuming anyone who would drive such a car to be rich and foolish — and hence fair game, turned into Black Barts in shop coats and indulged in outright banditry. ☐ In addition to this group whose contretemps with foreign thoroughbreds in the '50s and '60s reverted them toward Detroit iron, there was a much larger number with esthetic leanings but who were too firmly attached to the American way of motoring to consider an import. Walk-in doors, flower vases, lap warmers, and general stodginess of the home product were not qualities that endeared a car to a member of the latter group. It was things like reliability and durability, power accessories, air conditioning, and automatic transmissions that kept them buying American. ☐ The Luxury Specialty car that came to fulfill this market could, with a great deal of truth, be said to be the kind of car everyone would own provided it were cheap enough and there were no special space or use requirements. Motorists of just about any stripe can find among our test group a *now* car with pleasing and distinctive lines, good performance, and all the things that go to make a car enjoyable. ☐ The erstwhile exotic import fancier may give up a few mpg and, perhaps, some maneuverability for something otherwise much easier to live with. Likewise, the big luxury car driver will have to do with smaller luggage space and comfortable seating for four or five instead of five or six in some cases. But neither has to make any painful adjustments, and both readily agree that the Luxury Specialty car is an excellent compromise. ☐ The five cars in this class compete with one another in a sense but nothing like the head-on, feature-for-feature struggle we find in the Low-priced Specialty cars. Each has its own individuality or personality, so to speak. This holds true in spite of the fact that three of them — the Toronado, Riviera and Eldorado — share the same basic body shell and two — the Toronado and Eldorado — have almost identical fwd and suspension systems. ☐ Also there's a large price differential, depending on what optional equipment is ordered between the Grand Prix at the lower end and the Eldorado on top. So, strictly speaking, all don't compete pricewise, either. But this doesn't mean that one prospective buyer wouldn't consider all five before narrowing down his choice. In this class more than any other, buyers will unhesitatingly go up or down several

5 LUXURY SPECIALTY CARS

clockwise
from top left:
eldorado
thunderbird
toronado
riviera
grand prix
eldorado

thousand dollars to get the styling or some particular feature they want.

POWERTRAIN & PERFORMANCE

Since the Thunderbird and Grand Prix offer optional engines, we chose engines for them that were the nearest equivalent to sole engine offerings of the Toronado, Eldorado and Riviera. The resulting engine line-up is pretty evenly matched — within 5-cu.-in. displacement and 45 advertised hp. The Grand Prix, which comes standard with a 3-speed manual transmission and offers a 4-speed manual as an option, was ordered with the optional 3-speed automatic because all of the others have this type with no options.

The Riviera GS is the outstanding performer of the group, tested chiefly because of its 3.42 "performance" axle ratio. The standard 3.07 ratio produces performance more in line with that of the others. The Riviera lost none of its quietness, and the engine remained unobtrusive as ever in spite of the considerably higher numerical ratio. Undoubtedly the Star Performer would be a Grand Prix with the 428 HO engine (376 hp @ 5100 rpm). Maybe a GP with this optional romping, stomping powerplant and an automatic would still be tame enough to be considered in the Luxury Specialty class, but it definitely would be something else with a 4-speed and heavy clutch.

As can be seen from the spec table, all cars are highly satisfactory performers, although performance *per se* is not an overriding factor in this kind of car. Thunderbirds with the smaller 390, and GPs with the 400 engine, give somewhat improved economy and performance that is still more than adequate. With any optional or standard engine on any of the cars, relaxed cruising rpm with plenty of reserve power — both for accessories and passing — is the order of the day.

We almost forgot to mention that the Toronado and Eldorado do their driving with the front wheels. And that's a good indication of how noticeable it is. Only under unusual conditions like cornering much faster than normal do you feel anything different. Also, we noticed the fwd cars would move out smartly from a standstill on rain-drenched streets, while their conventional brethren tended to lag behind with churning rear wheels.

There was nothing in our experience with Ford's automatic transmission in the Thunderbird and GM's Turbo Hydra-Matic in the other cars to make us prefer one over the other. Each went about its business with quick, barely detectable shifts.

HANDLING, STEERING & STOPPING

With the exception of Thunderbird all cars in this group either come with stiffer-than-usual suspensions (Toronado and Eldorado) or offer some option in this department (Riviera's GS package and the GP's Ride and Handling package). Whether loyal T-birders would go for some sort of handling kit we can't say, but the car suffers in comparison to any of the others in this respect. It is *very* softly sprung and has almost no roll stiffness.

But such a suspension does have its virtues. At city speeds it smoothed out potholes, railroad crossings, etc., like none of the others. The Toronado and Eldorado suspensions tended to show their teeth under similar conditions.

The Grand Prix with standard suspension had an excellent ride, yet was stable and had reasonable steering response. To our way of thinking, the handling kit would make it more fun to drive, but the car is quite acceptable as is.

We can't decide whether the Riviera GS or Toronado has the best ride/handling combination, but the two of them are clearly ahead of the others in this regard. Both are truly superb road cars that beg to be cruised around 100 mph. They feel very secure and stable at high speeds and are practically immune to crosswinds, undulating surfaces, and other perturbations.

The Eldorado's suspension differs from the Toronado's in that it has lower rate (less stiff) rear springs paired with a load-leveler as standard equipment. Thus riding height and natural frequency stay pretty much constant with varying loads. Because tires are as much a part of the suspension as the springs, there's another difference. The Toronado uses a special low-profile tire while the Eldorado uses the same tire as the rest of the Cadillacs. The Toronado tire has a wider tread, and the low section height is more stable. Hence this tire puts more rubber on the road and keeps it there. The Eldorado has noticeably less cornering power and all-around traction than the Toronado for this reason. Disc brakes are practically a necessity on the Eldorado as stops from 60 mph in less than 200 feet are hard to come by with drums and these tires. The drum-braked Toronado stopped in about the same distance as the disc-braked Eldorado due to the difference in tires. From all indications a Toronado with discs should be a super stopper. Also, the rear wheels on the Eldorado had an annoying tendency to lock very early and cause fish-tailing when braking on wet surfaces, and again we can think of no reason except the tires.

The standard Thunderbird disc/drum combination is very well balanced and produces the ultimate in stopping power. What we've said that discs could be expected to do for the Toronado applies to some extent to the Grand Prix and Riviera, too: a further improvement in stopping, even though performance of their drums was very creditable.

SPACE, COMFORT & SAFETY

Space and comfort for a stated number of passengers is practically the name of the game with this class of car, and taken as a group they are probably safer than the average car on the road today. They are very kind to occupants — especially the driver — on extended trips, and it's pretty generally conceded that the fresh, alert driver is a safer driver.

Either fastback design and/or smallish rear windows tended to limit rearward visibility on all except the Grand Prix. But none was, in our opinion, restricted to the point of being hazardous, and with use of outside mirrors and the pivots in our neck, we had no difficulty determining when the coast was clear for lane changing.

BEST & WORST FEATURES

Trying to be objective about these cars proves to be as elusive as trying to do the same with another class of beguiling creatures — women. In looking back on our encounters with them we tend to remember not so much which was best or worst, just that in some ways some were better than others.

The big doors of the Riviera, Toronado and Eldorado qualify for both categories. They give good access to the rear seat, but need lots of room to swing open.

The best feature of the Eldorado, which has many nice accessories including a fine AM-FM Multiplex Stereo, has nothing to do with any of these. It's the awesome respect and prestige value accorded it by persons from all walks of life. After observing the effect it had on a great many onlookers we're convinced that, in this country at least, there's no car made anywhere at any price that equals it in this respect. Its worst features are the tires and the bent rear window that puts a sinister sneer on the grille of any car approaching from behind.

The T-bird's flabby suspension is its biggest drawback, and the good brakes and availability of a smart appearing 4-door are the best things it has going for it. The Grand Prix is the only one of the bunch offering a full choice of engine and driveline options as well as a convertible body style.

Flow-through ventilation (which we're sold on) and absence of front vent panes was a feature on all five cars. The missing vents and placement of the door-locking buttons on some of the cars probably won't stop a determined thief, but it will tend to separate the professionals from the joy-riders.

ELDORADO GRAND PRIX
THUNDERBIRD RIVIERA
TORONADO

Leather buckets are optional on Eldorado but bench shown here has fold-down center armrest, serves same function and has proved most popular. Grand Prix, shown with standard buckets, offers bench option. T-bird 4-door brings you luxurious expanded-vinyl tufted fabric, vinyl trim. Vinyl-interiored Riviera comes standard with tilt wheel — a needed option on others for complete comfort. Toronado in leather-textured vinyl has neat, designed-for-this-car look about its interior furnishings.

PHOTOS BY BOB D'OLIVO, GERRY STILES

	Eldorado	Grand Prix	Riviera GS	4-Door Thunderbird	Deluxe Toronado
PERFORMANCE					
Acceleration (2-aboard)					
0-60 mph (secs.)	9.5	8.4	7.8	9.0	8.9
¼-mile (secs.)	17.0	16.1	15.9	16.8	16.6
Speed at end of ¼-mile (mph)	81	87	86	86	85
Mph per 1000 rpm	23.7	27.0	22.6	25.0	25.3
Stopping Distances					
From 30 mph (ft.)	41	40	38	40	38
From 60 mph (ft.)	165	167	165	143	168
Speedometer Error (%)	+3	+2	0	0	+3
Gas Mileage Range (mpg)	10-13	10.5-14.5	10-13.5	10-13.5	10-13
SPECIFICATIONS					
Engine Type	V-8	V-8	V-8	V-8	V-8
Bore & Stroke (ins.)	4.13x4.00	4.12x4.00	4.19x3.90	4.13x3.98	4.12x3.97
Displacement (cu. ins.)	429	428	430	428	425
Horsepower @ rpm	340@4600	360@4600	360@5000	345@4600	385@4800
Torque (lbs.-ft. @ rpm)	480@3000	472@3200	475@3200	462@2800	480@3200
Compression Ratio	10.5:1	10.5:1	10.25:1	10.5:1	10.5:1
Carburetion	1 4-bbl	1 4-bbl	1 4-bbl	1 4-bbl	1 4-bbl
Transmission Type	3-spd. Auto	3-spd. Auto	3-spd. Auto	3-spd. Auto	3-spd. Auto
Final Drive Ratio	3.21	2.93	3.42	3.00	3.21
Steering					
Type	Variable-Ratio Power	Power	Power	Power	Power
Turning Dia. Curb-to-Curb (ft.)	41.3	42.8	42.3	42	43
Turns Lock-to-Lock	2.6	4.2	3.57	3.68	3.4
Wheel Size	15x6JK	14x6JK	15x6L	15x5.5JK	15x6JK
Tire Size	9.00x15	8.55x14	8.45x15	8.15x15	8.85x15
Brakes	Opt. Disc/Drum	Drum	Drum	Std. Disc/Drum	Drum
Fuel Capacity (gals.)	24	26.5	25	24.1	24
Usable Trunk Capacity (cu. ft.)	13.46	19.4	10.32	12.3	14.1
Curb Wt. (lbs.)	4680	4400	4420	4640	4800
Dimensions					
Wheelbase (ins.)	120.0	121.0	119.0	117.0	119.0
Front Track (ins.)	63.5	63.0	63.5	62.0	63.5
Rear Track (ins.)	63.0	64.0	63.0	62.0	63.0
Length (ins.)	221	215.6	211.3	209.4	211.0
Width (ins.)	79.9	79.4	79.4	77.3	78.5
Height (ins.)	53.8	54.2	53.2	53.8	52.8
PRICES AND ACCESSORIES					
Manufacturer's suggested retail	$6277.00	$3549.00	$4791.88	$4858.25	$4869.00
Optional Engine	—	(428 V-8) 78.99	—	(428 V-8) 90.68	—
Air Conditioning	515.75	419.60	421.00	421.49	421.28
Automatic Transmission	Std.	226.44	Std.	Std.	Std.
AM Radio	161.60	82.25	NA	NA	86.89
AM-FM Radio	187.90	124.20	175.24	89.94	173.78
AM-FM Stereo	287.90	225.00	266.81	163.77	238.03
Stereo Tape	NA	116.00	115.00	128.49	128.49
Vinyl Roof	131.60	105.32	115.78	Std.	110.59
Power Windows	Std.	104.00	105.25	103.95	104.00
Power Seat	83.15	94.79	94.73	97.32	94.79
Power Steering	Std.	105.25	Std.	Std.	Std.
Disc Brakes	105.25	110.50	78.94	Std.	78.99
Speed Control	94.75	44.95	63.15	129.55	84.26
Tinted Glass	50.55	42.10	42.10	47.49	47.39

NEW CADILLAC AND OLDSMOBILE

There are few external changes to the front-wheel-drive Cadillac Eldorado but a completely new 7.7-litre engine under the hood

FOLLOWING the Buick and Pontiac styling and engineering changes for 1968, General Motors have now released details for Oldsmobile and Cadillac. Chevrolet's new models will be announced next week.

The main story from both the prestige (Cadillac) end and the popular (Oldsmobile) ranges concerns engines. Cadillac have increased the capacity of their vee-8 from 7,031 c.c. to 7,736 c.c., making it the biggest unit in production in the world for passenger cars. Maximum gross power is up from 340 to 375 b.h.p. and torque is increased from 480 to 525 lb.ft.

Every part of the engine except four small components is new and it has taken three years and over two million test miles to develop it for production. To comply with the new Federal controls on pollution the new unit has an integral distribution system for air injection into the exhaust: Mountings for air conditioning equipment are also built into the structural castings for the first time. Last year 88.4 per cent of Cadillacs were ordered with air conditioning.

Cadillac buyers expect a few gimmicks and the latest is a buzzer which sounds in addition to a red tell-tale lighting if the engine temperature rises for any reason.

Much of the construction of the new engine has been simplified to reduce the number of joints and gaskets, and the bottom end has been generally beefed up with stiffer crank and a 24 per cent increase in bearing surface area. The camshaft has been designed by computer.

Unlike Rolls-Royce and Mercedes, who compete most closely with Cadillac in the large, luxury car markets of the world, Cadillac production is high and last year nearly 200,000 were built of which some 72 per cent were the DeVille models.

Externally the new Cadillacs have only small changes to grilles and lamp clusters, with new internal fittings on the general safety theme. Wipers park out of sight and there are the new GM side marker lamps on each front wing.

OLDSMOBILE

There has been an integrated design policy carried out by Oldsmobile for two years to design a complete power train from engine to wheels. The objectives have been better economy, more usable performance, less noise and vibration and a reduction in exhaust emissions. The way to this end has been to raise overall gearing and design the engine to rev less. To gain performance, engine size has been increased from 6.9 to 7.5 litres and final drive ratios are raised from 3.08 to 2.56 to 1. This cuts the revs at 90 m.p.h. from 3,400 to 2,840 r.p.m. and at 30 m.p.h. the 1968 model is revving at only 950 r.p.m.

In order to make this reduction a special "low duration" camshaft has been designed to bring the peaks for the torque and power curves down a few hundred r.p.m. This plus the capacity rise brings the values down from 365 at 4,800 to 365 at 4,600 for b.h.p. and from 470 at 3,200 to 510 at

3,000 for the torque in lb.ft.

To give better acceleration as well, the torque converter ratio of the automatic gearbox has been raised from 1.8 to 2.3 to 1. This puts the maximum bottom gear ratio up from 13.7 to 14.6 to 1 despite the change in final drive.

To reduce exhaust emissions Oldsmobile are using their "climatic combustion control", with pre-heated air and careful carburation and ignition regulation. This was introduced as an option last year.

Other changes to Oldsmobiles are of a styling nature with a new front for the Toronado and some major revisions to the Vista Vision estate car. ∎

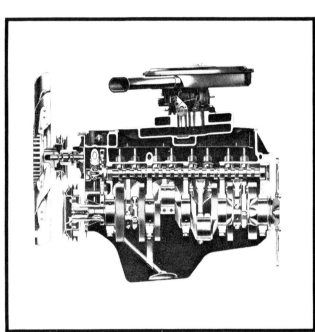

Top right: This is the high-performance Oldsmobile 4-4-2 with restyled body and side stripes. Above: Section through the new Cadillac engine showing the stiff crank and generous bearings. Below: Striking new front for the Oldsmobile Toronado

CADILLAC FOR 1968

Biggest engines in the industry and subtle styling changes for newest "standard of the world"

CADILLAC'S ALL-NEW 472-cid engine is the firm's big news for 1968. The new engine is rated at 375 bhp, with an astounding 525 lb.-ft. of torque. Both displacement and torque are new highs for passenger cars. Accompanying the new powerplant are detail improvements in drive train, including abandonment of variable-pitch torque converter and lower ratio, and stronger final drive gears. Apparently, the added torque available from the new engine makes it possible to use a fixed-pitch converter without sacrificing flexibility. Also, a 2.94:1 axle ratio is utilized, permitting high-speed cruising at lower engine speeds.

Styling changes follow the traditional Cadillac pattern. Changes are in the form of minor evolutionary developments, rather than sweeping revisions. Overall length is increased by 0.7 in.; all other major dimensions remain the same as in 1967. Standard Cadillacs receive all-new grilles, and a 6.5-in. longer

STANDARD-SIZED 1968 Cadillacs incorporate minor styling changes. New hood is much longer than 1967, accommodating concealed windshield wipers and projecting longer, more pointed grille shape.

FENDER-TIP parking lights replace steel blockoff plates in 1968 Eldorado front fenders. Turning lights and rear-quarter medallions provide side illumination required by 1968 federal safety legislation.

hood. Hidden windshield wipers increase visual hood length and clean up overall appearance. New rear bumpers, side trim and wheel covers complete 1968 facelifting.

Cadillac's front-wheel-drive Fleetwood Eldorado has been restyled with a lengthened hood which accommodates concealed windshield wipers, provision for side illumination at night, and new taillights.

Inside the 1968 Cadillacs, the picture is similar to the rest of the domestic industry. Safety considerations dictated all-new instrument panels, incorporating crushable structural components, extensive application of padding, and recessed controls. Padded windshield pillars, breakaway inside rearview mirror, and new-for-Cadillac molded door trim panels with recessed door and window controls complete major interior changes.

But the major change for 1968 is the new 472-cid/375-bhp Cadillac V-8 engine. This engine incorporates several clever innovations, primarily aimed at improving durability, decreasing noise and vibration, and reducing the total number of engine parts. The impressive displacement figure is rumored to be only a hint of the true potential of the new engine, with a maximum of 600 cid supposedly possible through bore and stroke increases. Surprisingly, although the new engine obviously is much larger internally than the 1967 engine, exterior dimensions remain nearly identical. Engine weight is up approximately 80 lb., largely because of increased cylinder wall thickness. The new heavier wall sections reportedly decrease noise transmittal from the engine.

Bore and stroke dimensions of the new engine are 4.30 and 4.06 in., respectively, compared to the 1967 engine's 4.13 in. bore and 4.00 in. stroke. The 43-cu. in. displacement gain yields 35 bhp and 45 lb.-ft. of torque over 1967. Peak power is developed at 4400 rpm, 200 rpm lower than in 1967. Thus, the new engine appears capable of providing a higher performance level while remaining quieter and smoother.

Major castings have been completely redesigned to include emission control air injection passages within the basic cylinder head, and incorporate coolant crossover and thermostat passages in the cylinder block casting. These changes, along with the utilization of GM Research's new hydrodynamic oil seals, provide a large measure of insurance against fluid leaks. Interior components of the engine reflect current metallurgical developments, highlighted by a cast ductile-iron crankshaft and cast Armasteel connecting rods.

Since air conditioning is ordered on a very large percentage of Cadillacs, the division has cleverly included compressor mounting brackets in the basic cylinder block casting. A new temperature warning device that senses metal, rather than coolant, temperature provides much earlier warning of excessive engine temperatures. The new sensor allows engine shutdown before major damage occurs, an advantage not enjoyed by previous water-temperature devices.

Crankshaft stiffness, bearing area, and piston skirt length were all increased in the new engine, promising exceptionally long life and minimum noise level. Oil economy has received attention in the new Cadillac engine, both in redesigned piston rings and in a cylinder bore finish developed through the radioisotope oil economy test program developed by GM Research and Cadillac.

Improved serviceability has been achieved by a self-contained, single unit oil pump and oil filter mounting directly on the cylinder block. Also, the distributor is now mounted in the front of the engine, easing service and installation. Camshaft design is computer-determined, for minimum valve train noise and maximum operating efficiency. All 11 of the 1968 Cadillac models use the new engine, in a single state of tune.

Thus 1968 is a year of major change for Cadillac, but the change is largely invisible to the casual observer. To the serious examiner, however, it will be apparent that Cadillac has incorporated myriad refinements and radical changes that promise substantially longer life, superior comfort and safety, and greater freedom from noise and vibration. All in all, these add up to a worthwhile set of modifications to an already excellent passenger car line. For 1968, even more than previous years, attention to infinitesimal details and utilization of latest technological advances should reinforce Cadillac's long-advertised position as the Standard of the World. ■

TREMENDOUS TORQUE is the prime characteristic of Cadillac's all-new 472-cid/375-bhp engine. Although internally huge, 1968 engine is externally compact, essentially identical to 429-cid 1967 engine. Many former bolt-on accessories are incorporated into basic block. New door trim panels, below, mark first use of 1-piece, molded panel by Cadillac. Panels are standard on full-sized models.

COMPARATIVE SPECIFICATIONS

	1968	1967
Displacement, cid	472	429
Horsepower@rpm	375@4400	340@4600
Torque, lb./ft.	525@3000	480@3000
Bore x stroke	4.30x4.06	4.13x4.00
Compression ratio	10.5:1	10.5:1

A lot of little additions and subtle styling changes add up to a new driving experience.

ELDORADO LUXURY-PLUS FROM CADALLIC

It's probably due to the volume of advertising over the years, but mention executive cars and Cadillac automatically pops into our mind. It's sort of a reflex action. Filling the bill again this year is the Eldorado, part of the Fleetwood series.

Our first reaction to the car was visual. The Eldorado is striking with clean, crisp, distinctive lines that blend classic and modern themes into a tasteful unit. There's a lack of unnecessary chrome bits that gives the Eldorado an elegant look, one of the major criteria for a luxury car. It's long (wheelbase is 121 inches) and big, but avoids looking bulky.

Inside, the Eldorado has a new dash layout that was prompted largely by Federal safety legislation. Padding abounds and adds to the soft, comfortable look associated with Cadillacs. There's lots of glass and a minimum of posts (no vent windows), yet a feeling of security is very much present.

Driving the Eldorado is effortless. A new engine standard on all Cadillac cars for '68 displaces 472 cubic inches and produces 525 foot pounds of torque, both figures the highest in the industry. Coupled with the excellent General Motors Turbo Hydra-Matic transmission and a 3.07 rear axle ratio, the engine puts out constant power for normal driving with plenty in reserve for highway speeds.

We enjoyed driving the Eldorado for a lot of little reasons. The new hood is 4-1/2 inches longer than last year to provide cover for the new windshield wiper system, one of the little things we liked. The new wipers cover a greater area of the windshield, particularly at the base of the windshield pillars. And there's a brake failure

executive swingers

New Eldorado has subtle changes: new parking lights at front of fenders, longer hood, side marker lights fore and aft. It's elegant luxury from beginning to end.

warning system standard on the Eldorado. Most Eldorado owners will never need it, but it's nice to know it's there. Same thing is true of the new metal temperature monitoring device. When the engine overheats, a buzzer sounds and a red warning light is activated.

Add front wheel disc brakes and anything you like from the long list of luxury extras (stereo, AM-FM radio, headrests, etc.) and you'll be off in the land of the "Executive Swingers." It's a great world to be in.

Potent engine is new for '68, displaces 472 cubic inches. Torque abounds (525 ft/lbs), is largest of any passenger vehicle as is displacement.

The Most Wanted Car In The World

From Papeete to Petrograd the Cadillac El Dorado is wooed like a beautiful woman. But is it that good?

The El Dorado is the concept of GM styling chief Bill Mitchell. Unlike other Cadillacs it doesn't try to disguise the fact that it is a car.

With headlight doors closed, the egg-crate grill presents a smooth plane. Leading edge of front fenders contain parking lights.

ONE CADILLAC DEALER we know hasn't been asked for a demonstration ride in his recent memory. Another reports that most of his orders are placed by phone. Nationwide, a vast majority of customers are repeat buyers and they repeat with cash. Most add at least $1200 worth of extras to a sticker that starts at $5500 plus tax.

We speak here of ordinary Cadillacs, cars that have ranged the gamut down through the years from bechromed, finny garishness to conservative versions of the same whale-like proportions. They have always sold well (70% of their market) and each year is better, saleswise, than the last. Owners may be typed in the sense of their $25,000 median annual income and their 53-year median age, but it's for sure that they can't be typed as automotive enthusiasts — that is, until now.

This isn't to say that enthusiasts haven't recognized and appreciated certain virtues common to all Cadillacs. First, the economics of owning one, once you absorb the shock of the initial fling, are easier on the pocketbook than most anything but a Volkswagen. Cadillac's re-sale value is second to none, percentage-wise. Then, there is the very large helping of superior engineering, items like the installation of balanced sets of pistons in an air-conditioned room, without which the beast would be a slug. Finally, there are the almost soporific standards of automation and quiet that must be admired although not necessarily desired by everyone.

The fwd Eldorado offers its full measure of all these qualities plus a styling extra defined by professionals as the "membrane effect." This is a GM-evolved configuration that might be likened to older private aircraft where the fabric skin was stretched over tubes that formed the fuselage. It's referred to as a "profile" rather than a "highlight" form, the Camaro being an example of the latter and the Mustang a blend of the two. The Eldorado, despite its size, is also a splendid example of the 2+2 pony shape, although here the long hood is a carry-over from the original engineering plan to power the car with two V-8's set in tandem. This idea was abandoned due to problems involved with transmitting the torque from one engine to the other. In any case, the project was GM chief stylist Bill Mitchell's first real chance to put the Cadillac nameplate on a true enthusiast's car since he created the original Sixty-Special back in 1938. Unlike other Cadillacs, the Eldorado doesn't try to disguise the fact that it is a car.

It is certainly the most sought after car on the U.S. market today and has been since its introduction in September of 1966. A measure of its scarcity is that each of Cadillac's 1600 dealers at any given time will have 4.5 days' supply of Eldorados on hand. This figure is an academic measure, however, because if each dealer sold Eldorados at this rate orders taken would exceed production possible by a factor of nearly five to one. The single assembly line in Detroit is capable of not much more than 20,000 units a year. The fact is that urban areas and most particularly Southern California account for the bulk of Eldorado sales.

Their popularity in the home of show business is as understandable as when years ago the likes of Clark Gable and Gary Cooper favored SJ Duesenbergs. While no one claims that the Eldorado is a suitable substitute for the luscious automotive hardware available in the classic 'thirties, it will certainly stand comparison to a current Rolls and it doesn't, like the Excalibur, pretend to be something it isn't. A standard Cadillac may still be a status symbol in Dallas but Hollywood is more concerned with image, however transient. A disproportionate share of the town's resident personalities may

While the El Dorado is 10 in. longer than the Toronado, trunk overhang is not excessive. Wheelbase is 120 in.

The El Dorado trunk is roomy but not cavernous. The low lip line permits easy loading. Capacity is 13.5 cu. ft.

fairly be called automotive enthusiasts but it is an enthusiasm that ignores "accepted" standards, past and present. Thus you'll find Jim Garner and Dan Blocker sponsoring race cars, Elvis Presley the owner of an interstate bus converted into a $40,000 motor home and Phyllis Diller, who is as genuinely eccentric offstage as on, incongruously garaging two Excaliburs.

Although many could afford it, few if any of the current stars seriously collect antique and classic cars any more than they would give house room to a bed once slept in by Rudolph Valentino. Cars are discarded with little more thought than last month's wardrobe. Ferrari and Lamborghini may still be *de rigueur* for the expatriates filming in Rome but in Hollywood the car of the moment is the fwd Eldorado. Just a sampling of owners includes Paul Weston, Steve Crane, Dick Martin and Jack Cassidy. Red Skelton wanted one but the Palm Springs Caddy dealer understandably refused to give him the Eldorado plus cash for his "pre-owned" Rolls. If pop music groups could cram their instruments into an Eldorado, demand would undoubtedly spurt even more, a factor that may have some influence on customizer George Barris's plan to begin limited production of a stretched Eldorado limousine.

As it stands, Southern California is absorbing 12% of Eldorado production and since there aren't nearly this many affluent actors and actresses about, a search for the explanation turned out to be interesting. It also indicated that if Cadillac is truthful about the claim that its owners have a median income of $25,000, then this group must be about equally divided between millionaires and ordinary folk — highly ordinary folk. For example, one Los Angeles Cadillac dealer, located some distance from the normal shopping orbit of the stars, reports a typical Eldorado transaction, this one to a working couple whose occupations were ambulance driver and clerk-typist, respectively. They received a $3450 allowance for their '65 Caddy, less the $785 still owed on it. Somehow the couple produced $1626 more in cash, took on two "pick-up" payments of $175 each and contracted to pay $185 a month for 36 months. The car stickered at $8890, a total about equal to the market value of their small home in Los Angeles' pin-neat but modest Wilshire district. Including this sale the same dealer has placed *eight* Eldorados on the *one block* where this couple live! At these prices and the resultant, obvious sacrifice of any other expenditure that might abet the good life for the next 36 months, it would seem apparent that Cadillac, and Eldorado in particular, enjoys a certain priority of desire in the hearts of working man and star alike.

There may come a day when Eldorados will be discounted like any other car, including standard Cadillacs, but it hasn't happened yet. In fact, it has only been recently that dealers are spared the temptation of "under-the-table" money offered by customers who wanted priority on the original two-month waiting list. It's more like a few weeks now, a relatively normal situation for a car that is essentially built to order. You have a choice between 21 different paints, five vinyl top options and no less than 147 upholstery combinations.

Buyers on the overseas black markets, though, will take any Eldorado they can get. In Brazil and Argentina the going price is $18,000 (U.S.), with about half representing the actual price of the car and half disappearing into the pockets of the enterprising individuals who somehow arrange these illegal transactions. The problem is not so much getting the car physically into South

The wide doors permit easy entry and exit for both the front and rear seats. Power windows, power seats and disc brakes are standard.

Luxury car owners, driving the El Dorado for the first time will never know by its feel whether he is being propelled by the front or rear wheels.

American countries that are trying to protect their own auto industries, but explaining its presence thereafter. In Switzerland or Iran, where it is just a matter of ponying up a legitimate tax, you might get an Eldorado for $15,000. Cadillac, however, is not pushing exports for a variety of reasons ranging from subtle State Department disapproval of any flamboyant expression of Yankee affluence (U.S. embassies in most poorer countries are now being supplied with Checker, not Cadillac, cars) to the very real problem of providing service and parts. Rolls-Royce counters the latter by dispatching a factory mechanic to the scene of the trouble, no matter how distant, but this is not the GM way of doing things.

The odds are very good that you will ride in a Cadillac at least once during your stay on earth for the reason that a great majority of hearses are mounted on an elongated chassis produced especially for this purpose. Accompanying you will be your survivors in Cadillac limousines, another commodity that's a Cadillac monopoly by default. Even the hearse, as if the occupant of honor cared, has standard electric windows, automatic transmission, power brakes and steering, and air conditioning. So, it is only fair to question how an exciting car like Eldorado was brought into being by an enterprise that in more respects than one, could be suspected of being operated by the Addams family.

Meeting the four men most responsible for the car, though, quickly gave the answer to this seeming paradox. Cadillac's general manager at the time, Harold Warner, had the critical task of selling the fwd Eldorado idea to corporate management. Weighing against it was the sales disaster of Cadillac's previous venture into the ultra-luxury field, the incredibly complex $13,000 Eldorado Brougham of circa 1957-59. On the plus side Cadillac's overall operations consistently down through the years have turned in a higher margin of profit than any division in the GM empire. Cadillac was in a position, in other words, to pretty much write its own ticket. Also on the plus side was Warner's own enthusiasm for esthetic and engineering superiority. Backing him in the Eldorado project was his head wrench, engineer Carl Rasmussen, who is one of the rare breed that can design a hearse or a Formula I racing car with equal skill and dedication. Finally, as we've said, stylist Bill Mitchell longed to place the Cadillac nameplate on a car aimed to attract those who were wont to say that the Lincoln-Continental was the only modern-day "classic" on the market. In this effort, his thoughts were ably translated to paper, clay and finally metal by the head of the Cadillac studio, Chuck Jordan.

Though there is a natural tendency for those interested in engineering to compare the fwd Eldorado with Olds' Toronado that preceded it into production by a year, the resemblance is more one of concept, not hardware. Both are sprung in front by torsion bars and both drive the transmission mounted along the left side of the engine with a special rubberized chain connecting to the flywheel end. They both share what GM calls its "E" body shell but none of this togetherness is visible. Here, the comparison ends. The Eldorado uses Cadillac's all-new 472-CID V-8, the world's largest, and in terms of torque (525 lbs-ft) most powerful production passenger car engine. Its Turbo Hydra-Matic transmission is geared and valved differently and more expensively than the similar design used by Olds. No exterior sheet metal or interior trim is shared. Even in character they differ. The Toronado reminds one vaguely of a

Center arm rest for the bench type seat provides comfort for front passengers on a lengthy trip. Temperature gauge on dash has warning light and buzzer.

Pedal placement and design are in harmony with the entire package. Absence of transmission hump adds to room and comfort.

female Russian athlete whereas the Eldorado appears lean and lithe. The Toronado is a muscle car whereas the Eldorado is deliberately set up so that its owner, presumably long loyal to Cadillac, will never know whether he is being driven by the front or rear wheels. The Eldorado is 10 inches longer, one inch wider and higher but only 160 lbs. heavier. The nearly $2000 difference in base price is somewhat harder to explain unless you note Eldorado's extras, like power windows, seats and disc brakes that are standard. And, like Mercedes' three-pointed star, you're paying a fair premium for that Cadillac nameplate and the higher quality trim, finish and production methods that it is claimed to assure.

Examples of the latter abound in the air-conditioned area where Cadillac engines are assembled. Cylinder bores are honed to a tolerance of 0.0002 (two ten-thousandths) of an inch, the entire range between the smallest and largest bore. Each bore is then matched with a piston of the same size. This is the why of the air-conditioning because if the temperature in the room was allowed to vary, the different metals would change sizes at a different rate and the fit under these conditions would not be as exact. Final reliance is placed on man, though, rather than machine. Each completed engine, after it has finished its many tests, is hand cranked by a veteran inspector. If it feels "wrong" to him — he doesn't have to explain why — the unit is summarily rejected.

The interior of the Eldorado is designed primarily for four passengers although the car will hold six in comfort due to its flat floor. Bucket seats, at a whopping $342 surcharge, would hardly seem necessary as there is an arm rest in the standard bench. As was mentioned, upholstery combinations are almost limitless, a charge being made only when all leather or vinyl is specified. The instrument panel is identical to conventional Cadillacs and as in all luxury cars with the exception of the Imperial, there is more emphasis on warning lights than gauges. There is, for example, a gauge for temperature but on the theory that the average Cadillac owner won't look at it, an auxiliary warning light and buzzer are provided as well. The panel really is just another extension of Cadillac's philosophy that the typical owner prefers to be automated to the ultimate degree. Two accessory ideas, both ultimately victims of human foible, show how much effort is expanded to this end. One was the "memory" seat, offered for a while but abandoned because it caused family problems. The main driver, presumably the one who wore the trousers, could position the seat where he liked it best and set the control. The little woman following could then adjust it to her preference, but as soon as she exited the seat would go back to the original setting. The arguments this generated are obvious. The other idea was a timer that could be set to start the car, say 15 minutes before the owner planned to use it. Thus, in the winter the car would be pre-warmed; in the summer, pre-cooled. Unforeseen, though, was the reaction of passers-by who invariably would try to locate the owner of that car parked there, locked, unattended and with the engine running. The device was never put into production.

The true enthusiast, attracted to the fwd Eldorado by its good looks and engineering uniqueness, may have trouble adjusting to all the power assists. But adjust he must because most of them are standard, and actually some, quite delightful. An example is Cadillac's exclusive variable-ratio steering system. This gives a rather good feel of the road at normal speed but permits fingertip parking. Another is the parking brake, not so much because it automatically releases when the engine starts but because it can be used as a foot brake in the unlikely event of the dual-master system failing. It won't lock up with the car in gear and the engine running. Cadillac brakes have always been good, but the power assisted front discs on the Eldorado deserve to be called excellent. So, too, is the working of the automatic load leveller, sensitive even to a single

Rear seat leg room is superior to most because there is no drive-shaft tunnel. Designed to carry four passengers, six may be carried in relative comfort.

passenger in one or the other corner of the rear seat.

Another complaint sure to be voiced but possibly due for correction as Cadillac ventures further into this new, for it, market is the almost total lack of power-train options. You can't even order an alternate ratio in the differential, much less an extra carburetor or bit of compression for the engine. A console with a floor shift, much less an optional Muncie four-speed, has not even been considered. If you want stiffer springs or shocks, or a sway bar or two, you'll have to fabricate them yourself. Any tire other than a two-ply, four-ply-rated 9.00 x 15 will have to be arranged after you have taken delivery of the car. This latter situation is unfortunate because while the factory tires may be tops for bottoms on the interstate or in the city, the Eldorado is not properly shod for maximum acceleration, braking or cornering, particularly in inclement weather. In fact, the loudest noise you'll hear in the car will stem from these tortured tires.

Starting from a standard base that's pretty luxurious in its own right, the degree of creature comfort that may be achieved in an Eldorado is limited only by your wallet. The $516 automatic air-conditioner uses strategically located thermistors to maintain a constant temperature throughout the passenger compartment. For another $89.50 you can get a steering wheel that will both tilt and telescope. A superb AM/FM stereo radio is offered at $288 and there's even a seat warmer at $94.75. If you add every non-conflicting extra in the catalog, the total tag will be $8869.70 excluding local taxes and transportation, and that's the way most Eldorados are sold, including the one that went to the ambulance driver and his working wife.

The big new engine is not there just to make the car go faster. Its purpose is to provide a reserve of muscle for existing and future power accessories. According to engineer Rasmussen, the previous design was just about stretched to its limit on this score. You give it too much work to do and you start getting into vibration problems. Still, the 5000-lb. Eldorado can hardly be called a sloth. The performance figures shown in the accompanying table should be considered approximations because they were recorded with just a calibrated speedometer and stop watch, but they indicate the potential. The longer than average stopping distances may be blamed more on the tires than the brakes. Never once was there evidence of fade or pull. Luxury car owners who must do a lot of their driving on ice and snow should give the Eldorado serious consideration on that basis alone. In one of its ads, Volkswagen asks how the snowplow driver gets to work and the answer, were these people better paid, could with equal justification be in an Eldorado. The weight of the engine over the driving wheels, whether it be at the front or the rear, offers traction unknown to conventional cars in really bad weather. Nor, surprisingly, do chains on the front wheels create much of a fuss. You feel a little wheel chuckle from them, but not to a degree that's annoying.

In summary, the Eldorado is enough car to perhaps woo a few aging enthusiasts away from their Corvettes and Shelby-Mustangs. Driven expertly, it will get across the mountain within a few minutes of any car. It has the advantage of not yet having attracted the suspicions of the insurance industry, and a high quality of service is far more readily available than can be found for any luxury import. Depreciation already shows signs of being less than the conventional Cadillac, the standard of the industry at least in that sense. The Eldorado is a prudent investment.

Cadillac El Dorado

Data in Brief

DIMENSIONS

Overall length (in.)	221.0
Width (in.)	79.9
Height (in.)	53.8
Wheelbase (in.)	120.0
Tread front (in.)	63.5
Tread rear (in.)	63.0
Turning diameter (ft.)	41.3
Fuel tank capacity (gal.)	24.0
Trunk capacity (cu. ft.)	13.5

WEIGHT, TIRES, BRAKES

Weight (lb. w/o accessories)	4680
Tires	9.00 x 15
Brakes, front	disc
Brakes, rear	drum

ENGINE

Type	V-8
Displacement (cu. in.)	472
Horsepower	375
Fuel required	premium

SUSPENSION

Front	torsion bar
Rear	leaf spring

PERFORMANCE
ACCELERATION (2 occupants)

0-30 mph (sec.)	3.0
0-45 mph (sec.)	5.2
0-60 mph (sec.)	8.6
0-75 mph (sec.)	12.4

PASSING (2 occupants)

40-60 mph (sec.)	4.9
50-70 mph (sec.)	5.4
Standing ¼ mile (sec.)	16.8
Speed at end of ¼ mile (mph)	84.00

BRAKING

From 30 mph (ft.)	41
From 65 mph (ft.)	186

A Nationwide Survey Based on
1,000,000 Owner-Driven Miles

Too Rough a Ride For the Soft Life

By BILL HARTFORD, Technical Auto Editor / Photos by Irv Dolin

CREATURE COMFORT is part and parcel of the Cadillac marque, but owner acceptance of the Eldorado +2 area is mixed. Individual, sculptured seats are luxurious and comfortable in themselves, but the rear passenger compartment draws complaints. Legroom is limited and visibility is severely restricted by the high front seats and hardtop roof line. Hard exit and entry and too low a seat are among other gripes

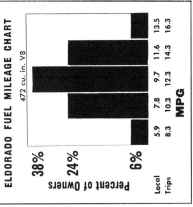

KNEE-KNOCKER bumper and taillight protrusions and the limited rear visibility are accentuated here

YOU WON'T FIND A CADILLAC ELDORADO in the starting line-up of an SCCA Trans-Am sedan race, but a lot of Eldorado owners might look for it. They think their car is that sporty in looks and ride. That's what's good about it and that's what's bad. It has the sports-car look that they like, but it also has a suspension that affluent owners find is a lot stiffer than the price.

Suspension stiffness, to most of us who drive a car just to get around, is a very subjective thing. One man's slush bucket is another man's flat-cornering F1. Eldorado owners' reactions to ride are subjective and relative: For almost 90 percent this is not their first Cadillac. Twenty-nine percent have had nine or more! They are experts when it comes to what this "Standard of the World" should be. And they sound off about Cadillac abandoning its ocean-liner ride with the Eldorado. You can actually feel the bumps! Used to limousines, owners attracted by the Eldorado's style didn't know they were getting a little more of a sports-car ride to go with the looks. And they can't forget what they've given up for it: "Riding comfort doesn't compare with a regular Cadillac," "not as smooth riding as the Coupe De Ville," "ride is too firm," "bumpy ride," "rough ride," "hard on bumps," "rides too hard," "needs softer springing," and so on go the remarks from owners of all ages, not just the many retired folks who own Eldorados.

Even first-time owners, like the young housewife and model from New York who says, "Not a smooth ride," voice a desire for a more sponge-cake car. Seems they want what an Iowan, a chairman of the board in his 60s, calls the Eldorado: "Really a two-passenger, old-man's sports car."

Most owners distinguish between the firm ride and great handling. An Indiana tool-and-die-shop owner, for example: Handling and cornering are what he likes even if he finds the ride "a little too rough." An Illinois restaurant owner speaks for most owners when he says "Front-wheel drive is terrific!" In the words of a Kansas banker, the Eldorado's merits are "feel of stability, lack of sway, excellent road holding in cross winds." And a retired Michigan man finds "safety on slippery roads" with his car and likes its "sports-car feel." An Indiana dentist, too, likes wet-weather handling, especially in snow: "Don't need snow tires, no fishtailing." And, front-wheel drive "eliminates skidding" for a Kentucky manufacturer.

The price owners pay for their cars is

SPORTY STYLING AND SIZE are well liked; some owners want smaller car, find doors too large and heavy

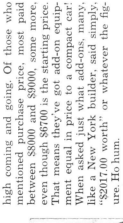

DRIVERS AND PASSENGERS like the flat-floor benefit of front-wheel drive, seating comfort and luxury; a few desire a larger glove box

FRONT-WHEEL DRIVE, available only on the Eldorado and Olds Toronado among mass-produced domestic cars, receives much praise from owners for contributing to good handling

LARGE TRUNK is not as deep as most, especially near edge of the lid, but owners are happy with it

ACCESSORY-LADEN ELDORADO with 472-cu.-in. engine gives no mechanical problems to 8 of 10 owners

DASH LAYOUT is disliked for tight grouping of controls around wheel and protruding dash divider

and taking notice of their all-too-active gas gauges to make fuel economy a chief complaint. A Washington, D.C. restaurant owner says, "Don't know what I'm getting but it's not many mpg.." Actually, 9.7 and 12.3 are the average local and long distance figures, respectively. Economy with a car like the Eldorado can't really be viewed objectively, however. An Illinois dentist getting six to eight mpg demands "an improvement." Yet, a New Hampshire insurance man getting about the same says his Eldorado "is a most economical prestige car."

A prestige car is certainly what any Cadillac is and that, quite a few owners confess, is the reason for getting the Eldorado. It's also the reason a California consultant *hasn't* bought a Cadillac up until now: "I can afford a fine car but I've been influenced by the stigma that goes with owning one. The Eldorado, with its front-wheel drive, etc. and its sports-car leanings, changed my mind."

And then, coming up with the last word, is a Texas owner who says, "There are too many of them on the road. The price should be raised to $15,000 to keep everyday people from owning them."

★ ★ ★

high coming and going. Of those who mentioned purchase price, most paid between $8000 and $9000, some more, even though $6700 is the starting price. That means they've got add-on equipment equal in price to a compact car! When asked just what add-ons, many, like a New York builder, said simply, "$2017.00 worth" or whatever the figure. Ho hum.

The price of the ride from tankful to tankful shouldn't matter much and it doesn't to a lot of owners—like the New Jersey wholesale business manager who gets five and eight mpg and doesn't even comment on the fact. A Texas real estate broker sums up the situation: "I have no idea of my mileage, I just fill it up once a day or so."

But enough owners *are* sitting up

Summary of 1969 Cadillac Eldorado Owners Reports*

Total miles driven	989,200
Average miles per gallon (472 cu. in. V8 [4 bbl. carb.], automatic transmission):	
local driving	9.7
long trips	12.3
Specific likes:	
Styling	49.4%
Handling	34.6
Comfort	26.5
Performance	22.8
Ride	18.5
Front-wheel drive	17.3
Specific dislikes:	
Economy	16.9%
Ride	16.3
Workmanship	10.8
Visibility	4.0
Dash layout	4.8
Tire quality	4.8
What changes would you like?	
Ride	14.5%
Dash layout	11.0
Styling	10.3
Rear visibility	9.7
Quality of materials	6.9
Had any mechanical trouble?	
No	80.3%
Yes	19.7
What kind of trouble?	
Windshield wipers	14.7%
Power steering	8.8
Ignition	8.8
Dealer repair satisfactory?	
Yes	70.6%
No	29.4
Why the Eldorado?	
Style	47.7%
Front-wheel drive	22.1
Past experience	11.4
Prestige	8.7
Quality	8.1
Performance	8.1
Is the Eldorado your only car?	
No	74.2%
Yes	25.8
Other cars owned:	
Chevrolet	26.0%
Buick	19.1
Pontiac	16.8
Oldsmobile	13.7
Ford	12.2
Cadillac	9.9
What options/accessories?	
Stereo tape	50.5%
Radio	49.5
Airconditioning	45.6
Cruise control	35.9
Tinted windshield	32.0
Power locks	30.1
Leather seats	21.4
Age distribution of owners:	
15-29	10.1%
30-49	47.1
50 plus	43.0

*Where applicable percentages may not equal 100 percent due to rounding and/or insufficient sample.

new cars 1969 ELDORADO
LUXURY SPECIALTY

NOW GOING into its third year, the Eldorado has established itself as a car for those who have always admired Cadillac's undisputed expertise in engineering but who don't particularly appreciate the barge-like proportions of the standard model. The Eldorado has a lithe, lean look to it that the similarly conceived Toronado is only now beginning to approach.

On the other hand it incorporates all of Cadillac's almost soporific standards of silence and automation. A perhaps unintentionally candid definition of this goal is contained in the section on "scientific soundproofing" of an elaborate product manual given out to Cadillac salesmen. This says: "The quietness of Cadillac interiors . . . is achieved through the Cadillac engineers' constant effort to design out any engine or chassis vibrations. However, the noise of thrown gravel and other vehicles' horns cannot be engineered out. Therefore, selected soundproofing is used at designated places . . ." Anyone who has futilely tried to use his horn to signal an air-conditioned Cadillac out of the way now knows the explanation.

Styling changes are limited to a new grille of a finer texture and a return to horizontally-dualled, exposed headlights. With a smugness that can only be afforded when you're No. 1 in your field by a margin of nearly 9 to 1, a spokesman explained: "We'll bow in with an innovation and then bow out. Too many cars have disappearing lights now. It's like the turn signal indicators on the fenders. We were the first to put them there but now nearly everybody has them so we've taken them off for '69 also."

Carryover styling features worthy of mention include ventless side glass, quarter windows that recess electrically into the roof panels, a "V"-shaped backlight, and articulated wipers recessed into the cowl. The standard cornering lights in the front fenders double as running lights, as do the illuminated Eldorado emblems in the rear fenders.

The instrument panel, while it continues Cadillac's tradition of square dials in the few instances where these are used, is completely new. The group-

ing is more driver-oriented with even the radio being moved to a position in front of him. The passenger side is bare padding except for air-conditioning outlets and some touches of synthetic wood trim. Use of the word synthetic is not meant to be disparaging. Anyone who owns an older Jaguar or Mercedes will confirm that the stuff from trees, no matter how well varnished, soon starts looking like a weathered orange crate wherever it is lengthily exposed to sun or wear.

Some Cadillac control concepts are exceptionally well thought out. The parking brake, which for years has automatically released when the engine is started and a gear engaged, also may be used as a true emergency braking system, a feature of which many present owners are probably unaware. As long as the engine is running and the car is in gear, the foot pedal in this system will not lock. It can be operated like the normal brake pedal to bring the car to a stop in the unlikely event of total failure of the main system. Another nifty item that is included with the electric door lock option is an automatic release for the front seat backs. This works on both seats when either door is opened.

Eldorado's front-wheel drive layout is quite similar to the one originally developed for the Toronado. The 3-speed automatic transmission is located

WHAT'S NEW: "Scientific Soundproofing"... finer textured grille... dual horizontally exposed headlights... driver-oriented instruments... sealed cooling system... 186 interior trim variations

❶ Lean and lithe is a fair description of the Eldorado profile. Backlite is sharply vee'd, quarter window retracts into the roof.

❷ This is a rare Eldorado without vinyl top, an option favored by most buyers in 1968.

❸ New grille, exposed headlamps and rich looking wheel covers are the extent of 1969 styling changes.

ELDORADO
ENGINE: 472 cu ins (375 hp).
TRANSMISSION: 3-spd auto std.
SUSPENSION: Torsion front, leaf rear.
STEERING: Power std, curb-to-curb 44.3 ft.
TIRES: 9.00 x 15 std, belted opt.
BRAKES: Disc front std, power std.
FUEL CAPACITY: 24 gals.
DIMENSIONS: Wheelbase 120 ins. **Track** 63.5 ins front, 63 rear. **Width** 79.9 ins. Length 221 ins. **Height** 53.7 ins. **Weight** 4700-4900 lbs. **Trunk** 13.5 cu ft.
BODY STYLES: 2-dr hdtp.

alongside the left of the engine where it is driven by a rubber and metal chain. A differential integral with the transmission at the driving end feeds power to each front wheel. After millions of miles racked up by both Toronados and Eldorados in owners' hands, there is no evidence of any premature U-joint failure such as once plagued Cords and other proponents of this design. Front suspension is by torsion bar, primarily in the interest of saving space, and single-leaf rear springs are all that are needed to support the car on a simple beam axle. However, 4 shock absorbers are used at the rear for optimum control, one set cushioning vertically and the other horizontally.

Eldorado continues to use the same engine as standard Cadillacs. Unless the Russians have added more cast iron to their Zis, this engine is the largest and from a torque standpoint, the most powerful of any stock passenger car plant in production today. The 472-cubic-inch design, all new in 1968, puts out 525 lbs.-ft. of torque at a usable 3000 rpm. It is, of course, a premium fuel engine with a 10.5:1 compression ratio and a single 4-barrel carburetor. One feature that greatly reduces vibration is a built-in mount for the air-conditioning compressor, a luxury that is practical because over 90% of Cadillac buyers specify this accessory. Another feature, new for '69, is a sealed cooling system. Coolant is added, if necessary, to a transparent plastic auxiliary tank which is under atmospheric rather than system pressure. Its cap may be removed without any danger of a burn injury from scalding coolant.

Cadillac operates a custom upholstery shop in the true sense of the word because no less than 186 trim combinations — 91 in cloth and 95 in leather or vinyl — are offered with only some of the leather versions costing extra. A choice of bench or bucket seats may be made, but the buckets are very expensive ($342 in 1968) and they negate the advantage of the completely flat floor. The standard seats are well-contoured and, of course, there is a folding center armrest. A thoughtful feature is a stowage area for unused seat belts. Outside belts automatically adjust to the girth of the wearer and retract when not in use. In addition, the buckles have been miniaturized to further reduce the clutter around the seats.

Most power assists are standard including steering and brakes, windows and shifting. As was mentioned you can automate the door locks and even the trunk. In addition to a normal air-conditioning system, a highly sophisticated unit that utilizes electronics to sense temperatures at various points in the car is available. This latter has been redesigned to give 19% greater air flow from a 100% increase in air outlet area. A special purging system prevents flash fogging that occasionally occurs at certain combinations of temperature and humidity.

Based on 1968 prices, you can easily add $3500 worth of non-conflicting options to the base $5500 price tag of the car, and most Eldorado buyers do. However, some items readily available with almost any other make are surprisingly absent from the Eldorado catalog. For example, no console is offered and therefore no floor mount for the transmission control. Trailer towers will have to make do with the existing suspension.

1975 Coupe

1976 Coupe

1976 Convertible

CADILLAC gets only trim refinement for '70. But has highest torque capacity axle in industry.

CADILLAC & ELDORADO

A PLAQUE on the grille of the Eldorado casually reads "8.2 litre." One liter contains 61 cubic inches and 8.2 times 61 equals 500. Five hundred cubic inches of engine, that is. Grand Prix may have the longest hood in the industry, but Eldorado has the biggest car engine in the whole world. Do not leave this car unattended in the paddock at a Can-Am race.

Other than the fact that it will be the no-budget Supercar of the year, the Eldorado is little changed from '69. Dimensions are the same, but a longer look is achieved via sculptured, knife edge front fenders. Subtle emphasis is placed on the bigger engine by confining the grille to the center of the nose, giving a classic car "power hood" look to the car. Slight trim changing around the lights and fender openings finish off the face lift.

Standard Cadillac changes are also confined to subtle trim refinement, with the accent on length. Cadillac's radio is the only signal seeking radio that seeks only *stereo* stations. How's that for snobbery? It can, however, be adjusted to stop at proletariat AM and FM stations as well. As on the rest of the GM cars, a windshield antenna is available (standard) as are rear window defrosters. Higher capacity air conditioning has been incorporated to provide quicker cooling.

The standard Cadillacs retain the measley 472-cid engine of '69, with 375 bhp, 525 ft./lb. of torque (versus 400 bhp and 550 ft./lb. of the 500 engine). A stainless steel flex-fan is new this year, to assist the bigger air conditioner and reduce noise. It also runs at a slower speed. Rear axle assembly is a completely new design, being quieter, having lower pinion input (for lower driveshaft mounting) and has the highest torque capacity of any passenger car axle. Are you listening, dragster builders? ■

500-CID makes Eldorado an anti-budget racer. Biggest automobile engine in the world.

Cadillac

Fleetwood Eldorado

ENGINE CAPACITY 472 cu in, 7,734.66 cu cm
FUEL CONSUMPTION 12.8 m/imp gal, 10.7 m/US gal, 22 l × 100 km
SEATS 6 **MAX SPEED** 120 mph, 193.2 km/h
PRICE IN GB basic £ 4,860, total £ 6,347
PRICE IN USA $ 6,693

ENGINE front, 4 stroke; cylinders: 8, Vee-slanted at 90°; bore and stroke: 4.30 × 4.06 in, 109.2 × 103.1 mm; engine capacity: 472 cu in, 7,734.66 cu cm; compression ratio: 10.5; max power (SAE): 375 hp at 4,400 rpm; max torque (SAE): 525 lb ft, 72.4 kg m at 3,000 rpm; max engine rpm: 4,600; specific power: 48.5 hp/l; cylinder block: cast iron; cylinder head: cast iron; crankshaft bearings: 5; valves: 2 per cylinder, overhead, in line, slanted at 45°, hydraulic tappets, push-rods and rockers; camshafts: 1, at centre of Vee; lubrication: gear pump, full flow filter; lubricating system capacity: 9.15 imp pt, 11 US pt, 5.2 l; carburation: 1 Rochester 7028234 downdraught 4-barrel carburettor; fuel feed: mechanical pump; cooling system: water; cooling system capacity: 35.55 imp pt, 42.70 pt, 20.2 l.

Front disc brake

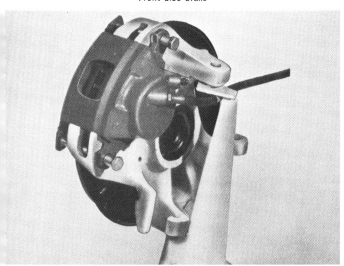

TRANSMISSION driving wheels: front; gearbox: Turbo-Hydramatic automatic, hydraulic torque convertor and planetary gears (driven through a chain from engine mounted convertor) with 3 ratios + reverse, max ratio of convertor at stall 2, possible manual selection; gearbox ratios: I 2.480, II 1.480, III 1, rev 2.090; axle ratio: 3.070.

CHASSIS integral, front perimeter box-type; front suspension: independent, wishbones, longitudinal torsion bars, anti-roll bar, telescopic dampers; rear suspension: rigid axle, single leaf semi-elliptic springs, automatic levelling control, 4 telescopic dampers.

STEERING bevel gears, variable ratio, servo; turns of steering wheel lock to lock: 2.70.

BRAKES front disc (diameter 11.30 in, 287 mm), internal radial fins, rear drum, dual circuit, servo; area rubbed by linings: front 224 sq in, 1,444.80 sq cm, rear 138 sq in, 890.10 sq cm, total 362 sq in, 2,334.90 sq cm.

ELECTRICAL EQUIPMENT voltage: 12 V; battery: 74 Ah; generator type: alternator, 42 Ah; ignition distributor: Delco-Remy; headlamps: 4, retractable, iodine.

DIMENSIONS AND WEIGHT wheel base: 120 in, 3,048 mm; front track: 63.50 in, 1,613 mm; rear track: 63 in, 1,600 mm; overall length: 221 in, 5,613 mm; overall width: 79.90 in, 2,029 mm; overall height: 53.70 in, 1,364 mm; ground clearance: 5.40 in, 137 mm; dry weight: 4,615 lb, 2,093 kg; turning circle (between walls): 44.5 ft, 13.6 m; width of rims: 6''; tyres: 9.00 × 15; fuel tank capacity: 21.6 imp gal, 26 US gal, 98 l.

BODY coupé; doors: 2; seats: 6; front seats: bench.

PERFORMANCE max speeds: 51 mph, 82 km/h in 1st gear; 85 mph, 136.8 km/h in 2nd gear; 120 mph, 193.2 km/h in 3rd gear; power-weight ratio: 12.3 lb/hp, 5.6 kg/hp; carrying capacity: 1,058 lb, 480 kg; speed in direct drive at 1,000 rpm: 27.4 mph, 44.1 km/h.

PRACTICAL INSTRUCTIONS fuel: 100 oct petrol; engine sump oil: 7.57 imp pt, 9 US pt, 4.3 l, SAE 5W-20 (winter) 10W-30 (summer), change every 6,000 miles, 9,700 km; gearbox oil: 9.15 imp pt, 11 US pt, 5.2 l, Dexron fluid type; final drive oil: 4.22 imp pt, 5 US pt, 2.4 l, SAE 90; valve timing: inlet opens 18° before tdc and closes 114° after bdc, exhaust opens 70° before bdc and closes 58° after tdc; normal tyre pressure: front 24 psi, 1.7 atm, rear 24 psi, 1.7 atm.

VARIATIONS AND OPTIONAL ACCESSORIES adjustable height and tilt of steering wheel; cleaner air system; air conditioning system; engine max power (SAE) 350 hp at 4,400 rpm, max torque (SAE) 500 lb ft, 69 kg m at 3,000 rpm, 9.2 compression ratio, 45.2 hp/l specific power, 92 oct petrol.

CADILLAC ELDORADO STILL

It was September, 1968 when ROAD TEST last looked at the Cadillac Eldorado. At that time we saw fit to proclaim it the most wanted car in the world. How do we feel a year and half later, now that the Eldorado has had nearly four years of market exposure? Well, with certain qualifications, just about the same. We'll bet that more people would still rather have an Eldorado than any other car in the world. There must be more frustrated non-Cadillac owners than non-owners of any other marque.

Several things are different about the Eldorado that combine to make it more desireable than other Cads. First, more attractive styling makes it the sportiest of Cadillacs. From any angle it's a darn good looking car. Second, front wheel drive contributes the dual benefits of a flat floor in the passenger compartments and remarkable handling for such a large car — the Eldorado weighs in at 4740 lbs. in fighting trim. Then, of course, limited production together with a stiff price tag — $9200 plus tax and license — provide a degree of snob appeal which is readily recognizable by the proles.

For 1970 the Eldorado retains the classic look of its predecessors. Exterior styling changes have been made to the grille, lighting, side moldings, and ornamentation. The Eldorado, despite its size, is a splendid example of the 2+2 Pony car shape. In automotive stylist's parlance it's a 'profile' form rather than a 'highlight' form. By way of comparison, the Camaro is an excellent example of the former, while the Mustang is a blend of the two.

Three major technical innovations are also introduced on the 1970 Eldorado — a new single piece ductile iron steer-

Profile retains classic Eldorado lines. Seating position is well back. Small quarter windows and rear window add up to limited side visibility.

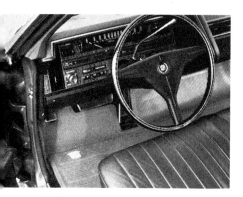

All instruments and controls are within ready reach and sight of driver. Small dark console near top of door is windshield wiper control — also within reach of driver's fingers without taking hands from wheel.

Slimmer tail lights give more finely sculptured look to rear of '70 Eldorado.

WANTED BUT WORTH IT?

ing knuckle which replaces a built-up assembly, a new signal seeking radio, and a new 500 cu. in. engine — largest in the industry.

The 1970 grille is all new and features a horizontal accent which gives emphasis to the engine compartment in similar fashion to the standard Cadillac. It is adorned with new Eldorado script plus a medallion reading '8.2 litre' to designate the new engine.

The exposed headlamps now assume a supporting role to the grille which dominates front end styling. New turn signals are highlighted by a vertical winged crest embossed on the lens. In the rear the tail lamps have been resculptured to give a more slender impression.

There are 21 exterior colors to choose from, 15 of them new, plus seven vinyl roof options. In the interior there are a total of 167 different combinations of vinyl, cloth, and leather.

Drive train

With the largest displacement of any passenger car engine in the world, there's plenty of reserve for the multitude of power driven accessories nestled under the Eldorado's skin.

The increase in displacement to 500 cu. in. has been achieved by lengthening the stroke of the 472 cu. in. engine used throughout the balance of the Cadillac line from 4.06 in. to 4.304 in. The bore is retained at 4.30 inches.

Using a single four-barrel carburetor and 10 to 1 compression ratio, 400 horsepower are produced with a maximum torque of 550 lb./ft., both figures up 25 horsepower and 25 lb./ft. from the 472 cu. in. engine.

For 1970, Cadillac engines will have a new cooling fan with flexible stainless steel blades. In addition to improving engine cooling and air conditioning performance, the new fan runs more quietly and at a slightly lower speed.

Although the view from the top when you open the hood gives a first impression of a plumber's nightmare, components requiring routine maintenance — plugs, points, oil filter, etc. are readily accessible. And there's the vaunted Cadillac reliability for the balance — things that don't need routine maintenance don't need much in the way of *un-routine* maintenance.

No Eldorado prospect will suffer agony with the transmission option list. It's either the Turbo Hydramatic with a 3.07 differential, or another car. The three speed transmission is mounted below the engine and chain driven from the torque converter which is directly

A little out of its natural environment, Eldorado still sails through quarter mile in 16.7 seconds.

Eldorado front passenger compartment is one of the few domestics with flat floor. Semi-divided bench seat permits maximum use.

coupled to the crankshaft. The front wheels are driven through short propellor shafts which have both inboard and outboard universal joints.

Power and performance

While hardly in the same context with the Muscle cars, the Eldorado is still no sloth. For freeway cruising the principal sensation is that of having something in the nature of a two hundred percent power reserve. Acceleration for normal street purposes is more than adequate. We didn't get any chance to verify top speed, but we don't doubt that the Eldorado would cruise all day at 80 mph with never a murmur.

As far as maximum acceleration is concerned, 400 horsepower applied to 4740 lbs. propelled the Eldorado through the quarter mile in a distinctly unslothly 16.7 sec. The trap speed was a less impressive 83 mph. It is always kind of a fun sensation to break the front wheels loose on take-off, though with the Cadillacs there is more sensation than fact. Even holding the brake while revving the engine until the car starts to creep and then standing on the gas won't produce much in the way of tire smoke. But in all honesty, with a car in this class, who cares?

Roadability and handling

Everyone ought to take at least one long trip in an Eldorado during his lifetime. There's positively nothing to com-

pare with the feeling of splendid isolation from the world achieved when cruising down the turnpike, with the cruise control set for a constant 64½ mph, the climate control set for a constant 72 degrees and the stereo tuned to whatever you can retain.

With everything taken care of except keeping the car pointed in the right direction, and the noise of the outside world well masked by an excellent job of sound insulation, the miles disappear effortlessly but the ease can make a careless driver drowsy.

Cornering behavior with the front wheel drive is excellent for such a large vehicle. We feel that it could be improved, though, with more robust tires. There's considerable body lean on very hard cornering, much less at normal cornering speeds. Aside from cornering there's no other sensation of having front wheel drive.

On a straight course we did notice a slight tendency to wander, particularly to the left. Perhaps this is only because with so many functions accomplished automatically we had a slight tendency to get lethargic about steering.

The Eldorado's ride is certainly all that might be asked. Pitch is well controlled and large bumps are well damped. Smaller bumps are apparent, but not objectionably so.

Independent torsion bars are used in the front suspension with hydraulic shocks. A 1-1/16 in. front stabilizer bar is also used. New in all Cadillacs for 1970 is an integral steering knuckle. This one piece ductile iron unit combines knuckle, steering arm, and disc brake caliper support plate into a single

Grille dominates front styling of '70 Eldorado, with headlights taking secondary role. '8.2 Litre' medallion in grille denotes engine displacement.

Spare tire placement contributes to large usable trunk volume. Low sill height simplifies loading and unloading.

the door panels provide a safety warning when doors are opened at night.

Comfort and convenience

If there are discrepancies in other areas of evaluation, the Eldorado rates high in this category. Everything inside is good from the standpoints of materials, arrangement and relationship. Opening the wide doors which swing on massive hinges like the entrance to a bank vault exposes an interior finished in leather with rich, grained wood trim inserts. Access to both front seats is simple, and the approach to the rear seat is simplified by an electric device which releases the seat back latches when a door is opened.

Once inside a six-way power seat unit with improved strength and reliability. It replaces an assembly which consisted of several finished parts, all hand assembled.

The rear suspension has a dead axle located by single, longitudinal leaf springs.

Belted bias tires are standard, with the only tire option being the choice of white sidewalls. 15 in. wheels with a six in. rim width are used.

Brakes and safety

The brake system offered on the Eldorado (there are no options) consists of power assisted front discs with rear drums. Both the drum and the vented disc are 11 in. dia. A metering valve at the front and a front/rear proportioning valve combine to apply 62-69 percent of the braking force to the front wheels.

The parking brake can only be set when the transmission is in neutral or park. It is automatically released by a vacuum device on shifting to either reverse or drive.

In the light of previous reports we were disappointed with the Eldorado's brakes in performance testing. The best deceleration we were able to record from 60 mph was a somewhat unimpressive 22 ft. per sec.^{2}; or 176 ft. and fade, accompanied by great clouds of smoke from the front brakes, came on in the third hard stop from 80 mph. It seems like the Eldorado has not enough brakes for a 4740 lb. car which has 60 percent of the weight on the front wheels.

Several features combine to give the lighting system an excellent safety rating. The twilight sentinel and automatic dimming turn the lights on and off as external lighting conditions dictate. It also dips the high beams at the approach of oncoming traffic, precluding the driver's overlooking this important action.

In addition, cornering lights on the sides of the front fenders are actuated by the directional signals. They project a beam of light from the side of the car to illuminate the roadside and signs for added convenience at night. Lights in adjustment theoretically permits anyone to select a comfortable position. The seats, while comfortably padded, don't offer much in the way of lateral support. Arm and shoulder room is spacious in both the front and back. With only two in front a broad center arm rest can be lowered.

Visibility is fair in all directions except to the rear quarters. A smallish rear window coupled with miniscule quarter windows leaves extensive blind spots beside the rear passenger's heads. Toward the front the principal visual impression is received from the hood, which appears to be only slightly less than an acre in size when viewed from the driver's seat.

Storage space abounds in the trunk, which must have been measured carelessly. It seems much larger than the

Body lean in a hard corner seems worse from outside than inside. Front wheel drive gives good cornering power and control.

quoted fifteen cu. ft. As an added bonus the rear styling concept allows a sill which is low so that the average owner, probably past his physical prime anyway, won't suffer a hernia lifting luggage in and out. For an extra $52 the lid can be opened from inside the car by pressing a release button inside the glove compartment.

The Climate Control system maintains a constant interior temperature with automatic actuation of either the heating or air conditioning system in response to strategically located thermistors. Just select the appropriate speed for the three speed fan, turn the control to automatic, dial the desired temperatue and forget it. In conjunction with the above system, a rear window defogger with its own two speed blower takes care of problems in that area.

Temperatures that are always in the comfort zone are achieved in near silence thanks to an excellent job of sound insulation, weather sealing, and silent operation of the moving parts.

When the silence is broken, it's best done by the AM-FM stereo radio, which performs with concert hall quality. A new innovation exclusive with Cadillac for 1970 is a setting on the station selector bar which limits the FM stations selected to those which are broadcasting in stero. The antenna is located in the front window. For some unexplained reason, when on AM, the radio emitted a loud 'screech' when passing under a bridge.

A strict rule of 'only if necessary for driving' seems to have been applied to the instrument display on the Eldorado. Consequently the driver can tell how much gas he has, how fast he's going, how far he has gone, and the time of day by looking at the dash. Abnormalities in other functions are announced by lights in the event that any should occur. In most cases by then it's too late. The degree of instrumentation and nature of display, however, are entirely in accord with the Eldorado's concept of taking care of as many details as possible for the driver.

Control placement is deserving of special mention. All are placed within easy reach of the driver, and most can be operated without removing either hand from the wheel. The wheel, with virtually no manual effort required to complement the power assist, has been reduced in size and is easy to whirl around. A choice of five vertical positions and three inches of in and out adjustments are offered. These adjustments, together with the range of seat positions permit a wide range of comfortable driving locations to be selected.

The GM 'Twilight Sentinel' which turns the lights on and off as required by lighting conditions, also permits leaving the headlamps lighted for up to 45 seconds after leaving the car — so that the boogie man won't get you before you get inside the front door.

Our favorite accessory control, and in our estimation the best buy on the automobile at $95, was the vacuum powered cruise control. It has an on-off switch on the dash, but is set by a button on the end of the turn indicator stalk to maintain a pre-set speed. This device is a great convenience on long trips, and equally so about town where it can be employed to prevent inadvertently exceeding the speed limit.

One interesting feature is the location of the controls for the three-speed windshield wiper and washer in a little consolette on the left door. Although this placement looks a little wierd with the door open it does assure that the wipers can be operated by finger tip control without removing the left hand from the steering wheel.

A. Auxiliary systems are accessible for service despite apparent clutter

B. Viscous drive fan reduces noise, aids cooling

C. Radiator catch tank prevents loss of coolant

D. A/C radiator in front of engine radiator

E. Good battery accessibility

Although it looks like a plumber's nightmare from top with all accessories, engine components are readily accessible for maintenance.

Massive 500 cu. in. power plant is largest in any passenger car. Tube crossing over left valve cover is for warm air, part of emission control system.

Economy

Although a look at the $9,147.80 total at the bottom of the window sticker would seem to negate any serious discussion of economy, the term is very applicable when value is considered. The base price starts at $6900. Climate control ($516), radio ($322), vinyl roof ($157), special paint color ($131), and leather upholstery ($184) eat up most of the cost of options, but it sure wouldn't be an Eldorado without them. That's why we would bet that not one Eldorado in a hundred goes out the dealer's door for less than $8000.

Depreciation on Cadillacs is historically low, though, and tends to soften the impact of the high initial price. Although there are a lot of things which *could* go wrong and require maintenance, most Cadillac owners have found that there are comparatively few which *do* go wrong. As for gas mileage, it works out to almost 10 mpg — pretty reasonable considering the gross weight and number of power accessories.

Summary

A very high price returns undeniable dividends in prestige, comfort, performance, and reliability. Eldorado owners are unanimously satisfied with the front wheel drive, styling, and performance they receive. Complaints arise on accessory performance — such as climate control, level control, etc. On tire wear, and on dealer service.

We feel that the Eldorado does an outstanding job of fulfilling the concept it is intended to meet. If your objective is a large, fairly comfortable, prestigious car with engine performance and handling suitable for its size, the Eldorado is probably a best bet. We wish it had better brakes. Cadillac has the largest share of its market.

In our ROAD TEST survey, present Eldorado owners list it as their probable next car without exception. Not too many others can make the same boast. ♠

Cadillac Eldorado

Data in Brief

DIMENSIONS

Overall length (in.)	221.0
Wheelbase (in.)	120.0
Height (in.)	53.3
Width	79.9
Tread (front, in.)	63.7
Tread (rear, in.)	63.0
Fuel tank capacity (gal.)	24.0
Luggage capacity (cu. ft.)	15.2

ENGINE

Type	OHV V-8
Displacement (cu. in.)	500
Horsepower (at 4400 rpm)	400
Torque (lb./ft. at 3000 rpm)	550

WEIGHT, TIRES, BRAKES

Weight (as tested, lb.)	4747
Tires	L78 x 15 belted bias
Brakes, front	disc
Brakes, rear	drum

SUSPENSION

Front	torsion bar with telescopic shocks
Rear	Longitudinal single leaf springs with telescopic shocks

PERFORMANCE

Standing ¼ mile (sec.)	16.65
Speed at end of ¼ mile (mph)	83.1
Braking (from 60 mph, ft.)	176

KING OF THE HILL

BY BILL SANDERS

Road testing the Lincoln Continental Mark III and Cadillac Eldorado.

At dusk, when the lights come on and the last vestiges of sun are still fighting the shadows, city and suburban neighborhoods give a more definitive presence to their being. Where material wealth reposes beyond well manicured lawns and shrub-lined drives, faint nuances of afternoon tennis and evening cocktail parties by the pool float delicately on the air. That's when you see them parked in the drives, at dusk. King of the Hill. A childhood memory of pulling, shoving, wrestling your way to the top, and the struggle to stay there. The struggle must have its rewards. In grownup reality the rewards are there. They're diverse and plentiful, luxurious and expensive. Whatever wealth can buy. And so you see them parked in the shadow of evening. A scene repeated a thousand times in a thousand movies so we lesser mortals can escape one reality and live another by osmosis. A symbol of how and how well a man has it made, his car is a mobile status beacon flashing the word to one and all. Many impressive marques have come and gone, many keep the pace today. In the good ol' U.S.A. two cars still live that retain an image of opulence and luxury that even their detractors must admit command a degree of attention not found very often. Two cars that still maintain an image of mystique that can't be matched on the Dow Jones affluence meter.

If you've got the American Dream, if you've made a pilgrimage to the Grand Canyon, Disneyland, Mt. Rushmore, or the Okefenokee Swamp, if your goal is to move all the way up from your Biscayne station wagon, then the Lincoln Continental Mark III and the Cadillac Eldorado are the end of status street. Top of the the heap. King of the Hill. But, which one? Is there a "King"? To settle this burning controversy that injects its indelicate presence into every social event and intimate tet-a-tete, *Motor Trend* has taken the reins and compared and tested both cars.

Just what is this opulent mystique that makes restaurant car jockeys ramble and doctors feel that they no longer have to make house calls now that they own one? Surely it's not a quarter-mile e.t. that would make a Mickey Thompson shudder. Definitely it's not such cornering prowess that a Mark Donohue would sigh in ecstasy. No, it's something much more intrinsic. Other cars may ride nearly as well and you can order most of the options for other cars that these two have. So, it's something more. They aren't limousines, but they have every attribute of comfort, ride, quietness, and smooth operation. They aren't sporty cars, but they impart an air of owner individuality that sets you apart if you have one.

Obviously, physical appearance has much to do with a final choice between these cars, but that's a personal matter of taste, the mystique is there in both. Most of us will accept a few minor hang-ups to get the car that outwardly reflects what we think is our alter ego. If outside looks are a matter of personal choice, inside is where you exist and that's what we can talk about: comfort and convenience, ride and steering, performance and braking, and finally (if you care) fuel economy.

Comfort is always tied up with ride characteristics, but seating comfort alone is a big factor in these cars. After long trips, our fatigue factor seemed to be increased in the Eldorado. The seating configuration just wasn't as comfortable as that of the Mark III. Sliding behind the wheel each time, too, we noticed the leather seemed to be of a better grade in the Mark III. Both cars have fold-down center armrests that are part of the lounge-type seats, and these add to easy, comfortable highway driving. Rear seats in both cars have limited leg room, which seems to be in vogue today in all U.S. cars. Because they've striven to get a "chopped" top look (watch out, Barris) the Mark III designers have lost a little in front seat headroom. Convenience, too, is somewhat a matter of personal taste, but we think the Eldorado has the most conveniently organized and driver-oriented switches, buttons, knobs, and other operative devices. Items such as the windshield washer-wiper controls are more convenient for the driver in the Eldorado, and the headlight sentinel that automatically turns on and off the headlights are little luxury touches that can be appreciated. Although the Mark III has full dash instrumentation, which the Eldo doesn't, they are laid out in square pods across the dash so it's difficult to check them all easily. Also, the Lincoln men have stuck their Cartier electric clock in the best location on the dash, directly ahead of the steering wheel. So, you know what time it is and the clock is by Cartier, but it's tough to find out if you have any oil pressure. Even the automatic temperature control in the Eldorado seems to be more thermostatically atuned to cause less human involvement. But, that is not to say convenience per se is *de rigueur*. David Pearson must realize great convenience with the dash of his NASCAR race car, but it is hardly the epitome of luxury. In total, the Eldorado dash and front seat environment is rather stark compared to the Mark III plushness.

The Mark III is more intimate, giving a taste of more luxury. The Eldorado still has power seat adjusting buttons on the lower portion of the seat, while they have been moved to the armrest on the left door in the Mark III, a much better location. Inside door handles are also a touch that counts. In the Eldorado they are under the armrests and you almost have to break your wrist to open the door. The same handles are on top of the armrest in the Mark III so you just squeeze and the door is open.

With weight factors somewhere just below a Union Pacific domeliner coach, both cars have quite similar ride characteristics because any harshness, noise, or road feel is cushioned out before it ever gets to the seat of your pants. Steering presents a different act. GM is hip to variable ratio, while Ford is still using straight power steering. The result is 2.7 wheel turns from lock-to-lock and a correspondingly lower overall gear ratio with the Eldorado compared to 4.03 wheel turns on the Mark III. Now, any clown who wants to take one of these cars to a road course and see what kind of violent under or oversteer he can force out of these immense, overly dampened, mushily sprung dinosaurs must be a little dingaling. Handling is what you'd expect... some roll steer and dip from the soft, soft

KING OF THE HILL

suspensions. Steering plays a significant role though, even on something as straight as an interstate highway across Nebraska. And, the Eldorado has steering response that overshadows its rival.

An engine seems to be incidental to these cars, as it should. They will cruise at 100 plus mph, but when they are idling you can't tell if the motor is running or not. They both have giant displacements; in fact, the Eldorado at 500 cubic inches (8.2 liters and don't forget it) has the biggest production auto engine going. But these engines are tuned to handle all the electric and vacuum power options and great weight of the cars. Acceleration is smooth and acceptable, nothing spectacular. The Mark III is rated at 365 hp and the Eldorado at 400, so even in that area they are close and acceleration times show it. Brakes on both cars appear to be adequate. Stopping distances weren't bad, but we noticed some fade after hard use. And from the smell of things, the brakes weren't too happy about the whole thing either. Both cars also have front disc brakes as standard. Fuel economy, or the lack of it, is another attribute both cars share. Gas consumption averaged out just about the same for both cars. In round figures, each car got between 10 and 12 mpg on both the highway and around town.

The Mark III has a very expensive option (that our test car had) which adds lots of fun and the psychological impetus designed into its mystique, a power sun roof. For $459.10 you can get the feeling of open freedom associated with convertibles and roadsters, but without the hang-up of stopping to put the top up or down. The same option is available on the T-Bird, but on the Mark III it's just more camp. Also, the Mark III can be equipped with Michelin radial tires, which our car also had. The Eldo had regular bias-belted tires. It's hard to tell how much added gripping power or stability the radials contributed because of the weight and suspensions, but after 30,000 miles or so the wear factor will probably come into play. Besides that, radials seem to give the Mark III a bit sportier handling, if that is possible.

So, who is King of the Hill? As long as there are Eldorado and Mark III owners around, cigar sales will continue to go up and no one will ever agree. The Eldorado has a lot of seemingly more advanced technical conveniences, but from a strictly plush, posh, luxury standpoint, the Mark III has the intimacy a car like this should offer. One thing, for a car you drive yourself, these two are about the ultimate today in computerized, programmed driving. Recently Mort Sahl and Sid Caesar were standing near Sid Caesar's Mark III discussing cars and driving. Mr. Sahl suggested Mr. Caesar get something a little more sporty, but Mr. Caesar felt that his Mark III did just about everything he wanted. Whereupon he opened the door and intoned in a deep voice to the steering wheel, "Take me to Beverly Hills." That's about as easy as it can be. /MT

Stark, sharp lines of Eldorado are followed through inside with austere looking dash and many automated instruments.

Posh, plush coziness of Mark III is apparent as you look up through optional sun roof. Lounge seats cater to comfort.

Cadillac Eldorado

Base price	$6,903.00
Special paint	131.60
Vinyl roof	157.90
Leather upholstery	184.20
Whitewall tires	40.00
AM/FM Stereo radio	322.10
Tinted glass	52.65
6-way power seat	89.50
Automatic temp control	515.75
Power door locks & seat back release	68.45
Tilt, telescope steering wheel	94.75
Twilight sentinel	36.85
Remote control deck lid release	52.65
Rear window defogger	26.35
Cruise control	34.75
Automatic headlight dimmer	50.55
Smog control	36.85

SPECIFICATIONS ELDORADO

Engine	90° OHV V8
Bore & Stroke	4.30 ins. x 4.30 ins.
Displacement	500 cu. in.
Max. horsepower	400 @ 4400 rpm
Max. torque	550 lbs.-ft. @ 4400 rpm
Compression ratio	10.0:1
Carburetion	1 4-bbl
Transmission	Automatic
Final drive ratio	3.07:1
Steering type	Variable ratio power
Steering ratio	16.1 to 12.3:1
Turning diameter (curb to curb)	41.3 ft.
Wheel turns (lock-to-lock)	2.7 ft.
Tire size	L78 x 15
Brakes	Power front disc, drum rear
Front suspension	Independent, torsion bar
Rear suspension	Long single leaf spring
Body/frame construction	Boxed perimeter frame
Wheelbase	120.0 ins.
Overall length	221.0 ins.
Overall width	79.9 ins.
Overall height	53.7 ins.
Front track	63.7 ins.
Rear track	63.0 ins.
Curb weight	4721 lbs.
Fuel capacity	24 gals.
Oil capacity	5 qts.

PERFORMANCE

Acceleration (2 Aboard)

0-30 mph	3.5 secs.
0-45 mph	5.9 secs.
0-60 mph	8.8 secs.
0-75 mph	13.1 secs.
Standing start ¼-mile	85.87 mph, 16.37 secs.

Passing speeds

40-60 mph	4.8 secs.
50-70 mph	5.2 secs.

Speeds in gears*

1st	46 mph @ 4400 rpm
2nd	75 mph @ 4400 rpm
3rd	91 mph @ 4000 rpm
MPH per 1000 RPM	22.7 mph

Stopping distances

From 30 mph	36.5 ft.
From 60 mph	144.8 ft.

Gas mileage

Range	10.0 to 12.8 mpg

Speedometer error

Electric speedometer	30 45 50 60 70 80
Car speedometer	30 44 49 59 69 79

*Speeds in gears are at shift points (limited by the length of track) and do not represent maximum speeds.

Continental Mark III

Base price	$7,281.00
Special paint	131.20
Leather and vinyl upholstery	164.00
Smog control	38.10
White sidewall radial tires	40.70
Power sun roof	459.10
6-way power seats & passenger recline	242.70
Tilt steering wheel	72.20
Remote control deck lid release	40.70
Rear window defogger	26.30
Automatic temp control	523.30
AM/FM Stereo radio	301.70
Tinted glass	52.50
Power door locks	47.30

SPECIFICATIONS MARK III

Engine	90° OHV V8
Bore & Stroke	4.36 ins. x 3.85 ins.
Displacement	460 cu. in.
Max. horsepower	365 @ 4600 rpm
Max. torque	500 lbs.-ft. @ 2800 rpm
Compression ratio	10.5:1
Carburetion	1 4-bbl
Transmission	Automatic
Final drive ratio	2.80:1
Steering type	Power
Steering ratio	21.9:1
Turning diameter (curb to curb)	43.1 ft.
Wheel turns (lock-to-lock)	4.03 ft.
Tire size	225 x 15
Brakes	Power front disc, drum rear
Front suspension	Independent, coil springs
Rear suspension	3-link w/coil springs & track bar
Body/frame construction	Seperate body/frame
Wheelbase	117.2 ins.
Overall length	216.1 ins.
Overall width	79.4 ins.
Overall height	53.0 ins.
Front track	62.3 ins.
Rear track	62.3 ins.
Curb weight	4866 lbs.
Fuel capacity	24 gals.
Oil capacity	4 qts.

PERFORMANCE

Acceleration (2 Aboard)

0-30 mph	3.5 secs.
0-45 mph	5.9 secs.
0-60 mph	9.2 secs.
0-75 mph	13.6 secs.
Standing start ¼-mile	85.63 mph, 16.50 secs.

Passing speeds

40-60 mph	4.7 secs.
50-70 mph	5.6 secs.

Speeds in gears*

1st	45 mph @ 4600 rpm
2nd	77 mph @ 4600 rpm
3rd	96 mph @ 4000 rpm
MPH per 1000 RPM	24.0 mph

Stopping distances

From 30 mph	35.7 ft.
From 60 mph	141.7 ft.

Gas mileage

Range	10.4 to 12.0 mpg

Speedometer error

Electric speedometer	30 45 50 60 70 80
Car speedometer	28 43 47 57 65 75

*Speeds in gears are at shift points (limited by the length of track) and do not represent maximum speeds.

OWNERSHIP IS NOT A SYMBOL OF SUCCESS, BUT SUCCESS ITSELF

CAR and DRIVER ROAD TEST

CADILLAC FLEETWOOD ELDORADO

As you ride smoothly along the American Way you can almost make out John Hancock's signature on the Eldorado's glovebox door. Life, liberty, the pursuit of happiness and Cadillacs are ideals that all converge on the horizon. Unless you're driving a Cadillac, you aren't really participating in America. In fact, the desire to participate in America the Beautiful is the only common denominator of Cadillac owners: You don't find Socialists making their journeys in Cadillacs, and Marxists would likely melt down every one in existence to reclaim enough iron for two Mavericks. Stature is added to Cadillac's owner list by corporate executives, oil tycoons and land barons, but they by no means make up the substance of that list. Wealth is implied but it's not mandatory. You see Cadillacs in the workers' parking lots at factories and you see Cadillacs parked in ghettos, solemnly awaiting their owners. With only a little prompting, service station attendants will tell you about their current Cadillacs and the ones they've owned before. Cadillacs are expensive but their owners are not necessarily wealthy. Each one does, however, have a conception of success, and owning a Cadillac is not a symbol of success but success in itself.

To get this Cadillac phenomenon straight in your mind you must first stop lumping Cadillacs together with Lincoln Continentals and Imperials in a vague luxury class. The Cadillac is not interchangeable with anything else. This becomes obvious when you check the yearly sales figures. Every year Americans indicate their preference by buying three times as many Cadillacs as Imperials and Continentals put together. And yearly Cadillac production, almost a quarter of a million cars, is not far short of the total efforts of American Motors. Clearly, a Cadillac has more significance than just an expensive car. It may even be that the Cadillac significance outweighs the Cadillac as a car. What are people buying when they buy a Cadillac? We suspect that in many cases it's much the same mindless reaction, on a higher plateau of course, that is responsible for the bountiful flow of VWs. Somehow you just know a Cadillac is a good car. Not from anything specific—you just know it. Everybody knows it, even those who have never ridden in one. So you can buy one with confidence—nothing to worry about. And a Cadillac has a certain social image that is conservative and responsible, even in low income situations where the payments will hungrily consume the family resources for the next three or four years. It's the halo of intangibles that makes the Cadillac especially desirable—the car merely has to avoid tarnishing the halo. The vastness, and at the same time the remoteness, of the Cadillac image is particularly well-framed when it is used as a reference for some other product. We've all encountered the "Cadillac of the lawn mowers" and the "Cadillac of the fishing reels." Frequently the designer of the device in question has incorporated some novel solutions to problems, but almost never does the Cadillac allusion indicate a functional superiority. All that description assures you of is price. This is apparently what the public mind thinks of Cadillac cars. If that is so, there is a need to refocus.

The Cadillac is, in fact, an exceptional automobile. It's the American equivalent of a Mercedes. The two have different strong suits but they are alike in that they are both highly developed for the driving conditions and the tastes of their respective countries. And each appeals to an equivalent section of society in its country. They are both establishment-oriented cars—and that is the key. So that you can see this distinction more clearly we need as contrast a non-establishment car in the same price class. The best example is BMW. BMW exists for the man who rejects the passivity and blind compliance with the status quo represented by Mercedes. The man who values automotive vitality rather than a safe, noncommittal facade steps out of the mainstream in a BMW.

The parallel with Cadillac in America is not nearly so straightforward. It doesn't exist in the Cadillac-Continental-Imperial triumvirate because the latter two are following as closely behind Cadillac as discretion will allow—hoping to travel the same path to success. But at least a skeleton of the parallel can be seen within Cadillac's own array of models. On one side are the traditional Cadillac sedans and on the other is the Eldorado. The division between the two is not a chasm—sedan buyers not infrequently switch to an Eldorado—but the Eldorado's appeal is more firmly based on the technical aspect of motoring and on automotive verve. Parts are shared between the two lines but the Eldorado is essentially a unique Cadillac. And the Eldorado buyers are unique. Cadillac feels it is significant that the average Eldorado buyer is 48 years old—four years younger than the average for conventional Cadillacs.

The Eldorado derives its mechanical personality from front-wheel-drive—an unusual arrangement for American automakers who, except for the Oldsmobile Toronado, have shunned it. Pulling with the front wheels does have a certain mystique —it's at least partially responsible for the fame of the Cords—but it is not without disadvantages in big, heavy cars powered by high-torque engines. And the Eldorado, with its 500 cubic inch engine, certainly falls into that category. All of this is a part of a very reserved performance image. A plaque in the grille is engraved "8.2 Litre" which is translated in the sales brochure as "the internationally recognized metric equivalent of 500 cubic inches."

You are also informed that this is the largest engine available in any production car anywhere. This enormous powerplant is new for 1970 and is a stroked derivative of the normal Cadillac 472 cubic inch V-8. It's used only in the Eldorado and thereby serves to strengthen that model's independence from the rest of the line. Unlike

Cadillac engines of the past, size is this one's only claim to fame. No Southern California torch artist will lose any sleep over a pressing urge to stuff one of these torque generators into some kind of Ford, and the idea that some latter-day Briggs Cunningham might campaign a Cadillac variant at Le Mans is out of the question for a lot of reasons. In fact, despite the omnipotent sound of 500 cubic inches, the new engine won't come near propelling an Eldorado to the performance superiority its ancestors enjoyed in the first half of the Fifties when Cadillac was invariably the production car winner at Daytona's Speed Week. That was in another era when power could be directly equated with dollars. Now Cadillacs, the Eldorado included, concentrate on smart transportation with the minimum of vulgar intrusions. And they do that very well. As expected, the armor required to shield the Eldorado's occupants from impinging vulgarities also boosts its weight up to 4895 pounds—a mass that would strongly suggest an immovable object to an engine less broad-shouldered than 500 cubic inches. With 400 horsepower and 550 lb./ft of torque the Eldorado jogs rather than runs and consequently requires 16.3 seconds for a standing quarter-mile, which it completes at 86 mph. It's not necessary to explain that this is modest performance by today's standards, for that is obvious, but for those of you not familiar with the athletic ability of Detroit's premium-priced automobiles, we should point out that the Eldorado is without a doubt the quickest one. And it does it with no loss of composure. The engine is so mild-mannered that you are aware of it only as you approach wide open throttle. Then it utters no more than a spirited hum. At normal cruising it's dead quiet and the idle is commendably smooth, even with the air conditioner on.

You would probably say the same about the front-wheel-drive system but that subject leaves more room for debate. Cadillac engineers are uniformly pleased with what they have wrought; they cite the glowing praise of customers—which they claim are the hardest in the world to please—but the fact remains that the Cadillac conception of handling and the C/D conception of handling are poles apart. If you assume, as *they* do, that a Cadillac needs only to maintain a stately pace on the freeways and to periodically shuttle from Grosse Pointe down to the Detroit Athletic Club, then the Eldorado is nearly without fault. However, if your idea of handling includes hurrying around corners, you'll find that the Eldorado has more than its share of thumbs and left feet. Front-wheel-drive cars invariably choose a markedly different path through a corner depending upon throttle opening—the more power, the more understeer—and the Eldorado does this to an extreme. In reality, you can expect very little else in a car so heavy, which in turn requires so much torque to attain a reasonable level of performance. We will concede that smoking around turns is a bit out of character for Cadillacs and not belabor the point any further. The normal advantages of fwd cars—excellent directional and crosswind stability resulting primarily from the forward weight distribution—are present in the Eldorado, but to a lesser extent than we expected. This was at least partially due—and we have the agreement of Cadillac representatives—to a poorly adjusted steering gear. We also noticed a tendency to drive left under power but we were assured by one of Cadillac's assistant chief engineers that, although incorrect suspension alignment could cause this quirk, it was certainly not a characteristic of Eldorados. We are inclined to agree with him, feeling certain that, considering Cadillac's position in the world, any predilection toward the left would be eliminated before the cars were allowed to leave the factory.

While we weren't particularly warmed by the suspension's contribution to handling, it deserves high marks for ride. The ride motions are very flat, there is no tendency to pitch and the body movements are very well damped. Partly due to fiber-

Specifications overleaf

CADILLAC FLEETWOOD ELDORADO

Manufacturer: Cadillac Motor Car Division
General Motors Corporation
Detroit, Michigan 46232

Vehicle type: Front engine, front-wheel-drive, 6-passenger coupe

Price as tested: $9003.60
(Manufacturer's suggested retail price, including all options listed below, Federal excise tax, dealer preparation and delivery charges, does not include state and local taxes, license or freight charges)

Options on test car: vinyl roof, $157.90; leather upholstery, $184.20; floor mats, $19.80; trunk mat, $8.35; white wall tires, $40.00; AM/FM stereo signal seeking radio, $322.10; tinted glass, $52.65; power seats, $89.50; door edge guards, $6.35; automatic temperature control, $515.75; power door locks and seat back release, $68.45; tilt steering wheel, $94.75; automatic headlights, $50.55; remote trunk lock, $52.65; rear window defogger, $26.35; cruise control, $94.75; twilight sentinel, $36.85; horn, $15.80; evaporative emission control, $36.65

ENGINE
Type: V-8, water-cooled, cast iron block and heads, 5 main bearings
Bore x stroke..4.30 x 4.30 in, 109.1 x 109.1 mm
Displacement...............500 cu in, 8200 cc
Compression ratio..................10.0 to one
Carburetion.....1 x 4-bbl Rochester Quadrajet
Valve gear.........Pushrod operated overhead valves, hydraulic lifters
Power (SAE)..............400 bhp @ 4400 rpm
Torque (SAE).........550 lbs/ft @ 3000 rpm
Specific power output........0.80 bhp/cu in, 48.9 bhp/liter

DRIVETRAIN
Transmission..............3-speed, automatic
Max. torque converter..............2.0 to one
Final drive ratio..................3.07 to one
Gear Ratio   Mph/1000 rpm   Max. test speed
I   2.48   11.3   56 mph (5000 rpm)
II   1.48   18.9   94 mph (5000 rpm)
III 1.00   28.1   112 mph (4000 rpm)

DIMENSIONS AND CAPACITIES
Wheelbase....................120.0 in
Track, F/R...................63.7/63.0 in
Length.......................221.0 in
Width........................80.0 in
Height.......................53.7 in
Ground clearance.............5.4 in
Curb weight..................4895 lbs
Weight distribution, F/R.....60.8/39.2%
Battery capacity.............12 volts, 74 amp/hr
Alternator capacity..........732 watts
Fuel capacity................22.0 gal
Oil capacity.................5.0 qts
Water capacity...............21.8 qts

SUSPENSION
F: Ind., unequal length control arms, torsion bars, anti-sway bar
R: Rigid axle, single leaf springs, two horizontal and two vertical shock absorbers

STEERING
Type.........Recirculating ball, power assist
Turns lock-to-lock...................2.75
Turning circle curb-to-curb............44.8 ft

BRAKES
F:.........11.0-in. vented disc, power assist
R:..11.0 x 2.0-in. cast iron drum, power assist

WHEELS AND TIRES
Wheel size..................15 x 6.0-in
Wheel type...........stamped steel, 5-bolt
Tire make and size............Uniroyal L78-15
Tire type..........fiberglass belted, tubeless
Test inflation pressures, F/R........24/20 psi
Tire load rating.....1970 lbs per tire @ 32 psi

PERFORMANCE
Zero to   Seconds
  30 mph.......................3.7
  40 mph.......................5.3
  50 mph.......................7.2
  60 mph.......................9.6
  70 mph.......................12.2
  80 mph.......................15.3
  90 mph.......................18.9
 100 mph.......................24.0
Standing ¼-mile........16.3 sec @ 86.0 mph
Top speed (estimated).............125 mph
80–0 mph..................266 ft (0.80 G)
Fuel mileage..9.0–11.0 mpg on premium fuel
Cruising range..................198–242 mi

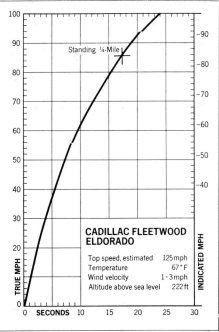

CADILLAC FLEETWOOD ELDORADO
Top speed, estimated   125mph
Temperature   67°F
Wind velocity   1–3mph
Altitude above sea level 222 ft

CADILLAC FLEETWOOD ELDORADO

glass belted tires, the ride tends to be slightly harsh (for a Cadillac, not for Chevrolet), and there is a surprising amount of low-frequency road noise, a kind of booming sound. But that's all you hear—no engine, no transmission, no wind, no clock—just road noise, and to put it into perspective the Cadillac is quieter than any Mercedes, with the possible exception of the 600 which costs several times more.

As we move along sifting the Eldorado's virtues and vices into ordered piles we are led to the not too surprising conclusion that it is meant more for touring than for sporting motoring. The performance of the brakes strongly reinforces that conclusion. It takes rather exceptional brakes to provide consistent stops for a car of the Eldorado's mass, and the car doesn't have them. It did make two stops from 80 mph in 266 feet (0.80G) but the fade was great enough so that after the first stop the test driver needed all the pedal force he could generate to make the second. The third try wasn't a stop at all but rather a smoky re-entry which took well over 400 feet. The stopping distances, as demonstrated in the first two tests, are adequate and directional stability is excellent, but the fade resistance is unacceptable for modern traffic situations. There just isn't the margin that you have a right to expect in a car of this quality and price.

Elsewhere you do get your money's worth. The Eldorado is very well finished: The paint is excellent, all of the trim pieces line up, the body is solid although not overly rigid, and high quality materials are evident throughout. And it's an easy car to drive. There are only two instruments as such, a speedometer and a gas gauge. The rest of the deeply hooded instrument cluster is given over to buttons and knobs for the activation and regulation of all sorts of marvelous devices. Easily the most enjoyable is the automatic temperature control which does its job with almost no noise. It's the best in the business. Of course there are other handy little labor savers that play music, turn on the lights, turn off the lights, lock the doors, lock the windows, open the trunk lid, etc., but they are all optional. Power steering and power brakes you get automatically, along with electric windows—everything else you pay for just like you would on a Chevrolet. "Want whitewall tires? That'll be $40.00, please, and we can put you in a trumpet horn for $15.80." And when you order up the optional leather upholstery you only get leather in the few discreet inserts that are most likely to end up beneath your backside—which doesn't show us any class at all.

None of these things detract from the Eldorado as a car, but they do tend to grind the luster off the Cadillac image. And after driving the Eldorado we are still convinced that image is Cadillac's most important asset. It's not a driver's car. Most of the development has been in the direction of isolating the driver from what is considered to be boredom inherent in over-the-road travel. And as the isolation becomes more complete the car stops being a car and instead becomes a kind of neutral transit capsule. And because there is no reason to prefer one transit capsule over another, identities have to be established for them so that the capsule once again becomes personal to its driver—even though, as a car, it has no character at all. Cadillac in general, and the Eldorado in particular, does this better than anyone else in Detroit. Knife-edge fenders covered with a mirror-like layer of acrylic lacquer, servants that dim the lights without being told, and vague, unsupported generalities about front-wheel-drive are the ingredients that constitute the Eldorado, and no one in the world is really concerned as to whether or not it goes around a corner, or stops on demand. The only thing that matters is what it appears to be—its image. Does it say the right thing?

Apparently it does. We tried extremes of American society, from Beverly Hills to Watts, and wherever we went the Eldorado was well received while, at times, we were barely tolerated. ●

THE STANDARD OF EXCELLENCE -REVISED

The more they change the Cad — the more it stays the same

They never *really* change the Cadillac from year to year, and perhaps that makes them one of the most sensible cars to come out of Detroit. Try and differentiate between the last five Cadillacs and honestly say you can tell which year is which. Most people can't, but the newly designed 1971 Cadillac will make it a bit easier next year.

The main view of the car, the one you see as it comes down the road at you, is basic Cadillac, but with a large egg crate grille and dual headlights that have been separated from each other. Overall it looks lower, a feeling derived from the new lower beltline for '71. The 472-cubic-inch engine is a low-lead fuel power plant. The interior is typically, elegant Cadillac.

Eldorado is also all new for '71 and also on low-lead gasoline for it's 500-cubic-inch engine. Styling is a complete departure from the Eldo tradition and the most noticeable feature is the fixed rear quarter windows, added to keep back seat riders from feeling like they're riding in a cave. The same back seaters were given due consideration on leg room and can nestle back into what feels like a big easy chair with plenty of room for their legs. They've even added an Eldo convertible.

The regular Cad and Eldo are new, but their grille treatments, clean uncluttered flanks, and slightly pointed vertical taillamps, along with the newly-revived hood ornament make them unmistakeably Cadillac. /MT

Above left and far left: Eldorado gets first complete facelift since inception. Front-wheel-drive remains, as does 500-cu.-in. engine, though it is now on low compression. Center left and near left: Regular Cads also get what is for them a radical restyling, though they are very obviously Cadillacs. Featured are new grille and interiors and lowered beltlines.

CADILLAC 1971 ENGINE AVAILABILITY

S = Standard

	Calais	De Ville	Eldorado	Sixty Special	Seventy-Five
472 cu. in., 4-bbl. V-8, 345 hp @ 4400 rpm	S	S		S	S
500 cu. in., 4-bbl. V-8, 365 hp @ 4400 rpm			S		

CADILLAC 1971 ENGINE SPECIFICATIONS

Disp. (Cu. Ins.)	No. Cyls.	Carb. Type	Hp @ Rpm	Torque (Lb.-Ft. @ Rpm)	Bore & Stroke (Ins.)	Comp. Ratio, Fuel Type
472	8	4-bbl.	345 @ 4400	500 @ 2800	4.30 x 4.06	8.5 R
500	8	4-bbl.	365 @ 4400	535 @ 2800	4.30 x 4.304	8.5 R

CADILLAC MAJOR OPTIONS & ACCESSORIES

1 = Standard, 2 = Optional, 0 = Not Offered

	Power Drum Brakes	Power Disc Brakes	Power Steering	Var.-Ratio Pwr. Strng.	Power Seats	Power Windows	Adj. Steering Wheel	Automatic Door Locks	Air Cond., Manual	Air Cond., Auto.	AM/FM Radio	AM/FM Radio	AM/FM Stereo Radio	Stereo Tape	Auto. Headlight Dim.	Headlight Delay	Cornering Lights	Automatic Ride Cntrl.	Rear Defrost in Glass	Luggage Rack	Sun Roof	Wagon Air Deflector	Tailgate Washer/Wiper	2-Way Tailgate	Antenna in Windshield	Styled Wheels or Covers	Vinyl Top	Disc Brakes	Ram-Air	Handling Package	Anti-Skid Control
Calais Coupe	0	1	0	1	1	1	2	2	2	2	0	2	2	2	2	2	1	2	2	0	0	0	0	0	1	0	2	1	0	0	0
Calais Sedan	0	1	0	1	1	1	2	2	2	2	0	2	2	2	2	2	1	2	2	0	0	0	0	0	1	0	2	1	0	0	0
Coupe De Ville	0	1	0	1	1	1	2	2	2	2	0	2	2	2	2	2	1	2	2	0	0	0	0	0	1	0	2	1	0	0	0
Sedan De Ville	0	1	0	1	1	1	2	2	2	2	0	2	2	2	2	2	1	2	2	0	0	0	0	0	1	0	2	1	0	0	0
Fleetwood Sixty Special Brougham	0	1	0	1	1	1	2	2	2	2	0	2	2	2	2	2	1	1	2	0	0	0	0	0	1	0	2	1	0	0	0
Eldorado Coupe	0	1	0	1	1	1	2	2	2	2	0	2	2	2	2	2	1	1	2	0	0	0	0	0	1	0	2	1	0	0	2
Eldorado Convertible	0	1	0	1	1	1	2	2	2	2	0	2	2	2	2	2	1	1	2	0	0	0	0	0	1	0	2	1	0	0	2
Seventy-Five Sedan	0	1	0	1	1	1	2	2	2	2	0	2	2	2	2	2	1	1	2	0	0	0	0	0	1	0	2	1	0	0	0
Seventy-Five Limo.	0	1	0	1	1	1	2	2	2	2	0	2	2	2	2	2	1	1	2	0	0	0	0	0	1	0	2	1	0	0	0

CADILLAC

The so-called "Standard of the World" is completely new for 1971 in both conventional and front-wheel-drive form. And, for the first time, bodies borrow a great deal from Cadillac's past. For example, fins are emerging once again and the Eldorado has a peculiar sort of rear quarter windows that Derham might have put in one of his customized standard bodies of the late Thirties and post-war Forties.

Mechanically, the cars are not changed much except that both engines have been tuned for regular gasoline and the Eldorado has a new, full-length frame with coil springs replacing leafs at the rear. A rear-wheel anti-skid brake system is an option for the Eldorado. Then, the gargantuan limousines on the 151.5-inch wheelbase are continued, and you will inevitably ride in one someday when a loved one passes away.

Calais as before comes in hardtop coupe and sedan form on a 130.0-inch wheelbase which is ½-inch longer than the '70 models. Very few Calais models are sold despite the fact that they are somewhat cheaper than a fully equipped Chevrolet Caprice. The De Ville 2-door hardtop, though, is Cadillac's biggest seller by far.

A student of this marque will note a reversion to the torpedo-like sculpture that marked the rear fenders of '61 models when fins were at their height. Whether the new ones have fins or not is arguable because while the fenders are straight along their tops, the trunk dips sharply enough to give them prominent display. At the front, the main styling difference is a rather wide spacing between each of the dual headlights. An intricate bumper with integral, rubber-inserted guards protects a vertical grille.

Roof lines are formal to an extreme and much attention has been paid to giving new expression to the commonly ordered vinyl top. On De Ville coupes, a trace of body metal follows up and over the side windows from rear to front. On the top-line Sixty Special Brougham, this theme is reversed with a trace of the vinyl material extending down the center pillar on each side.

The Calais series, as mentioned, consists of a hardtop coupe and sedan as does the De Ville. The convertible style has been transferred to the front-wheel-drive Eldorado, and both it and the coupe are technically a part of the Fleetwood series. This also includes the Sixty Special Brougham, a

CADILLAC 1971 BODY STYLE AVAILABILITY

SERIES	2-dr. cpe.	2-dr. sdn.	2-dr. hdtp.	2-dr. fstbk.	2-dr. conv.	4-dr. sdn.	4-dr. hdtp.	7-pass. sdn.	7-pass. limo.
Calais			X				X		
De Ville			X				X		
Fleetwood Eldorado	X				X				
Fleetwood Seventy-Five								X	X
Fleetwood Sixty Special							X		

CADILLAC 1971 CAR DIMENSIONS

SERIES	Wheelbase, 2-dr. (ins.)	Wheelbase, 4-dr. (ins.)	Length 2-dr. (ins.)	Length 4-dr. (ins.)	Width (ins.)	Height (ins.)	Track, Front (ins.)	Track, Rear (ins.)	Head Room, Front (ins.)	Head Room, Rear (ins.)	Leg Room, Front (ins.)	Leg Room, Rear (ins.)	Luggage (cu. ft.)	Fuel (gals.)	Weight, 6-cyl. (lbs.)	Weight, 8-cyl. (lbs.) (est.)
Calais Coupe	130.0	—	225.8	—	79.8	54.1	63.6	63.3	38.8	38.0	41.9	38.8	16.5	27	—	4750
Calais Sedan	—	130.0	—	225.8	79.8	54.1	63.6	63.3	39.3	38.1	41.9	39.9	16.5	27	—	4750
Coupe DeVille	130.0	—	225.8	—	79.8	54.1	63.6	63.3	38.8	38.0	41.9	38.8	16.5	27	—	4750
Sedan DeVille	—	130.0	—	225.8	79.8	54.4	63.6	63.3	39.3	38.1	41.9	39.9	16.5	27	—	4750
Fleetwood Sixty Special Brougham	—	133.0	—	228.8	79.8	55.5	63.6	63.3	39.4	38.2	41.9	43.9	16.5	27	—	5200
Fleetwood Eldorado Coupe	126.3	—	221.6	—	79.8	53.9	63.6	63.6	38.1	37.0	42.0	35.4	13.5	27	—	4700
Fleetwood Eldorado Convertible	126.3	—	221.6	—	79.8	53.9	63.6	63.6	38.1	38.0	42.0	35.4	13.5	27	—	4700
Seventy-Five Sedan	—	151.5	—	247.3	79.8	58.1	63.6	63.3	40.4	38.1	41.9	—	16.5	27	—	7000
Seventy-Five Limousine	—	151.5	—	247.3	79.8	58.1	63.6	63.3	39.5	38.1	40.9	—	16.5	27	—	7000

All dimensions based on 4-dr. sedan except where otherwise noted or style is not offered.

FLEETWOOD SIXTY SPECIAL BROUGHAM

CADILLAC
calais, de ville fleetwood eldorado

pillar sedan, and the Seventy-Five 7-passenger sedans and limousines which sell mostly to liveries and funeral parlors at the rate of about 7000 a year. The chassis for these are also widely used as a basis for funeral coaches and ambulances.

The 472-cubic-inch V-8 is continued but with an 8.5:1 compression ratio which lowers horsepower to 345 at 4400 rpm. Here it might be worthwhile to dwell a bit on the difference between gross and net horsepower ratings. Within GM, Chevrolet and Pontiac quote gross ratings, Oldsmobile net and Cadillac gives both. Gross is obtained from a bare engine operating on a dynamometer under ideal conditions. Net is roughly the figure produced as the engine comes installed in the car. With the latter system of rating, output for the Cadillac dwindles to 220 hp at 4000 rpm. Remember this when you get to the section on Oldsmobile and wonder what happened to the ram-air 4-4-2.

On the inside of the new Cadillacs a total of no less than 156 different trim combinations may be ordered in cloth, vinyl or leather or a combination of these. The instrument panel is new but still persists in depending upon warning lights. The hood release, though, is on the inside for better protection against theft. To solve a common complaint from buyers of recent Cadillacs, the front seats have lower backs for better visibility. Then, there's a new buzzer on the automatic headlight control to indicate that you've left the manual switch on and therefore, the twilight sentinel can't work.

The front-wheel-drive Eldorado has been given entirely new sheetmetal too, along with a new frame that now extends to the rear of the car. This allows the use of coil springs at the rear which are somewhat softer than the previous leaf variety. Front springing continues to be by torsion bars, and the method of driving those wheels is by a belt-activated Turbo Hydra-Matic mounted adjacent to the left side of the engine.

Standard Eldorado power is a 500-cubic-inch V-8 rated at 365 hp by the conventional gross method and 235 by the new net SAE procedures. We're not quite sure that this new honesty is ever going to sell because, unless you're technically minded, you might understandably think that low-lead fuels have brought us back to the days just after World War II. The new rating method just coincidentally relates to the new detuning of engines.

Styling of the Eldorado coupe is sure to be controversial but it does answer a fairly common complaint of present owners. The formal style of windowless landau tops may look fine from the outside, but rear seat occupants can't see much scenery. The new fixed rear quarter windows will help but they do look like an afterthought. A body style new to the Eldorado, but quite appropriate for this model is the convertible.

All Cadillacs have power-assisted front disc brakes as standard equipment along with almost every other form of power assist. Unlike Lincoln, though, they haven't standardized air conditioning even though almost every

SEDAN DE VILLE

FLEETWOOD ELDORADO

Cadillac made comes equipped with this option. Eldorado options include an anti-skid braking system that works on the rear wheels only and a most unusual addition to the battery of warning lights which tells you when the windshield washer fluid is reaching a dangerously low level. •

CALAIS/DE VILLE/SIXTY SPECIAL SEVENTY-FIVE
ENGINE: 472 cu ins (345 hp).
TRANSMISSION: 3-spd auto std.
SUSPENSION: Coil front, coil rear.
STEERING: Variable-ratio power std, curb-to-curb 46.0 ft.
BRAKES: Power front discs std.
FUEL CAPACITY: 27.0 gals.
DIMENSIONS: Wheelbase 130.0-151.5 ins. Track 62.5 ins. Width 79.8 ins. Length 225.8-247.3 ins. Height 54.1-58.1 ins. Weight 4750-7000 lbs. Trunk 16.5 cu ft.
BODY STYLES: 2-dr hdtp, 4-dr sdn, 4-dr hdtp, 7-pass sdn, 7-pass limo.

ELDORADO
ENGINE: 500 cu ins (365 hp).
TRANSMISSION: 3-spd auto std.
SUSPENSION: Torsion bar front, coil rear.
STEERING: Variable-ratio power std, curb-to-curb 44.8 ft.
BRAKES: Power front discs std.
FUEL CAPACITY: 27.0 gals.
DIMENSIONS: Wheelbase 126.3 ins. Track 62.5 ins. Width 79.8 ins. Length 221.6 ins. Height 53.4-53.9 ins. Weight 4700 lbs. Trunk 13.5 cu ft.
BODY STYLES: 2-dr cpe, 2-dr conv.

COUPE DE VILLE

CASA DE ELDORADO

"King of the Kustomizers," George Barris, scores again with this wagon built for Dean Martin.

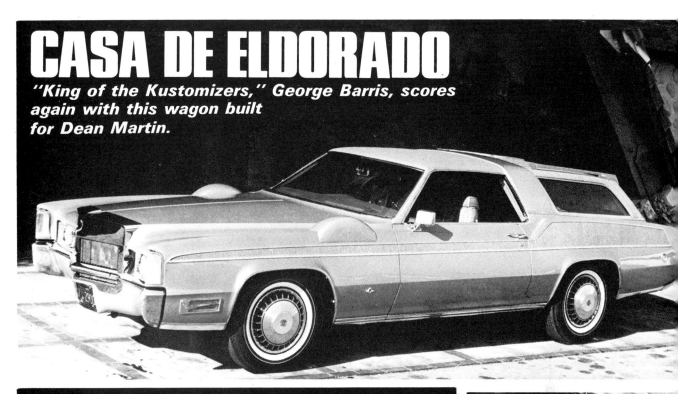

The fact that Cadillac is giving serious consideration to limited production of an Eldorado station wagon proves once again the Midas touch of George Barris, self-styled "King of the Kustomizers." His "Casa de Eldorado," built for Dean Martin in January, 1970, at a cost of over $18,000, is as far as is known the first of a kind that is now being made by several builders including Universal Coach of Detroit and Lehmann-Peterson of Chicago.

That $18,000 figure, of course, does not include the first cost of the Eldorado coupe from which the wagon conversion stems. Also, it is on the high side because Dean Martin characteristically ordered almost every extra in Barris's catalog, plus a few that weren't. The basic conversion can be had for $10,500, which includes the bodywork itself, a paint job in standard Cadillac "Fire-Frost" colors, matching leather vinyl upholstery with a Spanish motif, the Tambora vinyl exterior trim and the electrically actuated tailgate.

The use of standard Cadillac paint is a practical consideration to facilitate body repairs at a later date. Another very practical feature of this custom is that nothing is done to invalidate the Cadillac warranty. The only mechanical change performed by Barris is to adjust the rear air shocks (standard on the Eldorado) to match the slightly altered weight distribution.

The body is safer by far than the original because a double roll bar cage forms an integral part of the added wagon greenhouse, and all of the bodywork contributed by Barris is of metal. Extras available include an electric sun roof at $750, the Barris "Casa de Eldorado" grille and imitation spare tire pods shown on the car pictured (Dean Martin's) at $925 and $350, respectively, and the Vogue tires. Inside you can get a walnut entertainment console installed on the front center floor to house a 9-inch television, multiple track tape deck and telephone. A walnut cocktail bar can be installed in the glove box, containing decanters, glasses and the new canned mixed drinks. At the rear, vanity cases are standard.

The legality of the television is dubious and the illegality of the cocktail bar in use is certain, but these are still features of all Barris "Kustom" jobs. Perhaps you could get away with the latter while picnicking as long as all open containers were disposed of prior to operating the vehicle and, of course, the operator abstained from that phase of the picnic menu.

Barris dubs his creation a "luxury town and estate wagon" and certainly the plush carpeting throughout would dispel any inclination to use it for hauling gardening supplies. Four of them have already been built, with 12 orders currently on the books plus one based on a Mark III Continental for Glenn Campbell, the folk singer.

The car pictured is a '70 model and no '71s have been built as yet, primarily because of the re-tooling necessitated by the Eldorado's new frame extension at the rear.

Self-contained entertainment and business center is an option and a Barris trademark. Most states would require that the TV be angled away from the driver.

Customized luggage ordered by Dean Martin comes from Gucci of Italy. Plush carpeting in this area precludes use of the car for hauling gardening supplies.

Close-up shows the special Tambora vinyl body trim which matches only certain shades of Cadillac's standard "Fire-Frost" paint. Tailgate is actuated electrically.

Rear seats have been widened slightly from standard Eldorado dimensions. Vanity case in each "B" post is standard equipment and the roll cage is completely hidden.

KING

If you've got the American Dream, if you've made a pilgrimage to the Grand Canyon, Disneyland, Mt. Rushmore, or the Okefenokee Swamp, if your goal is to move all the way up from your Biscayne station wagon, then the Lincoln Continental Mark III and Cadillac Eldorado are the end of status street. Top of the heap. King of the Hill. But which one? Is there a King?"

That's the way we started our Mark III-Eldo comparison test last year, starting a controversy that still rattles between the walls of our office.

Your reaction was unexpected. We knew the "King of the Hill" test last July would ruffle some feathers, but not to the extent that it did. So the letters started, as did the controversy.

We got many notes obviously written by Mark III and Eldo owners, most of them neatly typewritten on business letterhead stationery with properly unreadable signatures. The majority set down nice, well thought out arguments why we were right or wrong. But then came a stream of letters we didn't expect, written by people who didn't own either of the cars, but who really cared.

The notes came typewritten on bond and illegibly scrawled on lined notebook paper. Some were logical arguments for or against us, but others were heated, obscene comments that not only questioned our judgement, but also our parentage. They called the Mark III the "Stinken Lincoln" and had similar, but unprintable, comments on the Eldo.

It seems that many owners consider the Mark III and Eldo extensions of their LTDs and Caprices, and if we say that Lincoln is better (as we did last year) an LTD owner considers his car to be better. But the interesting part is that these expensive, "high class" automobiles should spark so violent and heated a reaction.

With all that interest, and a new Eldorado, we decided to repeat the test and see if, perhaps, the Mark III must now take the back seat. The biggest difference in the new Eldo is styling and that is, of course, a personal thing. Regardless, we must say that the unchanged Mark III, in our opinion, still maintains a lead here. It has kept its smooth, clean, though boxy, appearance,

Styling is a personal thing, but Mark III (left) seems to come off cleaner and more formal looking than the new Eldo. Rear quarter window in the Eldorado breaks up a potentially dangerous blind rear-quarter. Eldo has its first convertible with clean, compact center-folding top frame.

OF THE HILL:
ELDO-MARK III REVISITED
Do not forget that for one brief, shining moment there was a magic place called Camelot and that a Mark III was parked in the driveway / By John Lamm

After a tremendous response to our Lincoln Continental Mark III vs. Cadillac Eldorado test last year, we decided to give the '71 Eldo a chance to redeem itself. It came close — closer than last year — but still falls short. And next year we get a new, secret Continental Mark IV.

while the new Eldo opted for a more cluttered design that involves extra bulges, a big chrome "scoop" on the side and that rear quarter window. If it is any consolation to the Cad fans, that rear quarter window is the newest rage in Detroit and you will see it on other cars in 1972. Along with design goes exterior finish and this again puts Lincoln ahead, though by very little. The padded vinyl top on the Lincoln is finished better, using a more luxurious looking material with extra padding. Cadillac uses more of the molded stitching and less padding, and the fit around the quarter window in our model had bulges where it should have been smooth. Eldo, like many GM products, has suffered because of the need of GM to catch up after the strike, thus producing some shoddily assembled automobiles. One Cadillac dealer remarked that for the first time ever, he has seen some of the poorly constructed "do-it-yourself" cars come into his dealership. No doubt the finish will improve as the production line smooths out.

Interiors are extremely important in a luxury car, since that is where the guy who shelled out $8,000-10,000 must live with it. The Eldo has a much better arrangement, especially in the dash area, where the instruments and gauges and switches are well placed and very legible. The Mark III's dash, with its instruments grouped in individual pods,

Above: Mark III interior won points on its luxury feel and aura. It lost, though, on placement of dials and switches and ease of use. Below: Eldorado was the reverse, with well placed, easy-to-read instruments and switches, but placing them in a colder, fabricated, all-GM atmosphere.

KING OF THE HILL:

is not as handy and gauges are much harder to read. But, in adapting the same fine layout and legibility of all GM cars, the Eldo inherits their sameness and so it looks like it could be any of 70 or 80 GM models. The Mark III stands alone.

The Mark III also won on back seat legroom, though there was a less than acceptable headliner fit around the back and the low profile top cuts into headroom. Both front seats are fully and electrically adjustable and while the Mark III kindly puts all the controls on the arm rest, making it very easy to whirr the seat up, down, forward, back tilted, etc., the Eldo will tilt and angle the driver into more comfortable positions. Seating comfort is strictly a seat-of-the-pants decision, with the materials doing a lot for the final decision. The Eldo had a bright fabric that did a nice job of holding you in place, while the Mark III had leather that let you slide a bit more and got hot in the sun, yet looked far more rich than the GM material. Both cars had an impressive array of the neat little trick gadgets that proliferate in these cars (though nowadays you can get them in most every model). There were full temperature controls so you just set the climate for your car and don't worry about it from then on. (They could offer rain and snow, but you know government regulations.) Fibre optics let you know if your taillights are working. The headlights go on automatically at dusk and then dim themselves when neces-

SPECIFICATIONS
ELDORADO

Engine	V8 —OHV
Bore & stroke — ins.	4.3 x 4.3
Displacement — cu. in.	500
HP @ RPM	360 @ 4400
Torque: lbs.-ft. @ RPM	535 @ 2800
Compression Ratio/Fuel	8.51/lead-free
Carburetion	1-4 bbl
Transmission	3-speed automatic
Final Drive Ratio	2.93:1
Steering type	Power — variable ratio
Steering Ratio	16.3:1
Turning Diameter (curb-to-curb-ft.)	41.3
Wheel Turns (lock to lock)	2.7
Tire size	L78 x 15
Brakes	Front disc/rear drum
Front Suspension	Independent torsion bars
Rear Suspendion	Beam axle, coil springs, shocks angled back to axle, twin locating arms
Body/Frame Construction	Separate body/frame
Wheelbase — ins.	126.3
Overall length — lbs.	221.6
Width — ins.	79.8
Height — ins.	53.9
Front Track — ins.	63.6
Rear Track — ins.	63.5
Curb Weight — lbs.	4,71
Fuel Capacity — gals.	27
Oil Capacity — qts.	5 + 1 (filter)

PERFORMANCE

Acceleration
0-30 mph	3.47
0-45 mph	5.93
0-60 mph	9.88
0-75 mph	14.55

Standing Start
¼-mile mph	83.0
Elapsed time	17.06

Passing speeds
40-60 mph	5.0
50-70 mph	5.7

Speeds in gears*
1st ...mph @ rpm	56.5 @ 4600
2nd...mph @ rpm	93.5 @ 4600
3rd ...mph @ rpm	100 @ 3500
Mph per 1000 rpm (in top gear)	28.5

Stopping distances
From 30 mph	32.5
From 60 mph	145.5

Gas mileage
Range	9.2 to 11.3

Speedometer error
Electric
 speedometer .30 45 50 60 70 80
Car
 speedometer 31 46 51 61.5 71.5 82

*Speeds in gears are at shift points (limited by the length of track) and do not represent maximum speeds.

SPECIFICATIONS
MARK III

Engine	V8 — OHV
Bore & stroke — ins.	4.36 x 3.85
Displacement — cu. in.	460
HP @ RPM	365 @ 4600
Torque lbs.-ft. @ RPM	500 @ 2800
Compression Ratio/Fuel	10.0:1/premium
Carburetion	1-4 bbl
Transmission	3-speed automatic
Final Drive Ratio	2.80 or 3.00
Steering type	Power
Steering Ratio	21.9:1
Turning Diameter (curb-to-curb-ft.)	44.6
Wheel Turns (lock to lock)	3.7
Tire size	225 x 15 Michelin radials
Brakes	Front disc/rear drum
Front Suspension	Independent, coil springs
Rear Suspension	3-link with coil spring, track bar
Body/Frame Construction	Separate body/frame
Wheelbase — ins.	117.2
Overall length — ins.	216.1
Width — ins.	79.4
Height — ins.	53.0
Front Track — ins.	62.3
Rear Track — ins.	62.3
Curb Weight — lbs.	5,038
Fuel Capacity — gals.	22.5
Oil Capacity — qts.	4 + 1 (filter)

PERFORMANCE

Acceleration
0-30 mph	3.50
0-45 mph	6.25
0-60 mph	10.25
0-75	14.95

Standing Start
¼-mile mph	82.5
Elapsed time	17.7

Passing speeds
40-60 mph	5.1
50-70 mph	6-1

Speeds in gears*
1st ...mph @ rpm	48 @ 4400
2nd...mph @ rpm	82 @ 4400
3rd ...mph @ rpm	105 @ 3800
Mph per 1000 rpm (in top gear)	27.6

Stopping distances
From 30 mph	30.4
From 60 mph	137

Gas mileage
Range	8.8 to 9.25

Speedometer error
Electric
 speedometer .30 45 50 60 70 80
Car
 speedometer .30 44 49 58 67 76

*Speeds in gears are at shift points (limited by the length of track) and do not represent maximum speeds.

KING OF THE HILL

sary, there are cruise controls, and rear window defrosters, a remote control for the right hand mirror (Eldo), front seat fold-down armrests, tilting and telescoping steering wheels, remote control trunk locks and radios — very expensive radios. The Eldo AM/FM stereo unit at $416.80 includes a tape deck that made a funny scraping noise and had a better sound than the Mark III's $307.00 stereo outfit. At that price they should both be superb.

To sum up interior environment, we could best quote from last year's test, "In total, the Eldorado dash and front seat environment is rather stark compared to the Mark III plushness." Perhaps the thing that sets the Mark III apart is the warm brown of the interior, rather like the dark, warm wood of a plush old estate house. But even when you look at Mark III and Eldo models with different interior colors, the Mark III still comes off like the family that has lived gracefully for years with its money, while the Eldo feels like "nouveau riche," trying so hard to tell the world it's wealthy.

"With weight factors somewhere just below a Union Pacific domeliner coach, both cars have quite similar ride characteristics because any harshness, noise, or road feel is cushioned out before it ever gets to the driver." Last year's observation on ride still holds true, though slightly modified. The Eldo has done an even better job of isolating the interior from the world and it is a bit quieter. However, road feel is eliminated in the Eldo, while you can still feel some of it in the Mark III. It's a matter of which you prefer. Neither of the cars is a good handling car and no doubt wasn't meant to be. They've been built to act safely in the terms of their manufacturer, but from that point it's all plush, quiet ride. Just a hint of engine noise and an occasional muffled rumble from the outside world, all easily covered up by the stereo. The Eldo rolls a bit more than the Mark III, in cornering, but takes the edge in wet-weather handling as that front-wheel drive does help out. Eldo also has an automatic leveling control that will allow for an extra 500 pounds in the back and still maintain an even attitude. Steering is an Eldo high point with that variable ratio unit making life less hectic when you have to turn sharply (and even in straight lines, for that matter) than the slow power steering of the Mark III. Both cars had front disc, rear drum brakes and trick braking systems intended to cut the possibility of a skid, Eldo with their Track Master, Mark III with their Sure Track, and while we never had a chance to try them in the wet ourselves, they are highly recommended.

Overall braking on the Mark III was disappointing both from the average 145.5 feet it took to stop the car from 60 and the way it wagged its tail in the last quarter of the stop. The Eldo stopped shorter (137 feet) and avoided locking up until the final 20 feet when it chirped the tires a bit as the back came out slightly.

Engines for both cars are two of the biggest around, Eldo being *the* biggest. That unit is 500 cubic inches and rated at 365 horsepower with its GM-type 8.5:1 compression ratio and the ability to drink lead-free gasoline (though one wonders how many Eldo owners can bring themselves to use it). The Mark III's engine is also rated at 365 horsepower (though it takes a back seat on torque — 500 lbs. ft. @ 2800) and has only dropped from 10.5:1 to 10.0:1 compression ratio, so it still needs premium. Acceleration of the two cars is almost identical, with only a difference of .4 second to 75 mph, though tighter smog regs have dropped them both back a full second from last year. That acceleration, though, is very smooth as is to be expected on this class of car, with no overbearing lurches as it drops to passing gear and no problems when you turn on all the "environmental control systems" that are hung on the engine. Both cars are very similar on gas mileage, Mark III just edging above the 11-mpg barrier and averaging closer to 10 mpg. Not that people who drop $10,000 for a car worry about those things — I hope. Now lets talk price, because if there is one thing both cars have a lot of, it's price. Interestingly enough, base for the Eldo is about $1,000 below the Mark III ($7,383 vs. $8,377), but comparably equipped models of both run about the same. Our Eldo listed out at $9,616, while the Lincoln ran about $9,137, with fewer options. Perhaps it all comes down to the fact that if you're in that price neighborhood and quibbling over pennies, you're buying the wrong car.

"So, who is King of the Hill? As long as there are Eldorado and Mark III owners around, cigar sales will continue to go up and no one will ever agree. The Eldorado has a lot of seemingly more advanced technical conveniences, but from a strictly plush, posh, luxury standpoint the Mark III has the intimacy a car like this should offer." That's how we ended the test last year and that's how we must end it this year, noting that margin between the two cars has been cut by the people at Cadillac but the Mark III is still our top prestigous automobile. Note also, though, that there is a new Mark IV coming for '72 and it is said to be something very special. For the prices they get for these cars, it has to be special. /MT

Top Luxury For Pennies...

It's not the $10,700 first cost but the $473 first year's depreciation that makes the Eldorado a best buy.

Webster defines soporific as "causing or tending to cause sleep" and thus, the word certainly may be used to describe the Cadillac Eldorado. The car, when equipped with all of its optional luxuries, is unbelievably complex but the package, and this is the design intent, needs merely to be aimed down the highway. About the only nicety lacking is a device to automate navigation.

The Eldorado is undeniably good looking and odds are that it like its only serious competitor, the Continental Mark IV, will be a collectors' car of the future. We wouldn't, though, care to contemplate the cost of restoration. It would be comparable in 1:50 scale to the raising and refurbishing of the RMS Queen Elizabeth.

The front-drive Eldorado, fashioned along lines pioneered by the Olds Toronado with which it shares basic body shells, first appeared in 1967 and for a car which can cost upwards of $10,000 when fully equipped, it has been a solid success. About 27,000 are sold each model year, the convertible added to the line in 1971 not having done much to increase the total.

The Eldorado has the dubious distinction of being powered by the world's largest passenger car engine, it being a 500 cubic-inch stroked version of the power plant used in rear-drive Cadillacs. It is exactly square with a bore and stroke of 4.30 inches, very smooth throughout the power range and not quite as thirsty as you would expect. A cruising economy of 12.4 mpg is about on a par with a big-engined Impala or Ford LTD.

The reason for what seems to be excessively generous displacement becomes apparent when SAE gross and net horsepower ratings are compared. The gross method measures output without any engine-driven accessories installed and on this basis, Eldorado output is 365 hp at 4,400 rpm. By the net method, which is closer to what is actually delivered at the driving wheels, the rating is 235 hp at 3,800 rpm. In other words, the accessories consume

While not standard, Eldorados look better with a vinyl top covering. The rear quarter windows are fixed but a sunroof is optionally available.

Instrument panel is plush even though it mostly consists of warning lights in extreme variety. Wide pedal is designed for two-foot braking should power assist fail.

130 hp or slightly more than one-third the total available!

There's still enough left, though, to pull the 4,750-lb car from zero to 60 mph in 9.4 seconds and through the quarter-mile in 17.4 with a terminal speed of 82 mph. Running the engine to about 2,000 rpm against the brake will draw protest from the tires and we have yet to get used to this originating from the front set. The average Eldorado buyer is not likely to run against the clock at Orange County International Raceway but if he so chose, he could do so in ultimate comfort, silence and safety.

We mention the safety aspect because it applies to conditions commonly encountered in winter. With front drive, even the slightest amount of forward movement gives you steering control. In the early fifties and on a smaller scale than the Eldorado, the Swedish Saab was quite popular in New England while all but unknown elsewhere in the country only because of its superior mobility in heavy snows and on ice. Volkswagen may have thought up the ad about how snowplow drivers got to work but it was front-drive Saabs that they used.

Theoretically, the Eldorado should be under power at all times while cornering on the premise that it's being towed through. In practice, however, the big beast is quite forgiving and surprisingly agile. It may need two lanes of road but allowing that or more, there seems to be no limit to the speeds at which you can go around. We don't suppose the technique is in any textbook but we found that a combination of continuous brake and throttle gave the highest degree of control while maneuvering a turn at speed.

It should be emphasized that overdriving an Eldorado could be dangerous because it is engineered, and exquisitely so, to not relate in any way to the road. It is not likely to give the driver any clear warning that the limit is approaching.

The ride is absolutely untroubled by any of the undulations on main thoroughfares or freeways. The Eldorado is not, however, a car to be driven at speed over rough surfaces or more particularly, over railway crossings or drainage gulleys. It can be bottomed easily and when that happens, frightening noises emanate from the vast side windows. There is also noticeable rebound from the soft shock absorbers. If we were to own an Eldorado, it would be equipped with adjustable Konis or the equivalent forthwith.

Variable ratio power steering by Saginaw Division is standard equipment and with 2.75 turns lock to lock, it is reasonably precise. Despite the fact that most are equipped with the optional tilt and telescoping feature, Cadillac has always favored a relatively tiny, 15½-inch steering wheel that further inhibits road feel. Granted, smaller ones are used on race cars but then, race cars aren't nearly 80 inches wide.

The Eldorado instrument panel, which is about the only item shared with rear-drive Cadillacs, is designed on the assumption that owners concern themselves only with ignition, speed and gas supply. Everything else registers on well-marked warning lights, enough of them so that even the most experienced driver would be well advised to study the owners manual before venturing around the corner.

There are lights for both the coolant

Vast rear window contains an electric defroster imbedded in the glass. Right-hand mirror is remotely controlled from the driver's position.

and engine metal temperature, the latter intended to indicate overheating that's serious versus a temporary condition. Along with the oil warning light, it perfunctorily reads "Stop Eng." There are also warning lights for brake failure, alternator, seat belts, trunk ajar and even the level of the fluid in the windshield washer bottle. Oddly, though, the more usual and useful door ajar and low gas warnings are missing.

A parking brake warning light is not provided because the brake releases automatically with a loud clunk whenever the car is started. Other clunks emanate from the automatic seat back latches and from the recycling of what Cadillac calls its "track master computer controlled rear wheel braking system" which we'll discuss later. The parking brake, incidentally, can double as a true emergency system operating on the rear wheels as it will not lock as long as the car is in any gear.

An optional lamp monitoring system that indicates via fiber optics when key exterior lights are operating invariably fascinates passengers new to the car. In each front fender, amber, green and red lights show turn signal, low and high beam, respectively. On the package shelf and visible through the mirror are monitors for the tail lamps which brighten when the brakes are applied.

With or without the above monitors, you can order devices to automatically dim the headlights and to turn them on or off automatically according to natural light conditions. The latter includes a time delay which keeps the headlights and the appropriate cornering lamp on long enough so that you can get out of the car and into the house. We've not been avid fans of automatic dimming, mainly because it's sensitive to light from other sources than oncoming cars, but Cadillac's latest system with intensity control admittedly works well if you practice the setting of it.

You also have to qualify as a buzzer expert to operate an Eldorado. There's one, of course, for the key being left in the lock. There's another if you start the car without you and your passenger fastening the seat belts. One sounds if you leave the car with the light switch on, something easy enough to do if you've become accustomed to their automatic operation which is automatic

Eldorado can occupy a couple of lanes while cornering fast but it's surprisingly stable for its size and soft suspension.

Our test car was equipped with an electronic anti-skid system that works only on the rear drums. Front discs grab harder, causing some dive.

only as long as the car is running. Finally, there's a buzzer for the "Stop Eng-Temp" warning system that you normally wouldn't hear except for the fact that it sounds off each time you leave the car. It takes some practice to arrive home overdue in the wee hours of the morning and get in the house without arousing the whole neighborhood.

Unlike most cars in the luxury-personal category, the Eldorado has adequate legroom in the rear when the front seat is positioned about midway and that in turn leaves room for a six-foot driver. In testing cars with split-bench power seats, we've learned to check the space (or lack of it) between the two sections for personal belongings that have dropped down out of sight. The haul this time was a pair of sun glasses, a case for another pair of glasses, a lady's handkerchief and a dollar bill — none of it ours. A few more items and the seat would have jammed.

Another minor complaint involves the design of the ash tray and lighter which are combined in the dash under the radio. It's on rollers and when you push in the lighter, you close the sharp-edged tray on your hand.

The stereo tape and AM/FM radio option is a superb instrument with a tonal quality that rivals some of the better home systems. The aperture for the eight-track tape hides behind the hinged radio dial and the speakers are hooked up diagonally front to rear. The radio does a good job of holding those flighty stereo stations in tune but unfortunately, the tape deck isn't equipped to handle the latest four-channel tapes. At a price of $417 one could rightfully expect this innovation but apparently GM's Delco Division was slow in obtaining the necessary licenses.

Also outstanding is the automatic air conditioning and heater system which, again, ought to be at $537. It has five settings and all but one will keep the interior at any temperature you select on the dial. It will defog the big windshield in seconds and handle the side glass at the same time. A separate unit with wires imbedded in the glass is provided for the rear window. Exclusive, we believe, is that the heater phase automatically refrains from operating until the engine reaches operating temperature which saves you that uncomfortable blast of cold air when the selector is inadvertently left in other than the "off" position.

Our test car was equipped with an

anti-skid system for the rear drum brakes and, of course, power assist for the overall system which includes front disc brakes. In normal operation, the brakes have a velvet touch but in repeated stops from 60 mph, fade is soon noticeable. On our third maximum effort stop from that speed, the rear drums wouldn't bite enough to actuate the electronic anti-skid control which you can clearly feel and hear when it's working. Thus, for both good and bad reasons, it's impossible to slide the wheels while braking an Eldorado. The brakes will recover rapidly, though, so the proneness to fade is not a hazard in normal operation.

The 174 feet recorded in our test data represents the average of these three stops and the first was a good 50 feet shorter than the last. In the National Highway Safety Bureau's standardized tests under light load conditions, the figure recorded is 196 feet but that

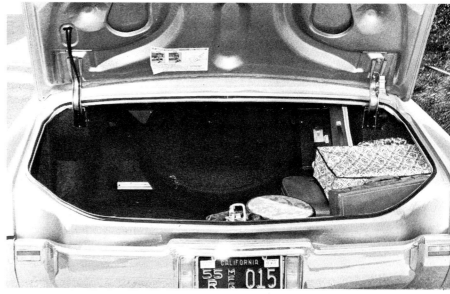

Trunk floor as well as spare tire are fully covered in genuine carpeting. An electric opener with switch in glove compartment is optional.

Super wide doors pose problems in parking lots but they have a neat electric lock which may be slammed closed. Caution: Don't leave key in ignition!

involves only 150 lbs pedal pressure which is about what the average woman is capable of applying. When the power assist was rendered inoperative in these NHSB tests, the stopping distance climbed to 508 feet from 60 mph with the same pedal pressure. Therein lies the reason for the tendency of Eldorado brakes to fade.

As the front wheels have the combined job of handling the major braking load, steering and acceleration, you can't expect much more than 8,000 miles from the front tires if you drive at all hard. Cadillac itself recommends rotating tires every 4,000 miles under these conditions.

Considering the complexity of the car, the attention to detail and finish must be rated as excellent. Fleetwood has been operated by Fisher Body Division for years but the name still has meaning because bodies so labeled are built in a separate plant. The line moves at a much slower pace than in other Fisher plants and the workers generally have been at their jobs for a longer period. In fact, tenure is the secret of Cadillac quality control for sales of this make seem immune to fluctuations in the economy. The same standards hold in Cadillac's own Detroit assembly plant and it has only been quite recently that a relatively small number have been built at a GM Assembly Division plant in Linden, N.J. All Eldorados still emanate from the home plant in Detroit.

For the enthusiast, the Eldorado offers a higher degree of mechanical interest than the Mark IV Continental. You get 10 inches more car for about the same money but that is not reflected in interior room with which the Mark IV is more generously endowed in most dimensions. The Eldorado is about 200 lbs lighter and is more powerful. At the

Wiper and washer controls along with the master window and door lock buttons are housed on the driver's door panel.

same time, one must consider such cars as the Jaguar XJ-6 and various Mercedes which sell for about the same money. Here, the value-wise buyer would rightfully give the nod to the American product although admittedly, those imports have much to offer the enthusiast that is not obtainable elsewhere.

Perhaps the biggest factor to favor any Cadillac is their exceptionally high resale value. Once you're over the hurdle of initial purchase, you can theoretically keep yourself in a new Eldorado for the astoundingly low sum of $473 a year. The comparable figure for the Mark IV is $853 which isn't bad either but it does place a premium on personal preference. Guide yourself accordingly. ●

A maze of plumbing and complex accessories live under the hood but items serviced regularly such as distributor, plugs and coil are accessible.

CADILLAC FLEETWOOD ELDORADO COUPE

SPECIFICATIONS AS TESTED

Engine . . . . 500 cu in., OHV 4V-V8
Bore & stroke . . . . 4.30 x 4.30 ins.
Compression ratio . . . . 8.5 to one
Horsepower . . . . 235 (SAE net) at 3800 rpm
Torque . . . . 385 lbs-ft at 2400 rpm
Transmission . . . . 3-speed, Turbo Hydra-Matic
**Steering . . . . 2.75 turns, lock to lock
46.8 ft, wall to wall
**Brakes . . . . disc front, drum rear
Suspension . . . . torsion front, leaf rear
Tires . . . . L78 x 15, belted
Dimensions (ins.):
   Wheelbase . . . 126.3   Rear track 63.6
   Length . . . . . . 223.2   Ground clearance . . 5.8
   Width . . . . 79.8   Height 53.9
   Front track . . . . 63.6   Weight . . . . . 4740 lbs
Capacities:
   Fuel . . . . . . 27 gals   Oil . . . . 6 qts
   Coolant . . . . 21.8 qts   Trunk . . . . . 13.5 cu ft

**Power assisted as tested

PERFORMANCE AND MAINTENANCE

Acceleration: Gears:
   0-30 mph . . . . 3.7 secs. 1st
   0-45 mph . . . . 6.2 secs. 1st, 2nd
   0-60 mph . . . . 9.4 secs. 1st, 2nd
   0-75 mph . . . . 14.9 secs. 1st, 2nd
   0-¼ mile . . . . 17.4 secs. at 82 mph
Ideal cruise . . . . 70 mph
Top speed (est) . . . . 112 mph
*Stop from 60 mph . . . . 174 ft
Average economy (city) . . . . 8.2 mpg
Average economy (country) . . . . 12.4 mpg
Fuel required . . . . Regular
Oil change (mos./miles) 4/6000
Lubrication (mos./miles) . . . . Life
Warranty (mos./miles) 12/12,000
Type tools required . . . . SAE
U.S. dealers . . . . 1620 total

*Anti-skid installed

BASE PRICE OF CAR

(Excludes state and local taxes, license, dealer preparation and domestic transportation): $7383 at Detroit
Plus desirable options:
$ 132 Firemist color
$ 161 Vinyl roof
$ 223 6-way seats L&R
$ 417 AM/FM stereo radio & tape
$ 537 Automatic air-conditioning
$ 211 Anti-skid rear brakes
$8864 TOTAL

ANTICIPATED DEPRECIATION

(Based on current Kelley Blue Book, previous equivalent model): $473 1st yr + $1144 2nd yr

RATING	Excellent (91-100)	Good (81-90)	Fair (71-80)	Poor (60-70)
Brakes		83		
Comfort	94			
Cornering		85		
Details	95			
Finish	94			
Instruments . . .		89		
Luggage		84		
Performance . .		90		
Quietness	95			
Ride		90		
Room		90		
Steering		85		
Visibility	91			
Overall		90		

Cadillac Eldorado vs. Lincoln Continental Mark IV

King Of The Hill

For the third year, **Motor Trend** holds up for comparison what are considered to be this country's top luxury cars. This time around, though, we take a deeper look, both at the cars and their rationale for existence.

Story and photography by John Lamm

You get philosophical driving through the desert at night. At 70 miles per hour, occasional pins of light balloon out of the distance into another dusty, paint-flaked gas station-and-cafe, then seem to burst in the far edges of your peripheral vision, snapping you back into the night and the darkness. That coming and going of light (life?) makes it easier to bare your soul and your thoughts and conversations take a philosophical bent. As we headed east from Indio, Calif., and entered the dark world, I punched up the speed limit on the Eldorado's cruise control, turned down the Gordon Lightfoot tape and A.B. Shuman and I let our thoughts pour out.

A.B. settled into the Eldo's leather upholstery a bit, stretched his legs out on the deep-pile carpeting and asked, "Do you think the Eldo and Mark IV do the job as luxury cars?"

I countered with something like, "Frankly, I'm not quite sure anymore just what a luxury car is supposed to be?"

In that brief exchange was created the perfect preface to the 1972 King of the Hill road test. For the third year, we are holding the Cadillac Eldo-

King Of The Hill

rado and Lincoln Continental up for close inspection. This year we have the Eldo in the second year of its second generation and the Continental in the first year of its latest edition, the Mark IV. In the past, though, we approached the two cars as the American ideal, not sure if that meant the most luxurious or, perhaps, just the most expensive domestic car. This year we are expanding our view, both in terms of actual testing, and rating of the two cars on the luxury scale.

Why change the system? For one thing, we are always, of course, trying to expand our tests and field of vision. More important, though, is that in the last year or so, we've tried to dig deeper into this sticky question of what is a luxury car. We have had the chance to drive more Mercedes, Citroëns, BMWs, Jaguars, Ferraris, Maseratis, as well as more cars below that line, like new Chevrolets, Fords, Peugeots, and the like. It has all unsettled our minds as to the true worth of American luxury cars and made us look into the foreign definitions of the same genre of automobiles. We know the *word* "luxury" means, basically, carrying "things" to a higher plane, but that gets muddled when you talk about the world's luxury automobiles. Eldo and Mark IV are quiet and soft, but don't handle particularly well. Mercedes handle and ride well but they can't seem to make the air conditioning or radio work, or the cars look exciting. The Italians can make the cars look exciting, but haven't figured out how to do that and still fit four people into one luxury car at the same time. The British can either build an undependable, good-looking luxury car or a dependable, ugly looking luxury car, but can't put them both together. The French are so newly returned to the luxury car field, they are still working just to make a statement on the subject. It is a jumble, and after hours of discussion on that dark highway east of Indio we could only come to the unfortunately rather simplistic statement that there are no international criteria for the "luxury automobile" and that each country's luxury cars are probably the ultimate statement of that country's attitude toward and definition of automobiles.

That would qualify our $10,000 Eldo and Mark IV as the final American words on automotive luxury, discounting the Fleetwood limo and limited production cars such as the Stutz Blackhawk. Granted you can option the price of a big Cadillac, Lincoln or Imperial up past a Mark IV or Eldo, but somehow paying that much money for a smaller "personal" car as opposed to a larger sedan shows a greater regard for spending money in a "luxurious" manner, i.e. getting less room for the same money. On the premise that the Eldo and Mark IV are "our" luxury cars, we first compared them in 1970, when the Eldo was in its more svelte first generation series and the Continental was still a Mark III. That year the Lincoln came out the winner and the letters came in droves. As I mentioned in the

Below: Somehow Lincoln has given the Mark IV's dash a look of quality Cadillac misses with the Eldo. Instruments may be harder to read, but they are easier to look at.

Above: Interior of Mark IV has a warm feeling, not so "corporate" as the Eldo. Leather in upholstery is sparse. Wheel looks "LTD." Left: Rear seat of Mark IV looks very inviting. Leg room in back is excellent, for a six-footer even with front seat all the way back.

King Of The Hill

opening to last year's test, the letters were not just ordinary comments or opinions, but violent (often vile) assaults on our integrity and parentage. Some even got personal. We were taken back by the whole response and so repeated the test in 1971, the last of the Mark IIIs winning the second contest. Again a rush of mail.

Now a person's soul tends to become hypersensitive under such violent verbal pummeling, but the fact that most of the letters were strongly in support of my choice of the Lincoln kept my head screwed on. This year we decided to analyze the two cars even further, establishing new tests and methods to delve not only into each vehicle's mechanical character, but also their *raison d'etre*. Instead of going for completely objective "numbers games" and abandoning the seat-of-the-pants subjective angle, I decided to improve on both . . . more numbers, as well as more time in the cars, more people driving them. So "we" begin, but with one warning to the bleeding hearts before we appraise the idols. We are commenting on them not as stylists or the final arbiters of good taste for the American people, but as we American automotive journalists see two American luxury kings.

PART I

I picked up the Eldorado on April 6th from the local Cadillac public relations contact, Ray Conners. The Continental Mark IV was ready about four working days later, after a close inspection and detailing by Bill Stroppe & Company. For about a week, the keys were passed around the office as I tried to get everyone in the cars either as a driver or rider. One staffer refused to drive either car. He preferred staying in a 5-speed Toyota Corolla, feeling it more relevant to today's traffic demands. Serious testing began on the 17th, as A. B. Shuman, Wally Wyss and I headed east on that trip through the desert to Phoenix and the government's crash-test of one of their $2 million safety cars. That round trip jammed some 800 miles of driving in 33 hours (half of it on the road) and quickly stripped both cars of their mystique.

First, the Eldorado seemed to have the best straight-line stability down the freeway. We can't prove categorically that it is a result of Cadillac's front-wheel-drive, but you'd have to invalidate decades of Citroën engineering to deny it. At legal highway speeds, the Eldo with its independent torsion-bar front suspension and four-link, coil-spring dead axle in back wallowed less than the Mark IV, which has an independent coil-spring suspension in front and a four-link, coil-spring live axle at the rear. Both cars bounced up and down and rolled mightily side-to-side over roadbed undulations, but the Mark IV also had a discomforting yawing sort

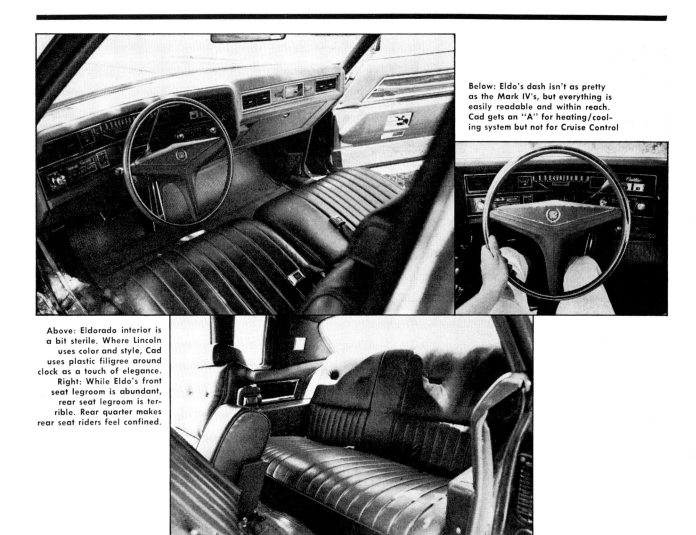

Below: Eldo's dash isn't as pretty as the Mark IV's, but everything is easily readable and within reach. Cad gets an "A" for heating/cooling system but not for Cruise Control

Above: Eldorado interior is a bit sterile. Where Lincoln uses color and style, Cad uses plastic filigree around clock as a touch of elegance. Right: While Eldo's front seat legroom is abundant, rear seat legroom is terrible. Rear quarter makes rear seat riders feel confined.

King Of The Hill

of twist to the ride. The sensation wasn't too disturbing from the driver's seat, but when I climbed in the back seat to ride a distance from that viewpoint, I found the bouncing and swaying problem markedly worse. In addition, the seats in both cars ground a tiring ache in the lower part of our backs, though we found the Eldo was the better of the two. The combination of a not-particularly comfortable ride, a tendency to react to crosswinds (which are abnormally high in the desert) and the seats, made it uncomfortable to drive either car for extended periods of time.

On the credit side, both cars were quiet at speed and made normal conversation no problem. One blight in the Eldo, though, was the continuing frustration of the GM embedded-in-the windshield antenna. They may be fine for GM's testing methods in Michigan, but are worthless in the western United States. I seriously suggest that anyone buying any GM product in this area tack on an external antenna. The warning goes double if you want FM or FM stereo.

Gas mileage for both cars was a very predictable 10-11 miles-per-gallon on the trip and both cars performed adequately on cheaper low-lead gasoline. Mechanically there were no problems with the cars and, except for one quart of oil the Eldo needed as we left Los Angeles, neither car required more than gas and a post-trip car wash. It was to their credit (and their national-

PRICE LIST CADILLAC ELDORADO			
Base price	$7,230.40	Automatic climate control	523.00
Firemist color	128.00	Power door locks and seat back release	69.00
Leather Up	179.00	Tilt and telescope steering wheel	92.00
Dual comfort seat	103.00	Twilight sentinal	40.00
Six-way passenger dual comfort seat adjuster	115.00	Remote control trunk lock	56.00
Two license frames	11.00	Rear window defroster	36.00
One-piece floor mat — front and rear	19.00	Cruise control	92.00
Trunk mat	8.00	Guidematic headlamp control	49.00
AM/FM stereo radio-tape player	406.00	Trumpet horn	15.00
Soft-ray glass	57.00	Custom cabriolet sunroof	1,005.00
Right side remote control mirror	26.00	Track master	205.00
Six-way driver dual comfort seat adjuster	89.00	Lamp monitors	48.00
Door edge guard (2)	6.00	Bumper impact strips	24.00
		Steel-belted radial tires — WW	295.00
		Total:	$10,926.40

SPECIFICATIONS
- Engine: OHV V8
- Bore & Stroke — ins. 4.3 x 4.3
- Displacement — cu. in. 500
- HP @ RPM 235 @ 3800
- Torque: lbs.-ft. @ rpm 385 @ 2400
- Compression Ratio 8.5:1
- Carburetion 1-4 bbl.
- Transmission 3-Speed auto
- Final Drive Ratio 3.07:1
- Steering Type Power-recirculation ball
- Steering Ratio 16.0-13.0 — variable ratio
- Turning Diameter (wall-to-wall-ft.) 46.8
- Wheel Turns (lock-to-lock) 2.75
- Tire Size LR78x15 adrials
- Brakes Disc/drum (anti-skid)
- Front Suspension Independent, torsion bar, auto level control
- Rear Suspension Four-link, dead axle, coil springs
- Body/Frame Construction Separate frame/body
- Wheelbase — ins. 126.3
- Overall Length — ins. 222.7
- Width — ins. 79.84
- Height — ins. 53.9
- Front Track — ins. 63.7
- Rear Track — ins. 63.6
- Test Weight — lbs. 5,105
- Fuel Capacity — gals. 27
- Oil capacity — qts. 5 (1)
- Trunk capacity 13.6 cu. ft.

PERFORMANCE

	A/C on High	
Acceleration		
0-30 mph	3.6	3.8
0-45 mph	6.2	6.6
0-60 mph	9.8	10.4
0-75 mph	14.9	15.7
Standing Start ¼-mile		
Mph	82	79.5
Elapsed time	17.6	17.9
Passing speeds		
40-60 mph	5.2	5.8
50-70 mph	5.9	6.6

Speeds in gears*
- 1st ... mph @ rpm 56 @ 4700
- 2nd ... mph @ rpm 78 @ 4700
- 3rd ... mph @ rpm 98 @ 4000
- Mph per 1000 rpm — (in top gear) 24.5

Stopping distances
- From 30 mph 32 ft. 8 in.
- From 60 mph 153 ft.

Gas mileage range — mpg 10 (city) — 11.9 (freeway)

Speedometer error
| Car speed | 30 | 45 | 50 | 60 | 70 | 80 |
| True speed | 31 | 46 | 52 | 62 | 73 | 83 |

MT Road Test Score 70.9

CADILLAC ELDORADO
SEATING COMFORT — Subject 6 ft., 190 lbs.
- Headroom — seat all the way up
  - Front ½ in.
  - Rear 0 in.
- Headroom — seat all the way down
  - Front 2 in.
  - Rear 2 in.
- Kneeroom — seat all the way back
  - Front 5½ in.
  - Rear −2⅞ in.
- Kneeroom — seat all the way forward
  - Front 0 in.
  - Rear 2½ in.
- Interior width — arm rest to arm rest
  - Front 4 ft. 9¼ in.
  - Rear 4 ft. 8 in.
- Interior compartment — length, dashboard to front edge of rear package shelf 6 ft. 4 in.

ity) that if something had happened on the way, either car probably could have been fixed in all but the sleaziest gas station. That means a lot in the middle of the desert or Tennessee.

After returning from Phoenix, the cars were driven by staff members around town and for short trips on weekends. Again, the Eldo came out on top. Here, though, the cars were more similar, tending to be something less than enjoyable *for us,* mainly because of their tendency to lean heavily in corners and wallow in dips. They made us feel too removed from traffic, a point we don't like, but at the same time the very thing for which many of their owners buy them. There was one inconsistency here I must admit to and that may take the measure of one myth about automotive journalists. It is fashionable in our profession to put down cars of this type, saying they are too fat and sloppy. But while some staffers did in fact question the Eldo and Mark IV's credentials, there was always someone coming in to borrow the keys so they could "Just take it to lunch." We could almost hear the L-M and Cad marketing departments snicker.

Anyway, the winner of this first portion of the test was the Eldorado, though neither car was an unqualified success on the long trip or the short haul. We have found a Mercedes 280SE or Jaguar XJ6 much more suitable for either type of driving, though I am sure I would be a bit wary about spending too much time in a desolate area with the Jag because of the repair problem should something go amiss. To generalize, if comfort is your desire, we would suggest opting for the big, imported sedans, but if you prefer peace of mind, go with the Americans.

PART II

There have been several recurring reader questions over the last two years that we decided to settle this time. These queries involved other aspects of ownership: Which of the cars needed the most frequent repair; how their resale value held up; which was the quietest car and, in terms of actual measurement, how did they compare in interior roominess. The repair question was prompted by several readers who complained that their Lincolns were

PRICE LIST	LINCOLN MARK IV
Base price	$8,897.00
Metallic paint	131.20
Leather upholstery	183.70
Calif. emissions package	16.00
Cornering Lamps	36.80
Automatic headlamp dimmer	51.20
Lock convenience group	95.80
Tilt steering wheel	72.20
Automatic speed control	94.50
Front bumper guards	19.70
Electric rear window defroster	85.30
AM radio/stereo tape deck	140.40
Intermittent windshield wipers	26.30
Vinyl insert body side molding	34.10
Appearance protection group	26.30
Total:	$9,910.50

SPECIFICATIONS
Engine:	OHV V8
Bore & Stroke — ins.	4.36 x 3.85
Displacement — cu. in.	460
HP @ RPM	212 @ 4400
Torque: lbs.-ft. @ rpm	342 @ 2800
Compression Ratio	8.5:1
Carburetion	1-4 bbl.
Transmission	3-Speed auto
Final Drive Ratio	3.00:1
Steering Type	Power-recirculating ball & nut
Steering Ratio	17:1
Turning Diameter (wall-to-wall-ft.)	46.7
Wheel Turns (lock-to-lock)	3.72
Tire Size	225 x 15 radials
Brakes	Disc/drum (anti-skid)
Front Suspension	Independent, coil spring
Rear Suspension	Four link, live axle, coil springs
Body/Frame Construction	Separate frame/body
Wheelbase — ins.	120.4
Overall Length — ins.	220.1
Width — ins.	79.2
Height — ins.	52.4
Front Track — ins.	63.0
Rear Track — ins.	63.1
Test Weight — lbs.	5,010
Fuel Capacity — gals.	22.5
Oil capacity — qts.	4 (1)
Trunk capacity	13.9 cu. ft.

PERFORMANCE
	A/C on High
Acceleration	
0-30 mph	4.2 .... 4.5
0-45 mph	6.9 .... 7.4
0-60 mph	10.5 .... 11.4
0-75 mph	15.6 .... 17.4
Standing Start ¼-mile	
Mph	80 78
Elapsed time	18.1 .... 18.8
Passing speeds	
40-60 mph	5.6 .... 6.1
50-70 mph	6.3 .... 6.6
Speeds in gears*	
1st ... mph @ rpm	49 @ 4600
2nd ... mph @ rpm	84 @ 4600
3rd ... mph @ rpm	100 @ 3800
Mph per 1000 rpm — (in top gear)	26.3
Stopping distances	
From 30 mph	32 ft. 8 in.
From 60 mph	152 ft. 6 in.
Gas mileage range — mpg	8.6 (city) — 11.7 (freeway)
Speedometer error	
Car speed	30 45 50 60 70 80
True speed	29 43 48 58 67 77
MT Road Test Score	67.6

LINCOLN MARK IV
SEATING COMFORT — Subject 6 ft., 190 lbs.
Headroom — seat all the way up	
Front	½ in.
Rear	2¼ in.
Headroom — seat all the way down	
Front	2¼ in.
Rear	2½ in.
Kneeroom — seat all the way back	
Front	1½ in.
Rear	¼ in.
Kneeroom — seat all the way forward	
Front	1⅞ in.
Rear	7 in.
Interior width — arm rest to arm rest	
Front	4 ft. 6 in.
Rear	4 ft. 5 in.
Interior compartment — length, dashboard to front edge of rear package shelf	6 ft. 1½ in.

KING OF HILL

not the mechanical equal of the Eldorado. There are few sources for such records, but after much hunting, it seems the two luxury cars are about equal in repair frequency. As with most automobiles, even Cadillacs and Lincolns suffer a bit in quality as each new model is introduced, but return to at least average quality as manufacturing processes are smoothed. Still, we are reminded of some griping from Eldo owners, confirmed by a local prestigious Cadillac dealer, that the quality of their cars coming through in the last 18 months has slipped. One reader, a staunch Cadillac *and* Lincoln owner, commented, "The Eldorado (1972) has several bugs but these could have and should have been corrected before delivery, but this just isn't done anymore it seems." We have comments on the general quality of the Mark IV, but couldn't substantiate them. As one last point on the repair question, we found that generally Cadillac owners think quite highly of their dealer and his service department. There is little comment from the Lincoln owners.

The Kelley Blue Book was the source for the next check, that being current resale value of "pre-owned" Eldos and Mark IIIs, IVs. The following retail resale values tell that story and the plot is a bit of a surprise. These values, by the way, are for fully-equipped hardtop models.

	Eldorado	Mark III/IV	Average mileage
1967	$2730	—	59,000
1968	$3470	—	55,000
1969	$4645	$5095	45,000
1970	$5805	$6155	35,000
1971	$7205	$7260	22,000
1972	$8125	$8125	6,000

(Figures from Kelley Blue Book, May-June 1972 Western Edition.)

All used car prices, of course, vary with condition of the car, mileage, options and the area of the country in which the buyer lives. The figures confirm the fact that the luxury cars do not lose their value quite as quickly as the average American sedan. A used 1969 Lincoln in 1972 is listed at 68.9 percent of original F.O.B. purchase price, while the Eldorado slips to 62.8 percent. As a comparison, a used 1969 Chevrolet Caprice 2-door hardtop is worth only 57.9 percent of original cost and a used 1969 Ford LTD 2-door hardtop is only 57.1 percent of what the first buyer paid for it. We suspect the 1969 Mark III's value is higher because that was the first full model year for the car and there were fewer produced (21,933 Mark IIIs, 27,214 Eldos). Remember that exclusivity is a valued quality in the luxury car market.

To get a truly accurate measurement of interior room this year, we decided to measure the room with me (6 feet, 190 lbs.) sitting in each position. You will find the chart has all the statistics, but the important point to be drawn from it is that both interiors are similar in basic dimensions, and Cadillac has virtually disregarded rear-seat legroom in favor of the front seat passengers, while Lincoln has done the reverse. The proof is in the "kneeroom" sections of the chart. Note also the rear seat headroom in both cars. It all comes down to this: The Eldo has the most front-seat legroom, the Mark IV has the most rear-seat legroom.

We ventured into another hereto unexplored area in this test, measuring interior noise to see just which car is quieter. We devised a 19-part test, the detailed results of which are in the statistics section. The gist of the findings is that the Eldorado won 9 parts of the test, the Mark IV won 7 and they tied on two.

The special trials wind up a tie between the two cars. Too many of the results are trade-offs, the winner being the buyer's approach to the subjects of noise (does he have the fan on most of the time?), interior space (does anyone ever ride in the back seat?), resale value (does he buy the car to own it or sell it?), and repair frequency (which local dealer is the best?) to declare a winner.

PART III

There has been more than enough information already written on the effect of the 1972 anti-smog equipment and the amount of power it drains from the present engines. The Mark IV is a case in point. There are still 460 cubic inches in the overhead valve V8, but where last year's Mark III engine was the equal of the Eldorado (365 hp to the Eldo's 360), this year's version has been humbled. The manufacturers list net horsepower this year so all the horsepower figures are down, but not like the Mark IV's. This year they report 212 hp at 4400 rpm compared to the Eldo's 235 hp at 3800 rpm. The story is repeated in net torque figures, the Eldo's 385 hp at 2400 rpm and the Mark IV's 342 lbs.-ft. at 2800. Cadillac retains its huge 500-cubic-inch V8. Both engines have low 8.5:1 compression (new for Mark IV this year), one four-barrel carburetor, a three-speed automatic transmission and similar rear end ratios (Mark IV, 3.00:1 — Eldo, 3.07:1).

Because of the popularity of air conditioning, both cars were put through their acceleration runs with and without the a/c's drag on the engine. A little cross-checking on the specifications chart pretty well tells the story: Mark IV loses by quite a bit. The Cadillac gets to 60 mph .7-second faster than the Mark IV with the air off. Turn the cooler on high and the Eldo gets there a full second faster. In the critical 40-60 and 50-70 passing tests the gap is not quite so bad, but the separation still gets as high as .4 second. Just as a comparison:

	0-30 (sec.)	0-60 (sec.)	40-60 (sec.)	50-70 (sec.)
1972 Eldorado	3.6	9.8	5.2	5.9
1971 Eldorado	3.4	9.8	5.0	5.7
1972 Mark IV	4.2	10.5	5.6	6.3
1971 Mark III	3.5	10.2	5.1	6.1

Braking was also a disappointment, though not with just the Mark IV. I was curious how each car would do, since both had their brakes fade on occasions before the test just in regular driving. The Eldorado was the worse of the two, even losing most of their efficiency on a normal downhill commuting section through Beverly Hills. How gauche. We weren't too surprised when the Eldorado "lost" its brakes twice during our normal acceleration tests in which we put on the brakes and try to preload the automatic transmission torque converter before accelerating down the track. We gave the brakes plenty of cool-down time between the acceleration runs and the braking tests and the car was able to make three panic stops from 30 mph and 60 mph with little fade. That included a full mile cool-down run between panic stops. Apparently it is that slow build-up of heat that will cause the fading. During the panic stops, the car actually behaved rather well, the nose diving and the back end hiking up in the air, the anti-skid system keeping the back wheels from locking up and sliding the car out of its straight path. The right front locked up, but caused no particular control problems. The distance, at an average of 153 feet, is not spectacular, but then this is a 2½-ton car.

The Mark IV's brake test had to wait for another day, since on the morning before the test day, the car's right front disc brake began to scrape, growl and leave little metal filings on the inside of the wheel. I haven't gotten the final word on just what the problem was, but apparently a disc pad failed. Lincoln-Mercury coughed up another car which was tested with stopping distances almost identical to those of the Eldo. Unlike the Cadillac, though, the Mark IV's anti-skid system couldn't do its job properly, the rear wheels alternately jumping off the ground as the rear end came up and the nose dipped. The result was the car sliding out to the left to the extent that I found myself correcting for it. Four panic stops

KING OF THE HILL

and it happened every time. Not the performance you would expect from a $10,000 automobile.

The performance portion of the test is an easy one to grade, Eldorado taking the honors. In all fairness, I would have to say that both cars have as much performance as most of their owners would care to use. One lap on a road course and you know these aren't per-

Noise level test		
	Eldorado	Mark IV
Idle (In Park)	63 db	64 db
fan on "low"	63 db	70.5 db
fan on "high"	74 db	73 db
25 MPH (city)	72 db	69 db
one window open (right)	73 db	74 db
two windows open	76 db	73 db
sunroof open	76.5 db	—
fan on "low"	71 db	71 db
fan on "high"	75.5 db	73 db
40 MPH (city)	74 db	72 db
one window open (right)	82 db	80 db
two windows open	82 db	81 db
sunroof open	84.5 db	—
fan on "low"	75.5 db	77 db
fan on "high"	77 db	80 db
65 MPH (freeway) passing lane	75 db	75 db
one window open (right)	86 db	91 db
two windows open	93 db	94 db
sunroof open	93 db	—
fan on "low"	75.5 db	80 db
fan on "high"	77 db	82 db

The "db" behind each number stands for decibel, the unit of measure used to relate the intensity of a sound wave. For comparison, the average telephone ring is about 78 db from one foot away, the key warning buzzer in a Mercury Comet averages 78 db and the IBM Selectric typewriter I am writing this on, bangs out some 77 db during constant typing. A four-door luxury Comet put through the first three steps of this test measured an average 81 db at idle, 82.5 db with the fan on low and 84 db with the fan on high.

formance cars — they aren't even close. But that extra .6-second the Eldo shaves off the Mark IV's time to 30 mph is important, because that indicates the extra snap the Eldo has in the low-speed, around-town situation in which these cars are so often driven.

PART IV

Now for the really subjective section of the test. I polled the staff on which car they preferred to drive for part 1 and the Eldo won handily. Then I laid out the crucial question: "But which car is better looking?" Only one member opted for the Eldo, saying the Mark IV looked "unfinished." All the rest except for one "undecided cop-out" said that Lincoln was their favorite, the art director quipping that the Eldo looks "swollen." I agree and that feeling is doubled when you drive the car. This is a "personal" car, but feels as big as a public convenience. The Mark IV's styling seems a clean statement of "established wealth" where the Eldo's bulby rococo lines say "nouveau riche."

The interiors come across the same way and, as we said last year, while the Eldorado's dash arrangement is far more legible and logical, the Mark IV's has that richer, warmer feeling so im-

portant in this type of car. I guess Ford is just better with the fake wood. If nothing else, all accessory switches, buttons and knobs were relatively easy to get to in both cars. There was "leather upholstery" in both cars, but in 1972 that means real leather only on the actual sitting and leaning surfaces, while everything else, the sides, back, front and headrests are vinyl . . . a very nice vinyl, mind you, but *plastic* none the less.

There were two options that deserve comment. One is the Eldorado's $1,000 steel sunroof/landau top combination. For that price, you expect a superior sunroof, but it isn't. We've driven a half-dozen cars with sunroofs that were quieter, less breezy and cheaper. Both cars had their corporation's version of the automatic cruise control and while the Mark IV's could be smoothly engaged with some practice, the Eldo's remained a mystery to everyone, never really putting you at the speed you requested and failing to do so with a lot of slowing down and speeding up. This isn't the first GM car we've had with that same problem.

THE WINNER

Design considerations aside, because we're doing this test as automotive journalists and because of the Eldorado's superiority on the road and track, we award the Eldo our 1972 King of the Hill label. It won two of the sections, tied on a third and lost only one, the last, the styling section. So, congratulations, Cadillac.

But, there is another point to be made. Mark IV did win the last section on styling and general "luxury" appeal, the basis for its wins in the first two King of the Hill tests. Considering the average American's approach to this type of car, perhaps that makes the Mark IV the grass roots winner. This does not dilute Cadillac's victory, but face it, these cars are bought for their looks, and on that score the Lincoln is the winner. When you are driving these machines people don't walk up and ask what engine it has or if the front-wheel-drive is an advantage. They only say how beautiful the car looks and how badly they want to own one, perhaps trading in their Thunderbird, Riviera or Grand Prix. That is the problem with our American luxury cars and the way most Americans approach them . . . they are mostly veneer, because, in the past, that's what has sold.

You see, we didn't find either of the cars to be particularly luxurious. At the same time, we won't deny the obvious appeal the cars have for the average American car buyer: They are his nirvana, the goal of his automotive life, his notice that he has arrived. We still prefer the Mercedes, Jaguar or BMW-type automobile as a starting point, and

bemoan the fact that Detroit has denied this type of car to so many American buyers. Sharply rising Mercedes, BMW and Jaguar XJ6 sales in this country indicate at least a large minority want it. And, there's another thing. Granted, these imported sedans are sold throughout the U.S., but let's face it, if you are a businessman you can really only buy an import in our metropolitan areas, use them for work and get away with it. Approach my father's partner in Madison, Wisconsin, driving a Mercedes and don't expect to sell your wares. Be advised to go out to the airport and rent a Ford.

Why do we feel this way about American luxury automobiles? Because to us, as automotive writers, a luxury automobile must first of all be a *competent automobile*. It should then be refined—made properly opulant and elegant with fine leather on the whole seat, real wood (if there is to be wood), on the dash and a mechanical sophistication (not gadgetry) in line with its cost. The whole package should exude a feeling of wealth, appeal to the senses and surround itself with an air of exclusivity that quietly, but firmly, says to everyone else on the road that this is *the car* that belongs to *the man*. Move over peasants. We do give credit to the Eldorado for its front-wheel-drive and to both cars for their quietness, the anti-skid part of their braking systems and the radial tires, but that is not enough. Neither Mark IV or Eldorado can justify their price increase over the Monte Carlo, Caprice or LTD except with a bit extra quietness, slightly thicker carpets and a lot of charisma, mistakenly based only on their price and who pays it. They just haven't grasped the aura of style that lifts them to that plane in which they become, as a dictionary describes, ". . . a refinement of living rather than a necessity."

One last comment before I'm buried by the inevitable avalanche of irate letters. We found a direct parallel for this American obsession for automotive things that are externally "pretty" in the federal government's Department of Transportation. Throughout their work with the safety cars, the DOT's leader, "Governor" John Volpe has been so concerned with getting cars through a 50-mph crash with little visible damage. After the Fairchild car went into the barrier, the "Governor" almost glossed over the fact that at least two of the three dummies in the car would have been "killed" instantly and continued to comment on how good the car looked after the crash. Who gives a damn how the car looks if only those three "people" had lived? I fear the "Governor" is just a visible example of where, on the subject of cars, the luxury cars being the final statement, our collective national head is at. /MT

The Eldorado Convertible

As the only luxury convertible built in America, it is both dramatically beautiful and remarkably responsive. Every inch an Eldorado. Everything about it tells you this is the world's most elegant convertible. The boldness of its lines and the richness of its interior. The sure response of its 8.2 litre V-8 (world's largest production passenger car engine) and the sure maneuverability of front-wheel drive, variable-ratio power steering and Automatic Level Control. It even converts uniquely. With an ingenious inward-folding Hideaway Top and a new two-piece hard boot. The Eldorado Convertible: a unique experience.

FLEETWOOD ELDORADO CONVERTIBLE IN CORONATION RED WITH A 1903 CADILLAC RUNABOUT.

'74 Detroit Preview

Continental Mark IV & Cadillac Eldorado

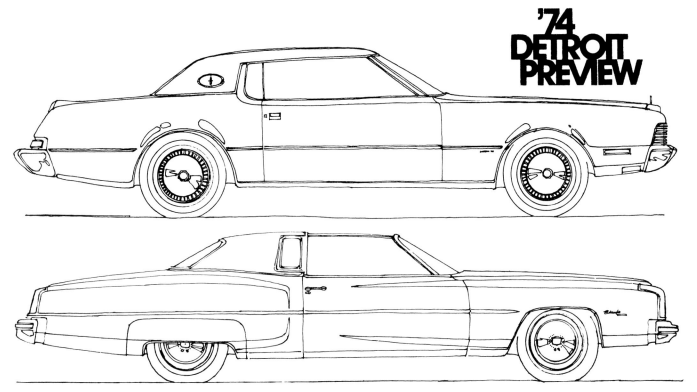

AND FOR '74 . . . FUTURE SHOCK? Well, almost. The Eldorado convertible, accounting for nearly one-third of sales, will be discontinued, replaced by a new Cabriolet version with lift-off panels like the Corvette. The Cadillac is the obvious GM choice to begin this innovation now that convertibles are a no-no in Detroit. Lesser priced personal luxury cars like the Monte Carlo and Pontiac Grand Prix will no doubt follow suit with "Parisienne" roofs of their own. Tail and parking lights, once an area of daring ingenuity at Cadillac, may grow vertically and cross to the fender top. Without question, the rear bumper will be pushed out slightly to accommodate 1974 5-mph rear bumper requirement. What it boils down to is that you'd better buy yourself an Eldo convertible now, before they become collectors items and begin escalating in value. The Lincoln Continental Mark IV shall remain very much as we know it today except that the rear bumper will be moved down some four inches to meet federal standards. Then, new wrap-around taillights will fill in the gap created. Spare tire bulge will be like the '73 but sides extend down to bumper, accentuating styling hallmark. ∎

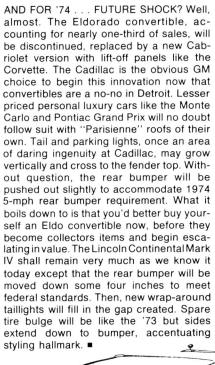

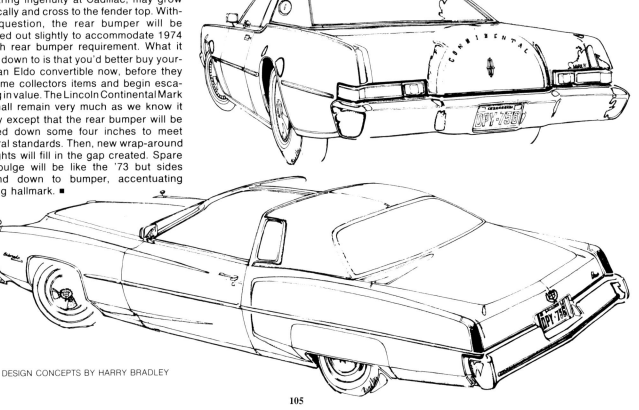

DESIGN CONCEPTS BY HARRY BRADLEY

CADILLAC
Calais, DeVille, Fleetwood, Eldorado

Although you have to study the illustrations closely to detect it, the grille, hood and bumper of the '73 rear-drive Cadillacs are new. In last year's model, the lower part of the grille was outlined by the bumper; this year, the lower part becomes a part of the bumper itself and the whole piece hinges upon impact similarly to the '73 Oldsmobile design. At the rear, the triangular-shaped taillights have been moved into the upper portion of the bumper extensions beyond the range of normal impacts. The reflex lens occupies the lower half and is protected by impact strips. The backup lights also have been relocated to the upper part of the bumper. The only change in side appearance is confined to the Sixty-Special Brougham, which has had the rear of its front doors extended to cover an awkward-looking extension of the "B" pillar into the body.

The front-drive Eldorado also has a new grille and bumper with the same hinging system described above. New fender caps sit above combined parking and turn lights that wrap around into the fenders, replacing last year's vertical design with separate cornering lamps. The decklid has been redesigned in the interests of minimizing the increase in overall length caused by the impact bumpers.

Cadillac uses Delco's air-hydraulic, impact-absorbing cylinders for the front bumper and its own design of urethane absorbing system at the rear. Both bumpers are of the recoverable type, meaning that they will return to their original positions even after repeated impacts. Heavy rubber tipped guards are standard in front, and horizontal rub strips are installed at both ends. These new bumpers are far less lethal (to other cars) and more attractive than past designs.

Nineteen of Cadillac's 21 exterior color choices are new, the total including 15 standard colors and 6 metallics of the "firemist" extra-cost type. To go with this assortment are eight different vinyl top choices and an amazing 153 different interior trims ranging from old-fashioned velour to genuine leather. A cloth called "Medici" is actually the most popular with customers. The more durable leather, though, brings back much of its extra cost at trade-in time.

Cadillac has joined the fancy clock bunch with a new one featuring Roman numerals on the dial. Hopefully, this bit of retrogression won't be expanded to other items such as the speedometer. Another anachronistic item for a car that is usually sold with automatic temperature control is an optional pillow and matching robe. Your wife will like the lighted vanity mirror on her visor, and Sixty-Specials have a neat reading lamp for the front passenger mounted on the right rear door plus the two already provided for rear passengers.

Wheelbase remains at 130 inches for the Calais and DeVille series, 133 inches for the Sixty-Special, 126.3 for Eldorado coupes and convertibles, and 151.5 for the massive 7-passenger Seventy-Five models. About 7000 of the latter are sold each year, mainly to funeral homes and car liveries, and half again as many bare chassis go out to builders of ambulance and funeral coach bodies. Although Toronados have become popular for converting into extra-long airport limousines, we know of no Eldorados that have met this fate so far. The Eldorado/Toronado chassis and front drive, incidentally, will form the basis for GMC Truck Division's forthcoming motorhome. As with the airport conversions, front drive

CADILLAC FLEETWOOD ELDORADO

allows the inexpensive addition of a second set of rear wheels.

Except for additional emission controls, Cadillac powerplants remain the same in design and ratings as last year. The 472 4-barrel of 220 hp is used for all cars with conventional drive, and a version of this stroked from 4.06 to 4.304 inches which is rated at 235 hp goes into front-drive Eldorados. These ratings may seem modest but they reflect the power absorbed by all of Cadillac's many standard accessories. The figures would be higher if a dual exhaust system were offered but here again, it's assumed that few customers will bother to compare horsepower ratings and fewer still will ever find use for all that provided.

Sixty-Special buyers will be offered the equivalent of the bridal suite at Miami Beach's Americana Hotel, an option which Cadillac calls in fractured Detroit French "Brougham d'Elegance." It includes a thickly padded roof in elk-grain vinyl, a stand-up wreath and crest on the hood, special wreathed wheel discs, pockets on the front seatbacks, and retractable assist straps for the rear passengers among other things. As might be imagined, your extravagance is spelled out to the world by script on each rear quarter panel.

First testimony that radio antennas imbedded in the windshield might not be the most efficient way of bringing in FM stations from a distance comes from Cadil-

CADILLAC FLEETWOOD SIXTY SPECIAL BROUGHAM

lac's revival of the automatic fender antenna as an option. Radial tires of American manufacture are available, each of the various brands having a 40,000-mile warranty which should make them attractive to Eldorado buyers. Get yours early because the tire companies will soon wake up to reality and hedge their warranties for heavy front-drive vehicles.

Automatic leveling is a standard feature on most Cadillac models, as are power seats and windows. Three-speed Turbo Hydra-Matic, power steering and power front disc brakes are also standard, with anti-skid for the rear wheels optional. Engineering changes are minor, mainly involving tuning the suspension and frame to accept the heavier bumpers.

CALAIS/DE VILLE/ SIXTY SPECIAL/SEVENTY-FIVE

ENGINE: 472 cu. ins. (220 hp).
TRANSMISSION: 3-spd. auto std.
SUSPENSION: Coil front, coil rear.
STEERING: Variable-ratio power std.
BRAKES: Power front discs std.
FUEL CAPACITY: 27 gals.
DIMENSIONS: Wheelbase 130.0-151.5 ins. Track 63.6 ins. front, 63.3 ins. rear. Overall length 228.5-250.0 ins., width 79.8 ins., height 54.1-58.1 ins. Weight 4835-7080 lbs. Trunk 16.5 cu. ft.
BODY STYLES: 2-dr. hdtp., 4-dr. hdtp., 4-dr. sdn., 7-pass. sdn., 7-pass. lmsne.

ELDORADO

ENGINE: 500 cu. ins. (235 hp).
TRANSMISSION: 3-spd. auto std.
SUSPENSION: Torsion bars front, coils rear.
STEERING: Variable-ratio power std., curb-to-curb 46.8 ft.
BRAKES: Power front discs std.
FUEL CAPACITY: 27 gals.
DIMENSIONS: Wheelbase 126.3 ins. Track 63.6 ins. front, 63.6 ins. rear. Overall length 222.0 ins., width 79.8 ins., height 53.9-54.3 ins. Weight 4820-5040 lbs. Trunk 13.5 cu. ft.
BODY STYLES: 2-dr. cpe., 2-dr. conv.

CADILLAC SEDAN DE VILLE

CADILLAC COUPE DE VILLE

Cadillac Eldorado: The King, Revisited

America's most change-less car goes through some changes
... and winds up feeling more like Cadillac *circa* 1953 / By Eric Dahlquist

The engineer swung the cream-yellow '73 Eldorado convertible into position in a little stand of trees just on the edge of the skid pad at the General Motors proving grounds. As the Cadillac's chrome took on the few glints of sunlight piercing the leafy canopy overhead, my mind shot back twenty years to my dad's '53 Cadillac convertible that we used to polish on Saturday afternoons in the open shade of three giant maples. I remembered how the thick chrome had a slightly bluish cast when you wiped off the polish and how smooth the curves of the body surfaces felt under the cheesecloth.

The car's interior was all two-tone real leather (blue) and every function was power operated except the brakes, an omission I never figured out.

That Caddy had what my parents

called the look of a big bug — solid, heavy, but yet somehow lithe. It lasted about 200,000 miles without a major repair, and may be still running for all I know.

The '73 Eldorado possesses a lot of the feeling of my dad's '53, and that's probably a good thing, because Cadillac sold every 1972 Eldo they could build. True, the grille has a more vertical theme to suit the bigger energy-absorbing front bumper, but essentially its the same car as a year ago, gargantuan 500 cubic inch engine, front-wheel drive, and all.

Of course, there are detail improvements. Vertical impact strips on the bumper ends for one thing and new wheel covers designed to improve air flow to the brakes for another. The Eldorado's rear suspension geometry has been modified to yield more precise handling and greater directional stability, improving an edge they already had over Continental Mark IV ("King of the Hill," MT July). Further, drivability on Cadillacs in general has been improved with an engine-speed-controlled distributor advance that allows lower transmission shift points than the previous transmission — controlled spark advance setup.

All very Nineteen-Seventies, right?
continued on page 117

Top, left and above: In keeping with tradition, there are some styling changes in the 1973 Eldo, most of them up front to accompany the 5-mph bumper. Biggest news lies under the sheet metal where frame changes, needed for the bigger bumpers, have strengthened the entire automobile making it more solid and durable.

Right-hand drive is not available on any American-built General Motors product. The Eldorado is quite a close-coupled four-seater with long bonnet and boot extensions. The engine (inset right) is mounted a long way back over the front-wheel centreline with a lot of body overhang in front. The huge size (18ft 7in. long by almost 6ft 8in. wide) is often an embarrassment on narrow country roads

CADILLAC ELDORADO

Brief Test

CADILLAC ELDORADO

Brief Test

Take the largest engine currently fitted to a passenger car, mate it to (of all the unlikely things) front-wheel drive, market the finished package through General Motors prestige outlets as a Cadillac, and the net result is something unique. In the USA each year some 235,000 people buy Cadillacs, so although there is a lot of prestige attached to owning one, it is not really in the same league as a Rolls or Bentley. Here, of course, there are only a handful imported, the sheer bulk of each car (coupled to left-hand drive, which is obligatory) making it pretty unsuitable for the conditions.

One of the rare Cadillac enthusiasts here is J. C. Bamford (of JCB excavator fame) and over the years we have been indebted to him for lending us his personal cars for assessment. The last one we borrowed was a Coupé de Ville in 1968 and these days he runs—amongst a fleet too large and impressive to list in detail—two Cadillacs, a Fleetwood Brougham and an Eldorado. When once again we were kindly offered the chance of a few days with one of these, we naturally opted for the latter with its 8.2-litre engine and front-wheel drive. Many of the JCB cars including the Cadillacs are actually used for investigation by JCB Research and Development Ltd., a company within the JCB group which does a lot of work on power transmission and hydraulics. Even for a novice in these systems, the power controls and gadgets fitted to the Eldorado can provide hours of entertainment long before he ventures out with the vehicle on the road.

Cleaner but less powerful

The Eldorado we tested was a 1972 car fitted with a detoxed engine capable of running on 91-octane lead-free fuel. From this huge cubic capacity the certified DIN output is therefore only a very modest 238 bhp at 3,800 rpm. When we tested the Coupé de Ville in 1968 the quoted power was 375 bhp (SAE) at 4,400 rpm from only 7¾ litres, so specifically and overall the emission controls fitted have caused a substantial power loss. Current regulations for emission levels of 1973 models are even stricter and there is talk in the USA of 1972 becoming the last year for cars with decent performance. The curator of the Ford Dearborn Museum, for example, has apparently bought three 1972 models which he will use in turn, hoping they will last the remainder of his lifetime.

Subjectively from behind the wheel the 1972 Eldorado feels as smooth and brisk as one would expect, bearing in mind the huge frontal area and kerbside weight of over 2½ tons. When running with the automatic choke in operation there is a slight lean patch in the carburation if the throttle is stabbed open too hard, and this can cause the engine to die in an embarrassing traffic situation. This characteristic apparently is the one which is much worse on the 1973 cars and occurs all the time.

When we put a fifth wheel on the Eldorado and timed its acceleration the results were extremely disappointing. Compared with the 1968 Coupé de Ville it took nearly a second longer to reach 60 mph and nearly 5 sec longer to reach 90 mph, but against the original 7-litre Oldsmobile Toronado we tested in 1966 it was a real sluggard. That front-drive Olds, from which the Eldorado was developed, reached 60 mph in only 8.7 sec and 90 mph in a remarkable 17.7 sec. Top speed was similarly reduced from 126 mph for the Toronado to no more than 110 mph for the Cadillac.

By the standards of today in Europe, the ride was very disappointing also. After cars like the Jaguar XJ6 and Ford Granada, the Cadillac feels a very poor engineering compromise. On sharp bumps there is much too much thump from the suspension and on long-pitched waves the car goes on oscillating in a most uncomfortable floating kind of way. We noticed some definite scuttle shake too when hitting broken surfaces or level-crossings and the only conclusion to be drawn is that the characteristic "boulevard ride" which impressed us a few years ago is now a myth, like the electrifying performance of the big vee-8 engines.

The best that can be said about the front-wheel drive is that most drivers will not be aware that this is anything other than a conventional layout, until it rains. The big difference then is that instead of slithering around with snaking slides every time full power is applied, the Eldorado simply pulls straight ahead. There is just as much wheelspin but the big car can be controlled much more easily. Statistically 60 per cent of the weight is on the front wheels, the engine being directly over their centreline. As power is applied some of this transfers rearwards, and on a dry road it is just possible to spin the front wheels moving off, but not for more than a yard or two. On a tight turn (into a main road, for example), it is rather too easy to go off with squeal and drama when trying to take advantage of a traffic gap.

Some of the gadgets and gimmicks seemed more worthwhile than others and in particular we liked the centralized door locking; remote control for door mirror adjustment including the offside one; automatic temperature control set by a single drum; dusk-sensing sidelamp switch and courtesy provision for keeping the headlamps on just long enough automatically to get your latch key in the front door; and the way the wipers were hidden when parked. Less good were the recoil seat belts (not nearly so easy to use as our own inertia-reel type), automatic headlamp dipping which cannot anticipate a car approaching round a curve; and reliance upon a rear window blower for demisting instead of electric wires. A radio antenna actually between the laminates of the windscreen was effective and fade-free except on FM stations.

What this Cadillac taught us most was that the great American safety and emissions campaign is definitely detracting from their products in terms of natural engineering progress and the latest models, judged in this environment, are not what they used to be. As the most expensive and ambitious car from the world's largest automobile manufacturers, the Eldorado falls a long way short of what it should be. Whether that is by design or Federal pressure we may never know.

PERFORMANCE CHECK

Maximum speeds

Gear	mph		kph		rpm	
	Eldorado	Toronado	Eldorado	Toronado	Eldorado	Toronado
Top (mean)	110	126	177	203	4,000	4,900
(best)	110	127	177	204	4,000	4,950
Inter	78	87	126	104	4,200	5,000
Low	47	52	75	84	4,200	5,000

Standing ¼-mile	Eldorado	17.4 sec	78 mph
	Toronado	16.9 sec	89 mph
Standing kilometre	Eldorado	31.8 sec	96 mph
	Toronado	30.0 sec	110 mph

Acceleration

Eldorado	3.6	4.8	7.6	10.7	14.2	19.7	25.9	
Toronado	3.8	5.1	6.7	8.7	11.3	14.0	17.7	
Time in seconds	0							
True speed mph		30	40	50	60	70	80	90
Indicated speed mph Eldorado		29	39	49	58	68	77	86
Indicated speed mph Toronado		31	42	52	62	72	83	93

Speed range, Gear Ratios and Time in seconds

Mph	Top		Inter		Low	
	Eldorado	Toronado	Eldorado	Toronado	Eldorado	Toronado
10-30	—	—	—	—	3.7	2.7
20-40	—	6.0	—	4.1	3.0	2.9
30-50	—	6.2	4.9	4.2	4.2	3.3
40-60	—	6.6	4.5	4.9	—	—
50-70	—	7.3	6.6	5.5	—	—
60-80	—	9.1	9.7	6.2	—	—
70-90	11.7	9.8	—	—	—	—

Fuel Consumption

Overall mpg	Eldorado	10.5 mpg (26.8 litres/100km)
	Toronado	11.8 mpg (24.0 litres/100km)

NOTE: Toronado denotes performance figures for Oldsmobile Toronado tested in *Autocar* of 14 January 1966

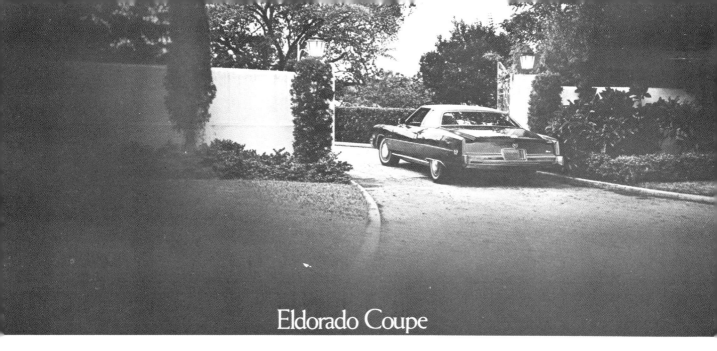

Eldorado Coupe

Here is our most elegant personal car—even more glamorous and exciting for 1973. The grille—bolder, more massive. The more horizontal hood further accents the jewel-like standup crest. There's new hood striping. New rear deck design throughout. New, improved bumper systems for 1973. And new side design, highlighted by the return of the lighted wreath-and-crest circular rear side marker. This is, without question, a unique American luxury car. The only one with  front-wheel drive, Automatic Level Control and an 8.2 litre engine. Variable-ratio power steering is also standard. And you may specify steel-belted radial tires; a Dual Comfort front seat; an electronic theft-deterrent system; a lighted vanity mirror; any of six radio systems and Track Master, Cadillac's skid-control braking system. Shown here is the Fleetwood Eldorado Coupe in available Saturn Bronze Firemist with White accent stripes and a White padded vinyl roof.

The King of the Hill

Mark IV vs. Eldorado

By John Lamm

This may well be "The Longest Surviving Comparison Test," our annual climb to find the King of the Hill. For four years now, we've held up the Lincoln Continental Mark IV (and III) and the Cadillac Eldorado for comparison. The Continental won the first two tests, and last year the Eldo took the honors. Each test was slightly different than the last. The first was straight road test, the second a sort of review of the first in light of a torrent of letters we received, while last year's test took on the look of a Consumer's Union test done by Cecil B. DeMille. Regardless, the reader letter fallout has always been the same, hundreds of missiles best characterized by such diverse descriptions as "unending praise," "outlandish charges," "deep sympathy" and "character assassination." The letters continue today, crayon scrawlings on cheap paper, brilliant longhand on typewriter paper, even dictated obscenities on expensive letterhead bond. This

is the test that seems to scratch at the heart of automotive emotions. The reason, very likely, is that in taking on America's premier luxury cars, we are taking on Camelot itself. When we declare one a winner, we've implied the other is a loser and we've taken a shot at that for which their owners (and dream owners) have been striving.

At the same time, we've seen, off in the periphery of the luxury car battle, certain forays we've suspected could step in and change the combatants. With luxury cars below the 10-mile-per-gallon point, we've wondered of the effects of the present fuel shortage. On one side we have the owner not able to buy gasoline, regardless of his wealth, just because there isn't enough for sale. On the other side is the view of the outsider who is bitter about (and in a mood to tax) anyone who seems to be gobbling up an inordinate amount of the precious fuel.

Safety and emissions regulations are particularly hard on luxury car builders, with the emissions equipment obliterating any thought of decent mileage, while at the same time strangling the life out of luxury car engines already overburdened with every option known to man. While luxury car buyers certainly aren't speed freaks, they demand above average performance. That's difficult, as luxury cars are larger and much heavier than those below them in the automotive pecking order. That extra bulk and poundage means larger bumpers fore and aft— massive bumpers that add even more weight and are as difficult to style as an Army tank. And, of course, style is one of the luxury car's very reason for existence. Those circumstances seem to threaten to turn the luxury car into an honest, rather than suspected, boat. The simple solution may be to make the luxury car smaller, to lob off a few pounds and make it the size of, say, a Mercedes.

Enter the other specter, the challenger from Stuttgart. There were some 41,000 Mercedes sold in the U.S. in 1972, and 75 percent of them cost $9,300 or more. That is Mark IV and Eldorado sales territory, so one could conclude Mercedes is a serious threat. We also had an inkling that a few important men in Detroit felt the same.

So we went to those men, the brains behind Lincoln and Cadillac, to sound them out. Will the luxury car continue as it is, large and heavy, or will the fuel shortage, combined with safety and emissions regulations cause it to shrink?

We first visited with Bill Benton, the new general manager of Lincoln-Mercury. Our timing was excellent, by accident, as we arrived on the day in mid-May when sales of the '73 Continental Mark IVs surpassed sales of the 1972 model year. That is the stuff of which division manager's dreams are made. Right off, Benton laid waste to one of our notions by playing down the influence of

Mr. Robert Lund, V.P. of General Motors and Cadillac General Manager, brings to the Division more youth and excitement.

Mercedes on the luxury car's public and future. He commented that the American automotive dream is based on a "price-size/hierarchy" that demands luxury automobiles be larger. That's not to give you the impression that L-M is ignoring the Mercedes, since they have to keep close tabs on any force in their price category that is ringing up sales of 41,000. But they also feel they have the evidence to show that the man who buys a Mercedes most likely would never buy a Lincoln (or Cadillac). Caught up in the "Mercedes mystique," that owner is

Mr. William "Bill" Benton, General Manager of Lincoln-Mercury, sells as many Mk. IVs as Continentals, sees no Mercedes threat.

In instrument design, you takes your choice. Cadillac, left, is easier to use and read but Lincoln looks more luxurious overall.

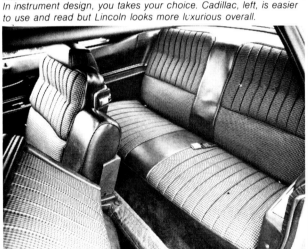

Eldo and Mk IV interiors are a study in contrast. Cadillac, above, uses ordinary looking houndstooth fabric and an imitation wood. With Lincoln, below, it's yards of super luxury real leather. That's class.

SPECIFICATIONS	Continental Mark IV	Cadillac Eldorado
Engine:	90° OHV V-8	90° OHV V-8
Bore & Stroke-ins.	4.362 x 3.85	4.3 x 4.304
Displacement-cu. in.	460	500
HP @ RPM	208 @ 4400	235 @ 3800
Torque: lbs.-ft. @ rpm	338 @ 2800	385 @ 2400
Compression Ratio	8.0	8.5
Carburetion	4V	4V
Transmission	Automatic	Turbo-Hydramatic
Final Drive Ratio	2.75	3.07:1
Steering Type	Power	Rotary valve-Recirculation ball
Steering Ratio	21.7:1	16.1-14.3:1
Turning Diameter (curb-to-curb-ft.)	43.0	43.48
Wheel Turns (lock-to-lock)	4.0	2.75
Tire Size	230-15	L78 x 15
Brakes	Disc-front-drum-rear	Disc-front-single piston drum rear
Front Suspension	Coil springs shocks axial strut stabilizer	Independent torsion bar shocks stabilizer
Rear Suspension	4 trailing control arms coils stabilizer	4 link coil suspension-dead axle shocks
Body/Frame Construction	Separate frame	Separate perimeter frame
Wheelbase-ins.	120.4	126.3
Overall Length-ins.	223.3	222.0
Width-ins.	79.8	79.8
Height-ins.	53.4	53.9
Front Track-ins.	63.01	63.7
Rear Track-ins.	63.09	63.6
Fuel Capacity-gals.	22.5	27
Oil Capacity-qts.	4(1)	5(1)

oriented toward foreign machinery in general, a parallel they can cite in the preference of some buyers for the more expensive Capri over the similar size-/power Comet.

Benton drew on the image of the American up from the Depression, working toward various goals, now perhaps more splintered than before, but with a luxury car taking up one segment. When the climber makes it, he deserves a soft, quiet luxury car and even if gas prices rise, well, that is just part of the dues one pays. As for being a gas hog in a day when fuel is short, one has to remember that the gas shortage will be resolved (all automotive general managers have ultimate faith in the *American System* to overcome any problem) and when you are living with a product that requires a four-to-six year lead time from conception to product, even a three-to-four year problem has to be considered as almost short term.

Even if the gas crisis escalates, perhaps the luxury car owner is exempted from the sort of Automotive New Morality that has developed from consumerism, fuel shortages and anti-smog regulations. First, he can afford it or he wouldn't (or shouldn't) be in the luxury car market and those looking at him from the outside may well exempt him because he's gotten to the level they want to reach.

Bill Benton doesn't see the luxury car reduced in size in the foreseeable future. His words were, "If we copied the Mercedes and put it on the market, the luxury car public would think we'd lost our minds." So much for Stuttgart. He did say, however, that there may be an evolution that could shrink the luxury size in the 1980s.

Sitting just outside this discussion, though, is something called the Ford Granada. The corporate luxury car in Europe, the Granada has admittedly been studied by L-M, but Benton claims they are not pursuing it right now. Perhaps they would like to see what will happen to Cadillac's small luxury car entry.

Fifteen miles to the east was Cadillac and their new general manager, Bob Lund. The attitude there was different, marked early in the discussion when Lund commented that anyone who sells cars in their market is a threat and he doesn't agree that any luxury car buyer is set on a foreign car. That led immediately to Cadillac's drive to get to the younger owner. "We are trying to enlarge our base of owners," Lund commented, then cited the use of the Eldorado as the 1973 Indianapolis pace car and recent ads spotlighting young professionals driving Cadillacs. Those two comments, combined with the fact that Mercedes owners are generally younger, would point up that Cadillac doesn't seem as willing to dismiss Mercedes, quite so easily as Lincoln. All this, of course, is backed up by the knowledge that even though Cadillac claims their new Mercedes-sized car, based on the Opel Diplomat, isn't even a sure thing, it is a very distinct possibility.

Much of what Lund said after that, though, was similar to Benton's comments. There was the picture of the man working his way to the top and finding a luxury car waiting there for him. This is the reward and it should be quiet, plush, fully-optioned, big and heavy. Cadillac knows first-hand what can happen if you reduce the size of an American luxury car. They sliced eight inches off one model in 1962-63 after owners complained of not being able to close their garage doors. The model bombed, so any small Cadillac will have to be an addition to the line, not a redesign of current models.

And it thrives, this luxury car market. We mentioned the Mark IV's success earlier, while Eldorado, though behind in sales, is also enjoying a record year. Cadillac claims they just haven't the production capability to keep up with the Mark IV, while L-M just chuckles over the situation.

Both cars are holdover models from 1972, with just the additional length of the jutting 5-mph bumpers adding .7 inch to the Eldo, but 3.2 inches to the Mark IV. Neither car wears the bumper gracefully. This continuance of models is one of the reasons we have cut back on the normal road test this year. Since both cars tested last year were 1972 California smog cars, they were very similar, performance-wise, to all 1973 models, as can be seen on the specifications page. To sum up last year's results, Eldorado won the first part of that test with superior ride and handling on freeways and highways, although both cars were quite similar in the city. Part two, involving repairability, quality, resale value and interior room was a trade off and a tie. The interesting point was Lincoln gave less front seat legroom, but offered plenty of rear seat legroom. The Eldorado had sufficient front-seat legroom for most, but virtually ignored the rear seat. Acceleration, braking and noise level were the points of part three, the performance section. Eldorado won hands down, running faster, stopping quicker (though both cars had brake problems) and it was quieter overall than the Mark IV. Part four was the subjective section and here the Mark IV came into its own. No one particularly liked the looks of the "swollen" Eldo and felt its interior was too obviously stock General Motors. Mark IV, with its Cartier clock and hand-cut emblem on the opera window, was considered more unique, warm and, frankly, more luxurious—and that is the word it's all about.

There are detail changes for 1973, but none that would appreciably alter last year's results, so the Cadillac Eldorado continues as the King of the Hill. Of course that leaves Cadillac winning the battle, but Continental winning the sales war. It is a contradiction, but somehow they seem a common event in this business.

But I must carry over one other point from last year, to quote: "We still prefer a Mercedes-, Jaguar-or BMW-type of automobile as a starting point, and bemoan the fact that Detroit has denied this type of car to so many American buyers." We understand the great American luxury car tradition and the fact that Lincoln and Cadillac would be crazy to up and change what they have going—sales. But being *enthusiasts* we would still like to see an alternative. That is why we are awaiting the Opel/Cadillac (LaSalle, Mr. Lund?) as a serious second choice. There is one point on which we must side with Cadillac against Lincoln. We don't believe that the Mercedes buyer is totally unwilling to consider anything American. We oftimes appear to be overly pro-European in our opinions of luxury cars, but don't think for one minute we wouldn't prefer to be able to say the same words about Cadillac or Lincoln. ∎

CADILLAC
CONTINUED FROM PAGE 108

But the best news is that Cadillac has recaptured a measure of structural integrity they last had twenty years ago. As you may have suspected, the energy-absorbing bumper is largely responsible. The use of the Delco-built system demanded that frames be revised and strengthened. This, in turn, caused a general improvement of front suspension compliance, shock absorber control, and body mount tuning. What you wind up with is a better riding, better handling, *tighter* automobile.

And quiet. Mufflers, resonators and tail pipes have been acoustically tuned for lower decibel levels and this—coupled with quieter air conditioner, pulleys, radiator fan and AIR (air injection reactor) pump have rigged these '73 models for truly silent running.

Cadillac has done a lot of soul-searching in the last few years, trying to figure out where they lost a lot of their following to Mercedes-Benz, and if it was all a matter of just building a smaller sized car to get them back. The '73s are certainly not Mercedes-size but despite their bulk — or perhaps because of it — they feel like substantially better cars than before. And that, Cadillac may find, has been part of the answer all along.
/MT

KING OF THE HILL
Eldorado or Mark IV?

Commoners are judged by the distance they can achieve on a measure of fuel. Royalty is judged by the awe created in the eyes of those Commoners. By Jim Brokaw

For five years now, *Motor Trend* has been pitting the Lincoln Continental Mark IV against the Cadillac Eldorado to determine which is king of the luxury hill, and therefore, king of the domestic market. It has become quite obvious over the years that while very few may hope to own one of these gliding leather cocoons, there are large and vocal numbers who have an emotional attachment to the top of the heap. Regardless of choice, we receive letters praising our astute judgement and taste, countered by an equal number of communications damning our unforgivable blindness, crass lack of perception, taste and legitimacy.

When one deigns to examine a monarch, one does it with grace, dignity, and a courteous selection of positive superlatives. When one presumes to judge a king, one must remember that, unlike a presidential election, there is not merely a winner and a loser, although our last election left even this in doubt, in a contest of royalty there is the *ascender*

to the throne and the *pretender* to the throne. Kings don't finish second, they become Dukes.

Ergo, it is with a distinct sense of honor that we present the two combatants in this joust for the symbolic title of King; the defending champion, His Royal Majesty, El Dorado de Cadillac, son of Field Marshal Motors, Knight of Grosse Pointe, Emperor Emeritus Beverly Hills, Order of Greenwich, K.G., O.B., E.P.A. vs. the challenger, His Royal Highness, Mark Lincoln IV, son of King Henry III, Duke of Dearborn, Knight of Grosse Pointe, V.C., D.S.O., E.P.A.

Their Graces are battle-hardened veterans of the Teutonic Wars with the dwarf warriors of the Baron Mercedes. They have endured many tests at the hands of the evil Viceroy of Smog from the Californian Empire, their armor has been solidly tested by the Federal Hammer of Thor. It is only their august sense of obligation to the peasant masses that their Highnesses have temporarily absented themselves from a punitive expedition against the minions of the Bavarian Prince, Motorische Werken.

Lord El Dorado de Cadillac, known affectionately to his knights, squires, and pikemen simply as Prince Eldo, is splendidly attired in curved armor by Fisher. Front and rear impact bars, referred to as "bumpers" by the field soldiers, have been skillfully blended into the front air grille and dual illuminators. One would scarcely believe that they have been smitten by the Federal Hammer at the blinding velocity of 5 mph. (Many Poundings from the Hammer.)

Eldo's armored shell is lined with a soft but durable Sierra grain leather, tinted a medium jasper (green) to match the outer colour. Eldo has resolved the difficulties arising during the heat of battle by installing an automatic climate control system to provide heating, cooling, and air dehumidifying to maintain a constant temperature pleasing to the royal hide.

Prince Eldo mounts a monstrous steed rumored to be as large as 500 cubits in displacement. It requires four barrels of carburetor to feed the steed from a tankard of some 27 gallons capacity. In the Prince's absence, his men are wont to boast of his great thirst, claiming that his Highness will only travel 13.7 leagues on a gallon of low-lead mead.

So powerful is Prince Eldo's steed that Field Marshal Motors has installed a high-energy ignition system with a magnetic impulse distributor, high-energy coil and integrated-circuit electrics for more reliability in leaving the lists on chill mornings as well as maintaining a comfortable canter on the highway.

Eldo's steed is shod with CR78-15 steel-belted radial shoes, by Uniroyal, of course.

Prince Eldo has craftily incorporated many refinements to his Fisher armor. There are power locks for the entry hatches, six-way power adjustment for the royal saddle, tilt-telescope saddle horn, AM/FM signal seeker communicator, fiber optic lamp monitors for night combat, and for viewing rocky crags, the Prince has cleverly installed a sliding panel in the helmet, which he calls a "sun roof."

In order to keep Prince Eldo fully informed and in complete control during periods of transport, there are also installed a digital sundial, decks of tape, variable ratio power reins, automatic hitching post release, automatic saddle level control, and cleverest of all, remote controlled right and left side mirrors that permit rearward vision. One may observe the line-of-march behind without appearing too strict.

Eldo's worthy opponent, Prince Mark Lincoln IV, affectionately dubbed, "The Mark" by his loyal lieutenants, selected gleaming battle armor from the House of Ford. Inasmuch as The Mark has been narrowly defeated in the two prior tournaments, his Lordship is attired from helmet to stirrups in glossy black.

KING OF THE HILL

Although The Mark has armor of moon-dust and diamond fire colours, his princely humility forbade a gaudy display. He also didn't want to mess up his parade armor if he caught another lance in the grille.

The Mark's steed is also of gargantuan proportions—to wit, 460 cubits. Though not of equal mass to Eldo's steed, The Mark claims that his is longer of stride.

The Mark's taste is as equally demanding as is Prince Eldo's. The armor is lined with quilted leather, has a six-way adjustable saddle, illuminated visor mirror, power entry hatch locks, but only a tilt control for the saddle horn.

Mark also has a complete climate control system for automatically heating, cooling and dehumidifying, the last of which is particularly gratifying during early mornings on the moors of Scotland. Actually, in regard to comfort and convenience, both princes have virtually identical devices. Some vary, in name, some vary slightly in function. For example, Mark also has a sliding panel in his helmet, but it is cleverly made of glass, enabling The Mark to see out, but forbidding the peasants from looking in. The Mark calls it his "moon roof."

The jousting grounds are brightly arrayed with colorful banners and pennants whipping in the breeze. There is a multitude of fine ladies in attendance.

Since a monarch must host a great deal of entertaining, drinking is a critical part of his kingly duties. Drinking is measured in a device called a "mile." The imbiber is gauged in his prowess by the number of "miles" he can perform while quaffing a gallon of low-lead mead. Prince El Dorado cleanly captured the first event by doing 13.27 "miles" to his gallon, while the best Mark Lincoln IV could manage was 11.99 "miles" per gallon. While these are certainly lofty performances, ugly umors float about of base-born archers achieving as many as 25 to 30 "miles" on a gallon of mead. These tales are given less credibility than the outright blasphemy of foreign born mercenaries and stable hands doing 35 "miles" on a gallon. What can you expect from someone who wears vinylle garments, and must use a "stick" and a "clutch" to shift his steed? When the wind is right, it's easy to tell *they* don't have dehumidifiers.

The Master of the Games announced the next event—the wounded knight rescue. In this contest, the rider must bring his steed to a full halt from a canter and from a gallop to simulate rescuing an unhorsed knight. From the canter, which is 30 "speeds", Mark stopped two feet shorter than Eldo, but from the gallop or 60 "speeds", Prince Dorado halted a full 19 feet shorter than Mark. The non-skid rear shoes failed to work properly, causing Eldo's rear to lock-up and giving Mark tail hop.

After a refreshing leg of mutton and a flagon or two of ale, the princes commenced the simulated combat phase. Foot soldiers called "seconds" hide behind shields on a platform called a "clock." The object is to commence from a standing start to ride by at specified "speeds" and chop "seconds" off the "clock."

At 0-30 speeds, armed with a battle axe, The Mark emerged the victor with only 3.6 seconds left standing to Eldo's 4.0 seconds.

At 0-50 speeds, Mark again triumphed with the mace, 7.5 seconds to 8.3 for Eldo.

At 0-60 speeds, Prince Eldo came closer but Mark's broadsword outchopped the prince of Cadillac, 10.2 to 11.2 seconds.

The passing contest was next. Each contestant canters at 40 speeds past a shelter known as an Ak-cell. The Ak-cell is filled with archers who shoot flaming arrows called "rays" at the riders. The riders must chop "seconds" off the "clock" while shunning the rays. This is called the *Ak-cell or Ray-shun Test*. In the 40 to 60 speeds portion, Prince Mark chopped all but 5.2 seconds, but Eldo had 5.5 seconds on the clock.

The next *Ak-cell or Ray-shun Test* started at 50 speeds. The black armored prince of Ford again had fewer seconds left on the clock, 6.2 to 6.9.

The final-showdown combat contest was a full gallop, flat-out run at the "clock" with lances from a standing start. The knights have to stand in a hole a quarter of a mile away from the clock. (The Knights have added incentive in this event since the winner is permitted to smite the loser with the flat of his sword in the area in front of the royal box known as the traps. This is called "beating him through the traps.")

Knights are allowed to have a squire in the hole to help him onto his horse. The crafty squires used a shovel to fashion steps for the knights. For years the fastest riders out of the hole were called "diggers."

Mark shot out of the hole first, opening a bit of a lead on Eldo. As they piked off the "seconds", Eldo began closing on Mark. The result was very close. Mark defeated Eldo, but Eldo refused to slow down so Mark barely beat him through the traps.

The two remaining events were the agility course and the grand finale, the stately-riding contest. In the agility test, the rider must weave through poles implanted in the turf at great speed, pluck a goat skin bag from the ground with his lance, drain the wine at a full gallop and hand the bag, called a Ling, to his squire riding at full gallop in the opposite direction. Inasmuch as the princely contestants were a bit winded at this point, Prince Eldo knocked two poles down while turning and Prince Mark knocked a peasant wench up into a hay cart while quaffing, the event was declared a tie since both managed to hand a Ling to his squire. In fact, to this day, the agility test is called the Hand-a-Ling course.

The stately riding event was declared in favor of Mark Lincoln IV since his courtliness was performed in complete silence, while El Dorado's steed emitted a barely audible "road noise" causing the ladies-in-waiting to giggle.

Although the symbolic crown was placed on the hood of the Mark Lincoln IV, who shall reign for one year as King of the Hill, El Dorado received the crowds' cheers when he personally handed the crown off to Mark. This was the first time anyone got a hand-off from an audible. ■

The King's Ransom Road Test

We look at big bucks from both sides now, and the intercontinental contenders are: BMW 3.0, Jaguar XJ-6, Mercedes-Benz 450 SE, Imperial LeBaron, Cadillac Eldorado and Continental Mark IV.

THE IMPORTS
By John Lamm

If you happen to be a fan of imported luxury cars and expect this to be a tirade against their American rivals, you will be disappointed in this portion of our road test. It's not because I secretly prefer the U.S. luxury cars (which I don't) or have been disappointed with the present offerings of BMW, Mercedes-Benz or Jaguar (which I am not), it is just that the domestic versus imported luxury car question makes an interesting discussion, but a terrible argument.

That is because the difference in luxury cars goes much deeper than "imported" or "domestic" labels. Any automobile is a direct reflection of its home environment. Everything from local laws, gasoline prices and national attitude to how history and geography dicate that any one automobile will somehow differ from its counterpart from another nation.

Let's use the obvious comparison of the U.S. and Germany. Right after World War II, we were able to get back to full automobile production relatively quickly; out went the bombers and in came the cars. Cadillac had a restyling in 1948 and introduced the overhead valve V-8 in 1949. BMW wasn't able to build their first post-war car in Munich until 1952. Even when the factories were humming, Europeans were selling to a public still grappling to rebuild their cities and their lives.

Out of these contrasts grew the divergent lines of luxury cars. American machines gobbled gas because it was cheap; the European cars had to nibble. Suspension engineers knew American luxury cars would be driven predominantly on wide smooth roads with gentle curves, while their overseas collegues had to reckon with narrow village streets, Alpine roads and vision-blurring cobblestones. A more specific example: Mercedes-Benz went for years with less than adequate air conditioning, a problem aggravated,

THE DOMESTICS
By Jim Brokaw

Our annual King of the Hill road test has been a pleasant and entertaining little face-off for the last five years between the Cadillac Eldorado and the Lincoln Continental Mark IV.

The Eldo and the Mark IV symbolize more than any other vehicles sold in the U.S. the traditional Great American Dream of "making it," both financially and socially. The Imperial is, of course, a co-equal status symbol, however, the traditional image of the Imperial owner is that of the wealthy who "made it" a hell of a long time ago, and who prefer a little handling with their ride.

All three are big cars with high price tags and a design philosophy of luxurious isolation. Before you condemn them for sheer size (5000 pounds, 18 feet long) you should be aware of their evolution.

In the pre-WW II America, the Great Dream was to own your own home and a Cadillac. We had plenty of space for wide roads and big garages, but we also had some pretty rotten roads that broke up in the freezing winters. We had wide open countryside, but very noisy cities. We didn't have any smog, but an abundance of coal-soot and dust. We had no aristocracy, but a very stratified economic class structure. While we boasted of equal opportunity, we struggled for individuality. Proud of our "masses," we all strove to rise above them. While few people ventured into the "rich" section of town, the "rich" always managed to drive their long, sleek machines where the ordinary folk could see and envy.

The cars for plain folks; Ford, Chevy, and Plymouth, were small, noisy and rough riding. The only thing that could cope with frost heaves and pot holes was a combination of weight and a long wheelbase. Isolation from the road surface was obviously the first requirement of a luxury car.

THE IMPORTS

BMW—Ah, the smell of real leather permeates the 3.0 si. The seats they cover are the most comfortable of the group. The air conditioning didn't fare as well and was less than adequate. Entry and exit are simple, the seat belts among the best. The outside rear view mirror is motor-driven. Note the odds and ends tray on the dash.

JAGUAR—Coventry's redesign of the XJ dash (last year) is a vast improvement over the original. The burled walnut dash panel adds a warmth the German cars lack. Jag has an automatic temperature control and they were thoughtful enough to add a rear seat vent at the back of the center console. Unfortunately, though, the air conditioning broke.

MERCEDES—This is what the well researched interior is wearing. The shift lever knob is even designed so as not to penetrate the average eyeball socket. The seats are harder than many Americans are used to, but most could easily adapt to them. Note, as with the BMW, the complete lack of chrome. Everything has a non-reflective finish.

no doubt, because Stuttgart is at a coolish latitude equivalent to the western border between the U.S. and Canada.

There are a good many other qualifying factors, all meant as an explanation, not an excuse. They make it fruitless to point up how imported luxury cars may be better than the Americans . . . or vice versa. In fact, none is necessarily better, just different.

The very fact that I am writing the European half of this dual test makes it obvious I favor their sort of luxury car. That opinion begins with size. Despite the fact that we, as a country, have had the natural resources and the psychological rationale to build and buy large luxury automobiles, I never could enjoy those massive Cadillacs or Lincolns. I just don't believe you need a Lincoln Continental's 232 total inches and 2½ tons to make an automobile luxurious. The BMW 3.0 si's 195 inches or the Mercedes' 205 inches seem sufficient, particularly considering the interior room achieved within those dimensions.

Then there is interior design. We American's have always put a high price on an automobile's curves and chrome. Europeans, particularly the Germans, have stressed func-

BMW—Another neat display, though this one eliminates the oil pressure gauge. Those four levers to the right of the wheel are the rather confusing heater/vent controls. The a/c buttons are below, above the radio. It is all well thoughtout, but the complete lack of color in the interior gives the BMW a cold, almost unfriendly feeling.

JAGUAR—You certainly can't complain about a lack of instrumentation. The gauges are all simple to read, though the simple steering wheel through which you view them appears to have come out of an economy car. The wide center console cramps the footwell area. Other than that, we all enjoyed the rather American feel of the XJ-6 L.

MERCEDES—We found this instrument panel the easiest to live with, though some claim the one instrument grouping on the left to be confusing. The heating/ventilation/air conditioning system is superlative, once you master the four-lever two-dial controls on the center console. As with Jaguar, the power window controls are on the console.

THE DOMESTICS

ELDORADO—Quilted leather seats, six-way power adjustments for both occupants, reclining seatback for the passenger. Multiple air conditioning outlets ensure an even flow of automatically heated or cooled air to the entire interior. In spite of loops and keepers, the shoulder strap is an obstacle to rear seat entry.

MARK IV—Cut pile carpeting and quilted leather seats are similar to Eldo, but Lincoln shields the dash with a padded cover while Eldo recesses it away from the passenger. Mark IV seat and window controls are both located on the armrest. Stereo speakers are located in bottom door section.

IMPERIAL—If you want to see a seat, that's a seat. Individual compliant seat and back cushions covered with delightfully wrinkled kid glove leather. Imperial places shoulder restraint to the rear of the door opening to fold back out of the rear seat passenger's path. It still gets in the way somewhat.

As roads improved, so did the base cars, bringing Ford, Chevrolet and Plymouth size, isolation and comfort. The mechanics of luxury were available to everyone. Only size, price tag and the mystique of the magic names remained to serve as public notice of "success."

Eldorado, Mark IV, and Imperial; the personal luxury cars, still got the job done to the tune of 40,412, 57,316, and 14,426, units respectively, in 1974, one of the worse sales years in memory.

Approached from the outside, all three domestics present a formidable image of protective mass that invites you to view from a distance rather than saunter up and peer into the window, which is precisely the evolutionary statement our luxury cars have been seeking. Look, but don't touch.

Eldorado is distinctly Cadillac, bearing a strong family resemblance to the de Ville line. Mark IV is longer and sleeker in image. Imperial projects a quite different aspect of being very wide and very strong. Eldo is protective, Mark IV is swift and Imperial is solid, formidably solid. You just don't race an Imperial across an intersection if there is any chance at all of losing.

ELDORADO—Horizontal control display places frequently used auxiliary devices, air conditioning, radio, to the outside, infrequently used devices, cruise control, rear window defog, to the inside. Minimal instrumentation is augmented by top-mounted warning light bar.

MARK IV—Clustered instrument pod is closer to aircraft philosophy. Light colored wood grain veneer is very well executed, forming good background to emphasize control clusters. Steering wheel spokes are cleverly curled away from pod. Wheel mounted speed control is easiest of all to use.

IMPERIAL—Balance of engine instrument gauges, stacked at the left, and warning lights, behind speedometer, is best of the domestics. Push button climate control is easier to use at night than traditional lever control. Tilt-telescope steering wheel is added comfort feature. Vent location could be improved.

THE IMPORTS

JAGUAR—Our test car was an XJ-6 L, the last letter signifying the long, 112.8-inch wheelbase, four inches longer than standard. The car has a very graceful look, especially for its size. With the 4.2-liter six, it managed 18.4 secs in a quarter-mile, though its V-12 counterpart would have been the fastest of all. Fuel economy was disappointing—15.3 mpg.

BMW—The 3.0 si looks smaller because it is, with a 106-inch wheelbase. Like all BMWs, it is as much a sporting sedan as a luxury car. The only one of the group available with a manual transmission, it scored best at the track, with a 16.98 quarter-mile time. The three-liter six uses electronic fuel injection giving the car excellent driveability.

MERCEDES—They tell us even the taillight corrugations have a purpose, that being to prevent dirt build-up. The 450SE matches the XJ-6 L's 112-inch wheelbase, though the 450SE has a more purposeful look. The electronically injected V-8 got the car through a quarter-mile in 17.5 secs, but M-B will lower that next year with a 6.9-liter version.

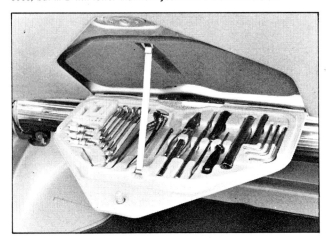

BMW—How very German, the fitted drop-down tool tray in the BMW's trunk. That is standard along with electric windows, air conditioning, the alloy wheels, power steering, leather upholstery, power brakes and one of the first great Becker radios we've heard. Only the metallic paint ($308) and electric outside mirror ($65) were added options.

tion in their designs. There isn't one crease or piece of chrome on the exterior of a 450SE that isn't there for some proven reason. The BMW's design is a little less, shall we say, scientific, but is still meant more to envelope an interior package than just provide visual satisfaction. The XJ-6 L follows that same thinking, if a bit more stylish. It is the refinement of several Jaguar sedan designs from the genius behind all Jaguars, Sir William Lyons.

To the staunch Caddy fan, the imports are plain and lacking in pizzazz, but I happen to prefer their purposeful design. It was architect Louis Sullivan who helped argue that "form follows function" and, for many eyes, that can also mean beauty. It's an old argument. One man finds the egg a package of beauty; the other would rather chrome it. I find the lean, taut concept of the imports preferable to the bulginess of the domestics.

American luxury cars exist, of course, as a display of wealth. In that direction, they do quite well with their interiors. Cadillac, Lincoln and Chrysler tend to utilize soft seats, thick carpets and gadgets by the dozen. All three of our imported luxury test cars are more restrained and have the same basic interior configuration—bucket seats up front separated by a center console with a bench seat in back. They lack the variety of materials and colors offered in American luxury cars, though they offer benefits such as leather seats that are completely covered with leather instead of the more common American mixture of leather and vinyl.

It is obvious that the dashboards of the imports were laid out by experts more concerned with ergonomics than economics. All three have sufficient instrumentation placed straight ahead on very readable dials. The same accessibility applies to all switches and knobs, though both German cars have heating, air conditioning and ventilation controls that take some getting used to. Jaguar's version of automatic temperature control does it quite simply with two dials.

However, the heating and ventilation systems offer another interesting contrast between the domestics and imports. The center of the point is gadgets, one area in which Mercedes, BMW and Jaguar don't match the American cars. The Cad, Lincoln and Imperial all have full automatic

MERCEDES—Our test 450SE included the corporate alloy wheels, though at a premium of $597 per set. That about runs the list of exterior options offered for the car. There is an identical-looking model, the 280S, which shares all the features of the V-8 models, but is powered by a carbureted dual overhead cam six. It is slow, but economical.

THE DOMESTICS

ELDORADO—Blunt front fender caps give the Eldo a fierce countenance at speed. Falling mid-way between the two domestics, Eldo had second best acceleration, second best fuel economy, 14.39 mpg, which isn't bad for 5000 pounds and second best stopping distance. Price, $11,744 was also between the two competitors from Detroit.

MARK IV—Lower belt line profile softens the Mark IV dimensions somewhat. Best in quarter mile acceleration, the Mark was third in fuel economy, 13.27 mpg, and best stop from 30 mph. Price as tested, which includes a moonroof the other two did not have installed, was the highest, $13,631, but less than all three imports.

IMPERIAL—Outwardly flaring side panels impart solid, durable, impregnable image to the Imperial. Lowest priced of the test, $10,530, Imperial achieved best domestic fuel economy, 14.89 mpg, and the shortest stop from 60 mph of all but the Mercedes. Full sail panel limits rear quarter visibility.

MARK IV—A common option for all three domestic vehicles is a sunroof.

All three curve around their occupants shielding them from the outside. There is no attempt at any image other than isolation. Genuine leather isolation.

All three are replete with illumination front, side and rear. The turn signals light up the side street for 50 feet. Here again, the emphasis is on subtly announcing the arrival of the occupants. You do not have to sneak a peek at the window sticker to be aware that the bottom line is well out of reach of the non-achievers.

Not so with the imports. Unless you happen to know that the BMW is a 3.0 si and what that means, the sight of a near $14,000 price tag on that little car is enough to induce cardiac arrest. All Mercedes look alike, from the outside and they do have a very distinct luxury image so you are already tensed up when you see the big numbers on the Stuttgart greeting card. A Jag is a Jag and if you don't recognize the car on sight, you do know that they are generally parked in wide sweeping driveways near the old man's Cad, somewhere on the other side of town.

Inside our domestics, the name of the game is isolation and environment control. Much of the 5000 pound test weight is used up in sound deadening material to isolate the outside noise. The U.S. is well ahead of the imports in this area, though the Jag does a very good job of keeping the sound out and the silence in.

Although we do not use a decibel meter to measure precisely the sound level, the collective staff ear gives the nod to the Mark IV as the silent one.

All three; Eldorado, Mark IV and Imperial, have leather covered, six-way power seats. The power controls all work with equal facility, but the Mark IV has a power lumbar control that really works. All three have a reclining feature on the passenger seat.

Seats on all are much firmer than in years past, but still yielding and very comfortable. They tend to get a bit squirmy on long trips, but Mercedes has the opposite problem. Their quite firm therapeutic seats are very comfortable on trips in excess of 100 miles, but a little hard on the buns for those short 30-mile commutes.

Instrumentation is sparse on all three with Mark IV having the least and Imperial having the most. All have a full array of warning lights.

Eldo's top mounted digital clock and fuel gauge on either end of the warning light bar is an excellent touch, as are the fender mounted light monitors.

Imperial's instrument and warning cluster is the most conveniently arrayed and gives the most information. Their push button climate control is easiest to use at night.

Imperial's seat leather is "kid glove soft," being superior in the pure sense of elegance to the competition. Eldorado uses the same type of "aged" leather appearance on their door trim.

Mark IV has a very light colored wood grain veneer

ELDORADO—Clever bit of one-ups-manship by Cadillac. They place an additional door handle to the rear of the passenger door, providing a means for the rear seat passenger to exit the vehicle without assistance from the front.

THE IMPORTS

SPECIFICATIONS	BMW 3.0 si	JAGUAR XJ-6 L	MERCEDES-BENZ 450SE
Engine	SOHC in-line six-cylinder	DOHC in-line six-cylinder	SOHC V-8
Bore & Stroke-ins.	3.50 x 3.15	3.62 x 4.17	3.62 x 3.35
Displacement-cu.in./c.c.	182/2980	258/4235	275.8/4520
HP @ RPM	176 @ 5500	162 @ 4750	180 @ 4750
Torque-(lbs.-Ft. @ RPM	185 @ 4500	225 @ 2500	220 @ 3000
Compression Ratio	8.1:1	7.5:1	8:1
Carburetion	electronic fuel injection	Two Zenith-Stromberg carbs	electronic fuel injection
Transmission	four-speed manual	three-speed automatic	three-speed automatic
Rear Axle Ratio	3.64:1	3.31:1	3.07:1
Steering Type	ZF power-assisted with ball nut, three-piece track rod	Power-assisted rack and pinion	Power, recirculating ball
Steering Ratio	18.4:1	16.4:1	13.92-14.02
Turning Circle-ft.	35.2	36	38
Wheel Turns (lock-to-lock)	3.5	3.3	2.7
Tires	195/70 HR 14 radials	E70VR 15 radials	205/70-14 radials
Brakes	Disc/Disc	Disc/Disc	Disc/Disc
Front Suspension	Independent—MacPherson strut and lower wishbone	Independent—Upper and lower A-arms, coil springs, tube shocks, anti-roll bar.	Independent—upper and lower A-arms, coil springs, tube shocks, anti-roll bar
Rear Suspension	Independent—semi-trailings arm, coil springs, tube shock absorbers	Independent—lower wishbone, fixed length halfshaft, trailing arm, two shock/coil spring units per side	Independent—diagonal trailing arms, coil springs, tube shocks, anti-roll bar
Body/Frame Construction	Unit	Unit	Unit
Wheelbase-in/mm	106/2692.4	112.8/2865.1	112.8/2865.1
Overall Length-in/mm	195/4953.0	194.7/4945.3	205.5/5219.7
Width-in/mm	68.9/1750.0	69.7/1771.6	70.5/1790.7
Front Track-in/mm	58.3/1480.8	58/1473.2	60.0/1524
Rear Track-in/mm	57.9/1470.6	58.6/1488.4	59.3/1506.2
Height-in/mm	57.1/1450.3	54.1/1374.1	56.1/1424.9
Weight as Tested-lbs.	3395	4130	4100 (advertised weight)
Storage Capacity cu.ft/cm3	22.8	17.0	17.7
Fuel Capacity-gals/liters	20.8/87.9	24/100.8	28.8/121.7
Oil Capacity-qts/liters	6.6/6.9	8.75/9.1	7.9/8.3
Base Price (West Coast)	$13,831	$13,100	$17,863
Price as Tested $	$14,347	$13,100	$19,166
PERFORMANCE			
Acceleration			
0-30 mph	3.8	4.5	4.5
0-40 mph	5.5	6.5	6.6
0-50 mph	8.1	9.6	8.8
0-60 mph	10.9	12.9	11.1
Standing Start ¼-mile Elapsed Time (sec.)	16.98	18.41	17.55
Speed (mph)	83.2	76.5	79.9
Passing Speeds 40-60 mph	4.0	7.4	5.8
50-70 mph	5.6	8.5	7.2
Stopping Distance (ft) 30-0 mph	25.9	29.7	29.7
60-0 mph	147.2	140.2	131.2
Fuel Mileage	18.4	15.3	18.7
Speedometer Error Indicated Speed	40 50 60	40 50 60	40 50 60
True Speed	37.8 47.1 56.4	40.1 50.3 60.0	35.7 46.3 56.3

temperature control ... just set and forget, if you will. Now I personally find it more impressive that you can cool the driver while warming the passenger in a 450SE, but as a buying country we love the complete climate control. Jaguar has now followed the American lead with "Automatic Temperature Sensing and Control" and Mercedes is working on it.

Our love of gimmickry shows up throughout the cars. There are "Moonroofs," six-way power seats (you can achieve the same variety of adjustment in the imports, but must do it manually), lights that shut off automatically, theft alarms and the tilt steering wheel. One reason for the lack of such "fun" in the imports can be seen in the angry answer of a Mercedes engineer when asked when they would have a tilt steering wheel, "We spend years to determine the perfect steering wheel position and now you want to change it?"

Apparently, the same attitude that keeps the cars lean and practical makes such options seem, well, frivolous. That same feeling puts less importance on such American necessities as total sound isolation and you would find all three imported luxury cars have a somewhat higher interior noise level than the domestics.

While the American luxury cars have sophisticated "luxury systems," the imports put the same emphasis on their mechanical features. Cadillac, Lincoln and Chrysler use overhead valve V-8s bolted to automatic transmissions for their luxury cars. The basic suspensions are no more sophisticated than those under an intermediate sedan. The imports, on the other hand, are a veritable festival of engineering. All have four-wheel independent suspension, though each shows a slightly different approach to the subject. The Jaguar has a dual overhead cam six (with an overhead cam V-12 in the identical-looking XJ-12), the BMW has a fuel-injected overhead cam six, while Mercedes uses the same sort of induction system on their 450SE's overhead cam V-8. Those refined mechanicals are one of the big selling points of this *genre* of car, though they do contribute to the car's prices and, in the case of Mercedes and Jaguar, add to the company's service headaches.

Again, it is a difference in need leading to a difference in philosophy. The Europeans need long range, high speed cruising ability, while the Americans prefer the brute torque to satisfy our love of acceleration and a wide variety of power-draining accessories.

The direction of their respective sophistication is most obvious when driving the cars—the Americans are best for luxuriating, the Europeans for driving. The Mercedes has the hardest feel of three, both in the seat and the suspension. It is only after at least 100 miles of driving that the firm support of the 450SE's seat softens and you begin to understand why it is there. The BMW is a much softer riding car that handles almost as well as the 450SE, but takes on a disconcerting lean in doing so. The Jaguar is just the short of the BMW's handling potential (though still quite good) and the combination of its seat, ride, handling and such factors and the feel of the brakes and steering give one the feeling that the XJ-6 would feel the most familiar to the average American. In fact, in many ways the Jaguar feels as though it could have been designed and built in Detroit. What comes home in all three is a well defined statement of how they feel about the usual compromise of ride versus handling. I have to agree with their staying on the handling side.

While we preferred the Mercedes ($19,100) it is also
CONTINUED ON PAGE 128

THE DOMESTICS

which is very well executed, brightening the interior considerably.

Eldorado falls short of traditional Cadillac excellence in their obviously substitute wood paneling.

Imperial relies on darkness and shade to put you in mind of multi-roomed stately old mansions with well polished mahogany or repeatedly varnished dark oak. Again, Imperial's image of established wealth.

Eldorado takes the blue ribbon for the extra touch with their dual handled doors. The rear mounted door handle to permit the rear seat passenger to exit without assistance from the front.

All three have optional sunroof or moonroof ceiling panels. All three have optional crushed velour velvet interiors whose elegance and sheer opulence can be exceeded only by something that moves and breathes by itself.

Interior appointments are two-thirds of what these cars are all about. Since this is not the market for nickel nursing and budget checking, the only decision that has to be made is, are you a leather person, a leather and cloth person, or a crushed velour person. You select your environment and how much of it you want to control.

Mechanically, there are more similarities than contrasts in the three domestics. All have large displacement, high torque, overhead valve engines. All have three-speed automatic transmissions. Imperial and Mark IV have conventional front engine rear drive configuration, the Eldo has a front engine front drive arrangment. Eldorado has front wheel disc rear wheel drum brakes, both Mark IV and Imperial have four-wheel disc brakes. All have an anti-skid feature. Eldo and Imperial utilize front torsion bar suspension, Mark IV employs front coil springs. Eldo and Mark IV have coils in the rear, Imperial uses leaf springs.

Ride and handling is the area where the diverging philosophies of the imports and domestics are most starkly contrasted. The Europeans place a priority on handling. The imports are closer to sports sedans utilized for long trips at high speeds on motorways and autobahns, on winding mountain roads and hedge-lined country lanes. The domestics emphasize ride. The prime difference is that the size of Germany and Britain (U.K.) are considerably smaller with much less contrast in terrain. Conversely every car built in the U.S. has to be saleable in every part of the U.S. from the narrow cramped roads of New England to the frost ravaged secondary streets of the upper Midwest, to the Rocky Mountains, through the Southwestern desert to the eternal dampness of the Northwest. If you expect to sell the same car in all areas, it has to be a compromise.

The choice was an isolated ride. It doesn't matter what condition the road is in, you won't be disturbed by it. Smooth they are, handle they don't, except in the strictest interpretation of the term.

All three can negotiate any curve, taken at a sane speed with plenty of lead time. All three can make an emergency lane change at freeway speeds without losing control.

On the handling course it becomes obvious that Eldorado's front drive set up is to eliminate the drivetrain tunnel. There isn't enough power to really pull the car out of a turn with the front drive.

Eldo exhibits pronounced understeer in an extreme turn and the isolation the produces the smooth ride also diminished road feel.

Mark IV, being a bit lighter up front, has less understeer in a corner, but not much less. It did have a bit more roll stability in the extreme, and a bit more exiting power.

Imperial was the best handling of the three with the most roll stability.

Braking is a testimonial to the engineers of all three manufacturers. Bringing 5000 pounds of anything to a smooth stop from 60 mph is a chore. All three do it well, but the brakes on the Imperial are a masterpiece. We made

CONTINUED ON PAGE 128

SPECIFICATIONS	ELDORADO	MARK IV	IMPERIAL
Engine	OHV V-8	OHV V-8	OHV V-8
Bore & Stroke-ins.	4.30x4.304	4.36x3.85	4.32x3.75
Displacement-cu. in./c.c.	500/8000	460/7360	440/7040
HP @ RPM	190@3600	223@4000	215@4000
Torque-(lbs.-ft@RPM	360@2000	366@2600	330@3200
Compression Ratio	8.5:1	8.0:1	8.2:1
Carburetion	4v	4v	4v
Transmission	Three-Speed Automatic	Three-Speed Automatic	Three-Speed Automatic
Rear Axle Ratio	2.73:1	3.00:1	2.71:1
Steering Type	Recirculating Ball (power)	Recirculating Ball (power)	Recirculating Ball (power)
Steering Ratio	20.0:1 to 16.2:1	21.8:1	18.9:1
Turning Circle-ft.	NA	43.3	44.78
Wheel Turns (lock-to-lock)	3.5	3.99	3.5
Tires	Uniroyal Radials LR78-15	Michelin Radials 230-15	Goodyear Polysteel Radial LR78-15
Brakes	Disc/Drum power	Disc/Disc power	Disc/Disc power
Front Suspension	TORSION BAR/SHOCKS/ STABILIZER	COILS/SHOCKS/ STABILIZER	TORSION BAR/SHOCKS/ STABILIZER
Rear Suspension	COILS/SHOCKS/ STABILIZER automatic level control	4-LINK/ COILS/SHOCKS/ STABILIZER	LEAVES/SHOCKS
Body/Frame Construction	PERIMETER	SEPARATE FRAME	UNITIZED W/ ISOLATED SUB FRAME
Wheelbase-in./mm	126.3/3157.5	120.4/3010.0	124.0/3100.0
Overall Length-in./mm	224.1/5602.5	228.0/5700.0	231.0/5775.0
Width-in/mm	79.8/1995.0	79.8/1995.0	79.7/1992.5
Front Track-in./mm	63.7/1592.5	62.9/1572.5	64.0/1600.0
Rear Track-in./mm	63.6/1590.0	62.8/1570.0	63.7/1592.5
Height-in./mm	54.1/1352.5	53.3/1332.5	54.5/1362.5
Weight as Tested-lbs.	5290	5430	5185
Storage Capacity cu.ft/cm3	12.5/1296	14.4/1493	19.6/2032.1
Fuel Capacity-gals./liters	27/108	26.5/106	25.0/100
Oil Capacity-qts./liters	6.0/6.0/ (with filter)	4.0/4.0	4.0/4.0
Base Price	$9935	$11,082	$8698
Price as Tested	$11,744	$13,632	$10,531
PERFORMANCE			
Acceleration			
0-30 mph	3.9	4.3	4.2
0-40 mph	5.8	6.3	6.2
0-50 mph	8.2	8.7	9.6
0-60 mph	10.9	11.2	12.7
Standing Start ¼-mile Elapsed Time (sec.)	17.60	17.56	17.77
Speed (mph)	78.19	80.50	79.92
Passing Speeds			
40-60 mph	5.8	6.5	6.0
50-70 mph	7.6	7.4	7.5
Stopping Distance (ft.)			
30-0 mph	34'1	29'8	35'11
60-0 mph	159'8	160'3	134'2
Fuel Mileage	14.39	13.27	14.89
Speedometer Error Indicated Speed	40 50 60	40 50 60	40 50 60
True Speed	40.12 49.86 59.84	40.55 50.87 60.97	38.39 46.92 57.39

THE IMPORTS

CONTINUED FROM PAGE 126

some $4500 more expensive than the BMW or Jaguar. Consider that fact and the 450SE and 3.0 si are on about the same level, with the XJ-6 L (at $1000 less than the BMW) a close third.

Of course that is still a lot of money compared to the American cars, even with all their options in place. So every time you see a BMW, Mercedes or Jaguar you are seeing another overt blow against American luxury cars.

There is the new option, Cadillac's Seville. While obviously a domestic, it doesn't really fit into either of the catagories we've worked up here. The Seville mixes the exterior and interior style of the domestics with the size of the imports. In fact, it is almost the dimensional twin of the 450SE both inside and out. The Seville stays more on the ride side of the inevitable ride-handling compromise, not achieving the precise handling of the imports. At that, it is still leagues ahead of its larger compatriots from Cadillac, Lincoln and Chrysler.

Add to this the larger-than-normal options list that Cadillac bestowed upon the Seville and you go a long way to honestly bridge the gap between the import and domestic luxury cars. There are still hard line advocates on both sides that will refuse to admit the qualities of the Seville, but they are playing a snob's game.

Any observer can see many of the economic conditions that caused Europe to build smaller luxury cars—expensive gasoline and precious resources—are now affecting us too. In the end, the more compact luxury car looms as the reasonable alternative.■

THE DOMESTICS

CONTINUED FROM PAGE 127

straight, consistent smooth stops shorter than any of the six cars except the Mercedes, which is outweighed by the Imperial by a 1000 pounds. And they were close enough to cover with a blanket.

Imperial is the best handling domestic and has the firmest ride. Eldorado is beautifully engineered to be driven by a person with slow reflexes and a tendency to overcontrol in perfect safety. Mark IV lies in between. None of the three will lure you up into the mountain switchbacks, but they are smooth as silk on the flat.

The two totally divergent philosophies have clashed head to head in Cadillac's new Seville. I can only add my concurrence to John Lamm's observations. We did not have the opportunity to give the car a full test, but a driving impression clearly indicates that the jump toward handling has been a long one. The Seville is a truly phenomenal balance of ride and handling in the achievement of a very reassuring agility without harshness. The kind of a car that will be comfortable on both the short hauls and the long ones.

We shall reserve final judgment until the complete test, but every indication is that the new king has just been born. The king of both hills.

Imperial, which performed remarkably well in all areas, has become the first victim of economic uncertainty and changing tastes. It is slated to become an option of the Chrysler New Yorker line for 1976. Perhaps what is passing into the archives is not the car, but the way we say, "I have made it!■

Cadillac Eldorado

The Eldorado is now the biggest standard Cadillac (outranked in length only by limousine models). The widely sought after convertible is gone from this silver anniversary year's lineup, but a special Custom Biarritz Option will help fill most of the prestige gap anticipated. This includes a fully padded elk grain Cabriolet roof, opera lamps, formal quarter windows and rear window, brushed chrome moldings, color-keyed wheel covers and special interior appointments.

All Eldorados benefit from a subtle restyle for 1977. The grille, headlamp and signal lamps are regrouped in a simpler layout and the tail-lamps have been moved to the vertical bumper members.

The Eldorado's sophisticated front-drive chassis layout is carried over unaltered for 1977, as well as refinements like four-wheel disc brakes and automatic level control on the rear suspension. The standard Cadillac engine—a 425 cubic inch V-8—is the only power choice available, but customers may decide between carburetion or electronic fuel injection.

Options seem to know no bounds when you're in Eldo Territory. A signal seeking AM/FM stereo radio with scan feature is base equipment, but C-B units may also be specified. Power seat recliners, power trunk locks, turbine vaned wheel discs and astroroofs may be built in as you wish.

Manufacturer: Cadillac Motor Car Division
General Motors Division
Detroit, Michigan 48232
Base price: $11,187
Vehicle type: front-engine, rear-wheel-drive
Body styles available: 2-door coupe

DIMENSIONS
Wheelbase .... 126.3 in.
Track, F/R .... 63.7/63.6 in.
Length .... 224.1 in.
Width .... 79.8 in.
Height .... 54.1 in.
Curb weight .... 5100 lbs.
SUSPENSION
F .... ind., unequal-length control arms, coil springs, anti-sway bar
R .... rigid axle, 4 trailing links, coil springs, automatic level control, anti-sway bar
BRAKES
F .... vented disc, power assisted
R .... vented disc, power assisted
ESTIMATED EPA FUEL ECONOMY
City .... 11 mpg
Highway .... 18 mpg

ENGINES / TRANSMISSIONS

Type	Displacement, cu in	Fuel system	Horsepower	Torque, ft-lbs	3-sp man	4-sp man	5-sp man	3-sp auto
V-8	425	1x4-bbl	180 @ 4000 rpm	320 @ 2000 rpm				X

Cadillac Eldorado

Be careful about being the first on your block to own an Eldorado. It could cause a scandal just parked in your driveway. It is still the longest non-limo Cadillac that eleven-grand-plus can buy. But order one this year if you like its behemoth proportions; the 1979 Eldo might be quite different than the car you're used to. There have been no alterations to its front-wheel drive chassis for 1978 and minor cosmetics to the grille constitute the styling changes.

If you're bored with the attention that base-equipped Eldorados attract, order the Custom Biarritz option. It will deliver an Eldorado decked out in opera lamps, formal quarter windows, brushed chrome moldings, and color-keyed wheel covers.

An electronic sensor has been added to the load leveling system to relieve the dreary task of manual activation. Cadillac has even found room in the instrument panel for a light to tell you that the compressor is operating. When you ask for luxury, you get it.

Manufacturer: Cadillac Motor Car Division
General Motors Corporation
Detroit, Michigan 48232
Base price: $11,921
Vehicle type: front-engine, front-wheel-drive
Body styles available: 2-door coupe

DIMENSIONS
Wheelbase .... 126.3 in
Track, F/R .... 63.7/63.6 in
Length .... 224.0 in
Width .... 79.8 in
Height .... 54.2 in
Curb weight .... 5100 lbs
SUSPENSION
F: .... ind, unequal-length control arms, coil springs, anti-sway bar
R: .... rigid axle, 4 trailing links, coil springs, automatic level control, anti-sway bar
BRAKES
F: .... vented disc, power-assisted
R: .... vented disc, power-assisted
ESTIMATED EPA FUEL ECONOMY
City .... 10 mpg
Highway .... 15 mpg

ENGINES / TRANSMISSIONS

Type	Displacement, cu in	Fuel system	Horsepower	Torque, ft-lbs	3-sp man	4-sp man	5-sp man	3-sp auto
V-8	425	1x4-bbl	180 @ 4000 rpm	320 @ 2000 rpm				X

1967 CADILLAC ELDORADO

It's What's Up Front That Counts

by Maurice Hendry
photos by Roy Query

THERE'S A WIDESPREAD misconception that the '67 front-drive Eldo is nothing but a reskinned Toro, conveniently added to the Cadillac line after rummaging around in the GM corporate parts bins. It is not. The fact is that the Eldo was an original and independent concept. Its development did not follow the Toronado—it paralleled it. At times it was ahead of the Toronado project. And even if the Toro had never gone into production, it is quite possible and likely that the Eldo would have proceeded on its own. It should be remembered that in the creation of these front drives, a lot of work was handled by other divisions of GM.

Olds engineering was directly concerned with the engine, front suspension and drive train of the Toro. Cadillac handled the rear suspension and subframe. GM styling and Fisher developed the Toro body structure; HydraMatic Division the transmission and drive train; Buick the planetary differential; Saginaw the fwd axles, joints and steering.

Front wheel drive experiments had been conducted at GM way back in the thirties (and, simultaneously, by Chrysler and Ford) but nothing much came of them. Interest revived postwar at GM with the V-6 LaSalle II sports car shown at the 1955 Motorama. The idea here was to develop a big fwd design, and the GM Engineering staff, via the Power Development and Transmission Development groups, evolved a compact unitized power package, embodying the V-type engine with automatic transmission and diff/axle assembly, and requiring no more space than a normal power plant.

By 1958, GM Engineering had developed a fwd package using a 429 Cadillac V-8 and resembling the later Toro/Eldo concept. It was around this time that Olds started looking into a "new concept" car, and within a year, Cadillac was doing the same thing. The first Olds work, incidentally, was with an F-85-sized car using the little Olds aluminum V-8, mounted transversely (an American Mini-Minor?)—quite a different design from the full-sized car which Cadillac favored from the start. And even after Olds switched to "full size" they persisted with a cross engine layout for a while.

At Cadillac in 1959 it was clear the Eldorado Brougham would be phased out within a year or so. Assistant chief engineer, Don Adams, and his assistant sales manager, Tom LaRue, worked out a concept for a personal car to succeed the fabulous Brougham (see SIA #2). General Manager Harold Warner approved the idea and authorized initial experimental and development work. The project was moving by fall 1959, and Cadillac staff engineer Lester Milliken, a specialist in vehicle dynamics and handling, was assigned to work with other GM engineers on the Unit Power Package. In the winter of 1959 tests were already underway at an airport at Grayling in northern Michigan. (Olds didn't have their experimental fwd built and tested until early 1960.)

It was here that fwd showed some advantages over rear wheel drive in ice conditions. Maurice Olley told me about one driver who, in testing, found he could safely travel at about double the speed of a rear drive car on glare ice. A V-12 with single ohc per bank (see SIA #64) was rumored to have been projected for the package at one stage, accounting for the fore-and-aft engine layout. Transverse mounting would have been impractical because of its length. Although the V-12 was abandoned, the north-south engine arrangement was retained for the standard Cadillac V-8 finally adopted.

By 1963, GM group executive Ed Cole ordered Cadillac, along with Buick, to join Olds in sharing the E-type body development program. GM Engineering Staff initially coordinated the pilot program. Weekly coordination

1967 CADILLAC

meetings were held to direct the overall design and expedite major decisions. Early in 1964 this phase was ended, and responsibility was handed back to the three divisions. Buick was originally to share the fwd design, and all three makes were to announce it simultaneously in 1966. But Buick decided to retain orthodox rear drive for the Riviera, and Cadillac felt the package needed more development, so delayed it a year. Thus Olds was first on the market.

While the engineers worked on chassis development, Cadillac styling section under chief designer Stanley Parker evolved designs suitable for either front or rear drive, in case the former failed to make good. They began in October 1959 with "XP-727." This clay mockup featured from inception the "neo-classic" long nose, short tail concept. The hallmark of the "Cadillac look," said Bill Mitchell, lay in its "powerful, sedate architecture, its sheer planes, and chiseled features." In its changes, or even in an entirely new model, it should try to subtly refine, rather than depart from these characteristics.

Within a few months, however, GM management indicated to styling they were heading up a false trail. Then followed design "XP-727-2," which reached finality in August 1961. This concept showed English influence in its rear treatment (foreshadowing Seville) and Lucas PL700 driving lamps figured in one of the various headlight designs. The V window also appeared on this exercise—as a windshield. Strong overtones of Buick Riviera were evident on the last of the original experimental series, XP-727-3. This was developed from December 1961 to November 1962. This had disappearing headlamps (high beam only) and four doors. When front drive was decided upon, XP-784 was begun and occupied the stylists during May to August 1963. This returned to two doors, and continued the non-divider windshield. But it looked a bit like a Thunderbird, and was promptly scrapped.

Next month came XP-820, which by December had evolved into XP-825, and a fiberglass version of this, virtually in final production form, was shown to the management in May 1964. This was approved and the next two-and-a-half years were spent getting it ready for production, tooling up and laying down a separate line—for the first time

Contemporary Comment on the '67 Eldo

The 1967 Eldorado was a car with a very definite personality. Had that personality been human, it would have been one of the most insufferably conceited in all autodom. Here is a sampling of how critics greeted the car:

"Our international jury of designers, engineers, racing drivers, editors and automotive writers reached overwhelming agreement on the significant contribution to automotive design and engineering made by the Cadillac Eldorado."
from *Automobile Quarterly*, who granted the Eldorado their Design and Engineering Excellence Award.

"Most luxurious personal car on the road... instantly recognizable as a Cadillac and a real attention getter, the Eldorado's crisp, tailored, almost razor sharp lines aroused admiration everywhere."
Motor Trend

"Sight and touch say Eldorado is a classic... brisk and solidly constructed, the Eldorado imparts the same sort of feeling as a carefully machined block of platinum."
Car Life

"Outstanding...the car is a masterpiece of automotive engineering...and the styling is pretty impressive too. In typical Cadillac fashion, it came to the market just as Cadillacs have done for years, a smooth, unobtrusive, nonetheless brilliant automobile."
Motorcade

"A status symbol...its success is assured. If a problem exists, it's because the car is so surefooted and agile for its size that we unconsciously tended to overdrive it...nearly barreling into 40 mph curves at a speed closer to twice that figure. I suspect if I had, we would have gotten round with the eerie silence of the car shattered only by squealing tires."
Don Macdonald

"Not since the V-16 has Cadillac produced an automobile so intrinsically attractive to the car enthusiast."
John R. Bond

Opposite page, top: Eldo has typically Cadillac egg-crate grille motif; distinctive front fender treatment helps give the car a low, wide, broad-shouldered appearance. *Below:* Rear bumper accents are carried up through taillamp housings. Bumper may look massive, but it's vulnerably close to the sheet metal for effectively fending off whacks. **This page, below:** Profile of the Eldo is chiseled and formal, yet touches like the curved bottoms of the rear fenders lend it a sporty air. *Bottom:* Peek-a-boo quad headlamps hide behind the grille when not in use.

in Cadillac history—in the former Clark Street foundry building. This move apparently fooled the skeptics who had argued against rumors that a new Cadillac model was in the offing by pointing out that the regular line already had as much as it could comfortably handle.

Although Oldsmobile's Toronado had grabbed the front-wheel-drive limelight a year earlier, the Eldorado still drew enthusiastic reception from the automotive press. More restrained, Cadillac's own publicity presented the car in a relatively low key from the start, even though chief engineer Carl Rasmussen had stated: "Throughout the development of the Eldorado, Cadillac engineers had in mind that this car had to be exceptional or there was no use in producing it. It was *not* to be just another car."

In true penalty-of-leadership tradition, Charles Adams of Cadillac's longtime ad agency (then McManus, John & Adams, now Darcy, McManus & Masius) said, "It was a temptation, but our advertising approach has always been that a Cadillac is a Cadillac whatever the model, whatever the year." After a couple of years' production, the Cadillac touch was evident. The extra year's development allowed Cadillac to refine its front wheel drive over that of the Toronado, making it softer riding and quieter, and with less teething troubles. The Eldorado sold 19,662 cars in 1967 and increased its sales in 1968, whereas the Toronado, after high first year sales (50,000), dropped off 33 percent in 1967. In 1968 Eldorado went up to 23,000 and Toronado fell again to 25,000. In 1969, the Eldorado climbed again to 25,000, while the Toronado

Below: Delicately styled vertical taillamps began a Cadillac styling theme that continues on the Eldo today. Right: Command post in driver's door includes controls for outside mirror, electrically operated windows and window lock.

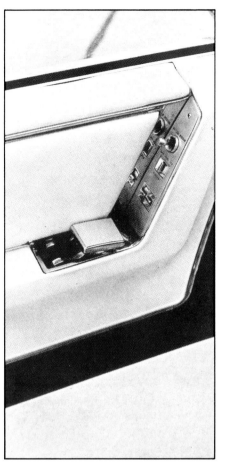

Eldo and Toro—The Subtle Differences

Caddy and Olds front drive and suspension components were common, but Cadillac had its own engine. The body-chassis base was the same Fisher E body and stub frame for both cars, and shared also by the Buick Riviera with complete frame and rear drive. (This series of E bodies was, in concept, exactly like the current GM front-drive X-cars introduced in 1979—GM spread development production and tooling among the three makes, thus reducing costs.)

Body outer panels were exclusive to Cadillac throughout. One is a notchback with V-window, the other has a swooping fastback. Instrument panel, steering wheel and interiors are different. The Eldo has a distinctive Cadillac grille with hidden headlights included, rather than in the hood like the Toronado. The Eldo's flow-through ventilation outlets were in the door frames and fenders, rather than under rear window a la Toro. The Eldo rear suspension had Cadillac's automatic load leveler, the Toro had to get along without one. Eldo had a one-inch longer wheelbase, was ten inches longer overall, one-and-a-half inches wider overall, 96 pounds heavier, and wore 9.00 x 15 tires versus the Toro's 8.85 x 15.

1967 CADILLAC

remained almost static. So, despite the Toro's head start and bigger volume, Cadillac retained its sure touch and got the success it wanted regardless of opposition. They aimed the Eldorado at ten percent of their own market and at a lower age group than the usual Cadillac buyer. Production and sales figures, and owner surveys bore this out in practice. Ad copy called it "the world's finest personal car," and in the Cadillac manner declared that it was the only car that could make a Cadillac owner look twice. Smugly, they showed one of the regular models and an Eldorado above a caption that read "The only real choice in luxury motoring." Playing it both ways, they said, "While longtime Cadillac owners, accustomed to the finest, may prefer one of Cadillac's traditional models, they have high regard for the spirited glamor, admire the bold concept of the Eldorado."

Even the skeptics were inclined to agree. Said *Car and Driver*, "The Eldorado's appeal is based on the technical aspect of motoring and on automotive verve...a certain mystique from front wheel drive." *Car Life* commented that the Eldorado went beyond the scope of contemporary luxury/specialty car concept—evoking instead the sort of visually distinctive, tastefully luxurious, enormously expensive, individualistic conveyance which characterized the classic era of automobile designs.

SIA research associate John R. Bond called the Eldorado "the most unusual Cadillac built in 30 years." What made it so special, he pointed out, was the front-drive power train, a close coupled sporting coupe body, and the same, long hood, short deck image that graced the older, classic Cadillacs. It was the unique styling of the Eldo that many observers found just as fascinating as the front wheel drive. Many preferred its looks to those of the Toronado. Don MacDonald wrote: "An Eldorado causes heads to swivel as it goes by. It's good looking by any standards—long, lean and formal—whereas the burly Toronado seems to be built more along the lines of a female Russian athlete." This no doubt pleased Bill Mitchell, who had said, "most of our inspiration comes out of what's inside the car—its precise engineering, its performance, its quietness. We try to make the car look the way it goes."

Driving Impressions

This Eldo wasn't the car for every actual or potential Cadillac owner. It looked quite different from other Cadillacs. That would have put off Mrs. Jellychin Gotrocks for a start. And even if old man Gotrocks wanted a board chairman's sports car, she, and possibly he, might have sounded off about actually being able to feel the bumps in this thing. There may have been more complaints about the poor rear visibility, lack of leg room in back, and so on. To which the bland Cadillac salesman's answer might have been, "Sorry Madam. Would you like to try our latest Sedan de Ville, or perhaps the 75 Limo, Madam?"

At this point I would have walked in and said, "I'll take it. How much?" Paper formalities complete, I'd have settled into the Eldo's front bench with its shaped bucket individual seating and pull-down armrest. The six-way power seat and tilt/telescope steering column would soon find me a comfortable position. I would have noted the nicely designed instrument panel with huge, easily read speedometer (white letters on matt black background), flanked on the left by a vertical stack of warning lights, clearly labeled fuel gauge and engine temperature, shown quantitatively, one each side of the speedometer. To the right an electric clock, silent in the Cadillac manner. All this beneath a concave non-reflective glass giving no panel glare, day or night. Electric window and seat controls are positioned conveniently on a

specifications

Illustrations by Russell von Sauers, The Graphic Automobile Studio

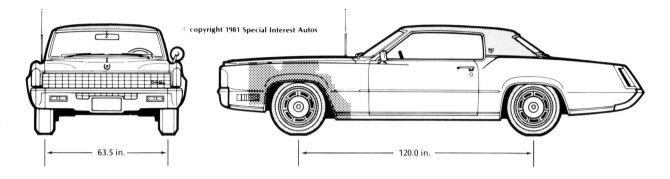

© copyright 1981 Special Interest Autos

1967 Cadillac Fleetwood Eldorado

Price new:	$6277.
Standard equipment	Power steering, power brakes, turbo-hydramatic, heater, defroster, automatic level control, padded vinyl roof with 5 color selections, retractable headlamps. Self releasing parking brake, 3-speed windshield wipers with washer, power seat, brake warning light, backup light, corning lights, hazard lights, trunk light, map light, courtesy lights, electric clock, remote control mirror, power windows, with lock.
Optional equipment	Climate control, rear window defogger, tilt/telescope wheel, cruise control, Guide-matic headlight control, Twilight Sentinel, AM-FM radio, stereo, power door locks, power rear windows, remote control trunk lock, front disc brakes.

ENGINE
Type	V-8 ohv.
Bore/stroke	4.13 x 4.00.
Displacement	429 cid.
Max. bhp @ rpm	340 @ 4600.
Max torque	480 @ 3000.
Compression ratio	10.5:1.
Induction system	Rochester 4-bbl carburetor.
Exhaust system	Dual, combining at muffler, single tail pipe, resonator. Muffler cross mounted at rear of car.
Electrical system	12-volt, battery/coil

TRANSMISSION
Type	Torque-converter, chain drive planetary gearbox mounted left side engine.

FRONT DRIVE
Ratios	1st	2.48:1.
	2nd	1.48:1.
	3rd	1.00:1.

DIFFERENTIAL:
Type	Planetary, front drive, four constant velocity joints.
Ratio	3.21.

STEERING
Type	Power, variable ratio.
Turns lock to lock	2.7.
Turn circle	41.3 ft.

BRAKES
Type	Hydraulic 4 drum or front disk, rear drum. Power assisted, separate circuits.
Total swept area	(disc/drum) 360 sq. in.

CHASSIS & BODY
Frame and body construction	Combined box-perimeter frame and integral construction.
Body style	All steel, 2-door coupe body.

SUSPENSION
Front	Independent front, SLA, ball joint, torsion bars, telescopic dampers, torsion stabilizer.
Rear	Beam axle rear, single leaf springs, horizontal and vertical telescopic dampers 2 per side. Self-leveling, compressor with load-sensitive switch pressurizes vertical shocks.
Wheels	15 x 6 JK, slotted disc.
Tires	9.00 x 15.

WEIGHTS & MEASURES
Wheelbase	120.0 inches.
Overall length	221.0 inches.
Overall height	53.8 inches.
Overall width	79.9 inches.
Front tread	63.5 inches.
Rear tread	63.0 inches.
Ground clearance	7.3 inches.
Curb weight	4790 pounds.

CAPACITIES
Crankcase	5 quarts.
Cooling system	18.25 quarts.
Fuel tank	24 gallons.

PERFORMANCE
Max speed	120 mph +.
Acceleration 0-30	3.1 seconds.
0-60	8.8 seconds.
Standing start - quarter mile	16.8 seconds.
Gas mileage	11-14 m.p.g.

1967 CADILLAC

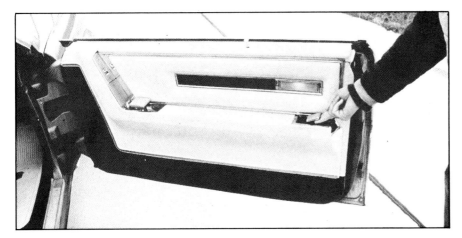

Above: Eldo is a marvelous highway cruiser; supremely comfortable, yet with remarkably good handling qualities. *Right:* Of course it has two ashtrays. It's a Cadillac, isn't it? *Below:* And it also has two handles in each door for the convenience of both front and rear passengers. *Bottom:* Loads of front compartment leg room and a flat floor thanks to fwd eliminating the transmission and driveshaft hump.

console on the driver's door, as is the power door lock.

Start the motor, select a gear, and the foot-stomper parking brake automatically releases. At moderate speeds the car handles like its rear drive brothers. But it doesn't ride like they do. It's firm, solid, sometimes even jiggly—more like a Mercedes. It has automatic self-leveling at the rear. And despite its beam rear axle, unsprung weight is actually *lower* than independent rear suspension rear drives. It corners flatter and more surely than any other Cadillac you've driven, and at higher speeds. Roll resistance is very good. Steering is precise, with excellent response and road feel. Generally the handling is excellent, although the car is not at its best in a "slalom" maneuver, probably because of the forward mass distribution. On the other hand, directional stability and resistance to crosswinds is excellent.

Apart from eliminating the transmission hump and driveshaft tunnel, giving a nice flat floor and lower built car, what else does front drive do? First, there's better traction. You always have the same adhesion weight on the drivers, unlike rear-drive cars where it varies according to passenger and baggage load. There can be no fishtailing when accelerating, and with power on, the car goes where you point it.

However, front drive does take some getting used to. As might be expected, the car sometimes behaves opposite to a rear drive car—it will understeer when the rear-drive oversteers, and vice versa. Yet most of the traditional and sometimes unpleasant characteristics of front-drive cars have disappeared in the Eldo. The old time feeling of being "yanked down the road by the steering wheel" has gone. Cadillac's variable ratio power steering gives nimbleness and agility, makes the car feel much smaller than it really is; and the excellent automatic leveling system maintains longitudinal poise when heavily loaded.

Let me quote Don Vorderman, automobile editor of *Town & Country* and for years editor of *Automobile Quarterly*. Don is not exactly a whoopeeing Detroit car fan—in fact he prefers to do his con brio driving in Italy. But that only makes his comments on the '67 Eldo all the more interesting.

"It is in the area of handling that the car shines brightest. Absolutely neutral at all but the highest cornering speeds, the car, when forced, will finally develop a mounting understeer under full power, but this is easily neutralized by backing off the accelerator, at which time the tail will move out in the classic fwd tradition. There is still complete controllability at this stage, and in fact, the Eldorado can be held in this mode and sent into and around bends at speeds that will send many so-called sports cars skittering completely out of control.

"An Eldorado driver truly travels Grand Luxe...underneath all these lavish surroundings is a thoroughly engineered, smoothly functioning, extremely impressive automobile...for the most outstanding in both design and engineering introduced for 1967."

I couldn't have said it better myself, Don. In fact I think that even that swashbuckling seventeenth century adventurer, Le Sieur Antoine de la Mothe Cadillac, would have been pleased to grace the interior of this elegant twentieth century *grand routier*. □

Acknowledgements and Bibliography
Cadillac: The Complete History *by Maurice D. Hendry;* Cadillac: Standard of Excellence *by Richard M. Langworth; various 1966-67 issues of Automobile Quarterly, Car and Driver, Car Life, Motorcade, Motor Sport, Motor Trend, The Motor, Road & Track. Our thanks to: John R. Bond, Escondido, California; Richard M. Langworth, Contoocook, New Hampshire; and members of the Cadillac-LaSalle Club. Special thanks to Gary Witzenburg, Troy, Michigan.*

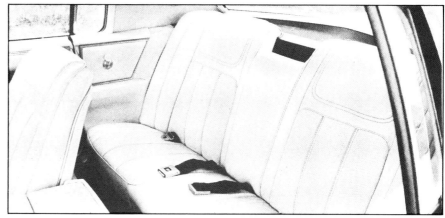

Top: Front end is as massive as it appears. Overall width is well over six feet. **Above:** *For all its size, Eldo offers somewhat cramped quarters for rear seat occupants.* **Below:** *Rear end styling is very restrained; an appearance of being sculpted from a solid piece of metal.*

But It's Not Supposed To Work!

"It has hitherto been accepted that it is inadvisable to combine front drive with engines of more than two liters capacity, as the effect of torque transmission on tire characteristics can cause difficulties in handling." So wrote British motoring writer and engineer Laurence Pomeroy in 1966. And the same year, The Motor said (but only after road-testing the Toronado): "There is an old European maxim that front-wheel-drive won't work with more than two liters. It is nonsense."

Nonsense or not, it *was* devoutly believed in Europe for years. Alec Issigonis, father of the Mini and British Leyland's great front drive guru, limited his front drive models to 1800 cc. When he designed a bigger car—the Austin three liter—he reverted to *rear* drive. Likewise Citroen, premier traction avant-gardists of Europe, who never strayed above the supposedly magic two liter limit. (See SIA #9.)

Why this ancient superstition and how come General Motors broke it? It's not an easy question to answer. A big fwd car meant heavy steering—but power steering, although an American development, had already been adopted in Europe by the late fifties. Steel-belted radials? They were already popular in Europe before they came on the American scene. Multi-link chain drive? The four-wheel-drive Jensen FF (see SIA #59) used a similar chain to drive the front wheels. Constant-velocity joints? Despite their own excellent Tracta joint, the Europeans lagged here: Minis and other fwd BMC models, for example, used only one C/V joint plus one cardan joint per axle shaft, causing violent engine shake, vibration and resonance under certain conditions. This drawback was shared by the majority of European front drives. In the General Motors design, with their lavish use of *four* constant velocity joints, there were no such problems.

Steering geometry? GM innovated with a steering pivot axis *outside* the tire centerline (instead of inside, or on the tire contact patch center), a revised Ackerman angle, and negative caster—all unusual, and quite effective.

Whether or not the reasons lie above or elsewhere, it *was* a fact that, to quote the venerable William Boddy in *Motor Sport*: "Up to now there is thought to have been a limit to the power it is prudent to convey to the road through the front steered wheels... the front drive Oldsmobile Toronado tended to foil this theory, for English motoring writers went into raptures over its handling and stability."

Maybe the reason General Motors was successful was their titanic technical resources. But there is another reason, I think, just as important—they had the guts to try it.

Cadillac Eldorado 1953-1973

RETROSPECT

FROM FINS TO THE 500-CUBIC-INCH V-8

by C. Van Tune

PHOTOGRAPHY FROM THE *MOTOR TREND* ARCHIVES AND COURTESY OF CADILLAC MOTOR DIVISION

Though it's hard to imagine in today's era of rebates and rent-a-car resales, there was a time when the name Cadillac conjured images of wealth, style, and luxuries beyond the dreams of most mortals. The division gloried in an enviable legacy built during the time of the Duesenberg and sparked by the magic of V-12 and V-16 roadsters, celebrity owners, and pricetags the equivalent of several new family homes. Its excellence in engineering and unrelenting quest for ever-quieter, easier-to-drive cars carried the self-proclaimed "Standard of the World" into the '50s with image intact. Cadillac was widely recognized within the industry as the cash cow of General Motors, earning huge profits per car, though annual production didn't exceed 150,000 units until 1956. Both Ford and Chrysler attempted to combat the enemy with luxury models of their own, but even the best years of Lincoln and Imperial sales *combined* didn't make more than a dent in Cadillac's wholesale market domination.

In 1949, Cadillac introduced its 331-cubic-inch OHV V-8, designed by Charles Kettering, father of the V-16. Producing 160 horsepower, this lightweight and fuel-efficient motor can be credited with starting the factory horsepower race of the postwar era. Combined with the Lockheed-P-38-inspired bodywork of stylist Harley Earl (who later penned the first Corvette), the '49 Caddy effectively became the icon of the burgeoning American Dream. With sales in 1950 marking a 100-percent increase from just two years previous, Cadillac's management was on a roll. Their follow-up trick was a limited-edition (only 532 produced) super-luxury convertible referred to as El Dorado in early press releases. Stuffed to the gunwales with luxo items and trimmed in GM Design's best dream-car styling, the pricetag was an equally stunning $7465 (the standard Cadillac Series 62 Coupe was $3571). Powered by a 210-horsepower version of "Boss Ket's" V-8, the first Eldorado was considered a real screamer. With a top speed of 116 mph, it wowed everyone from quarter-mile draggers to Bonneville racers and earned the televised honor of carrying Ike and Mamie in the 1953 Presidential inaugural parade.

A hardtop Seville model was added to the Eldorado line in '56, while the convertible was renamed Eldorado Biarritz. Lincoln's response to the ever-flashier Caddy was its $9966 Continental Mark II, a sleek two-door hardtop produced for only two years ('56-57) and selling just 2996 units. Chrysler attacked the luxo-performance arena with a vengeance, beginning with its 331-cubic-inch Hemi-head 300-Series (boasting 300 horsepower) in '55 that grew to a 392-inch/375-horse/dual-four-barrel fire-breather two years later.

By '57, Cadillac styling had accelerated into hyper-drive. Aeronautic themes were the rage of the day, and the era of the monstrous tailfin took off in response. The $13,704 Eldorado Brougham was created as the ultimate in luxury (its price was the highest of any postwar American car), replete with air suspension, memory power front seat, stainless-steel roof panel, and "suicide" rear doors. Less than 1000 Eldo Broughams were built during the model's four-year run, the '59 and '60 models partially constructed by Pininfarina, in Turin, Italy (just as the Allanté would be built some three decades later).

Performance took a back seat to flamboyance until '64, when the new 429-cubic-inch V-8 joined elegantly understated bodywork to produce one of the best-looking Cadillacs ever: the Biarritz convertible. Now focused on a more youthful market, Cadillac's execs moved ahead to launch the striking front-drive Eldorado coupe in '67. Though sharing basics with the Oldsmobile Toronado, this new Caddy was no cookie-cutter car. Eldo sales jumped from 2250 in 1966 to 17,930 just a year later, prompting Lincoln to respond with its lavish (but rear-drive) Mark III in '69. By '70, with the industry's largest passenger-car production engine (500 cubic-inches/400 horsepower) under its mammoth hood, Eldorado sales had swelled to comprise 10 percent of total Cadillac production.

Sadly, the performance Eldorado was but a memory as we entered the low-lead-gasoline phase of reality in '71. Wheelbase increased from 120 to 126.3 inches, and tonnage was added in ladlefuls. The convertible bodystyle returned that year and continued through '76, ultimately receiving worldwide media hype in a tearful farewell to "the last American convertible." (Never say never, was the lesson learned.) The downsizing trend took hold in '79, accompanied by the disastrous diesel and V-8-6-4 engine variations. Fortunately, after nearly a decade of turmoil, Cadillac has now risen to reclaim its title as one of the world's premiere auto makers. This article covers the Eldorado's glory years of 1953-76.

The Eldorado Years

1953-1960

It shared the GM styling limelight that year with the debut of the gorgeous Buick Skylark, Oldsmobile Fiesta, and, of course, the Corvette, but the '53 Eldorado helped bring Cadillac the enviable distinction of building the fastest cars in America. "In a little over a fifth of a minute, a '53 Cadillac will hit 60 mph from a standing start. In not too much longer, it'll top 115 mph," wrote an MT editor in the May '53 issue. Though commanding a tariff more than twice that of a "regular" Caddy, the Eldo was responsible for boosting the division's image through sheer awe-power: It was as close to a full custom car as could be bought from a factory. In '54, the price was dropped by more than $3000, and sales nearly tripled to 2150 units. By '55, GM's stylists showcased the first dramatically finned rear fender treatments, a design element Cadillac had used since '48, but only now began to push to extremes. This yearly growth would reach its zenith in '59, then begin a decline to eventual neutering in '65. All '56 Eldos lept to action with a 365-cubic-inch/305-horsepower/dual-quad V-8 and four-speed Hydra-Matic tranny, though only the new Eldorado Seville coupe was offered with a gold-anodized aluminum grille. The pretentious Eldorado Brougham "dream car" of the '56 GM Motorama show became a production reality the following year. Its four-headlamp system (pioneered by Cadillac) was technically illegal in several states.

Chrome and glitter took center stage in '58, but horsepower was raised to 330 with the optional triple two-barrel carbs. Cape Buffalo leather and "metallic" upholstery were used extensively in the giant interior. Fortunately, the '59 and '60 Eldos were blessed with far tamer styling than the regular Cadillacs and pulsated with the added thrust of the new 390-cubic-inch/345-horsepower engine. Massive, fuel-swilling, and ill-handling, they represented the pinnacle of GM's unabashed debauchery.

The '53 Eldo (left) was a big-buck boulevardier. In '56 (below), dream car styling was the rage. The '57 Brougham was luxo-lavish.

1961-1966

A changing of the guard in the styling studio saw the last of the Harley Earl influence fade by 1960 and gave rise to the lean and chiseled look favored by Bill Mitchell, whose future credits would include the '63 split-window Corvette and Buick Riviera. His more contemporary eye helped put Cadillac in step with the younger-thinking Kennedy-era rapidly awakening. For '61, the Biarritz convertible was the lone survivor of the Eldorado's multimodel barrage of recent years. Annual sales held steady between 1450 and 2250 units until the shocking front-drive Eldo rocked the establishment in '67.

The '61-63 Eldorados wore only minor exterior styling differences from the more traditional deVille ragtops (which outsold their most expensive brethren by a factor of 10 to one) though their interiors gushed with the special luxuries of leather bucket seats, real wood trim, and extra ornamentation. Cornering lights were pioneered by Cadillac in '62, and in '63, a new 390-cubic-inch/325-horsepower V-8 replaced the same-size/same-output engine used previously, but brought greater fuel efficiency and lighter mass.

"1964 Cadillac Designed with Youth in Mind," was the headline on the company's press release introducing the new models. The Eldo moved to become a part of the Fleetwood line, lost its rear fender skirts, and gained a gorgeous, one-year-only visage that remains striking today. The 390 engine was poked and stroked to 429 cubic-inches and 340 horsepower giving enough thrust to run 0-60 mph in 9 seconds and top out at nearly 125 mph. A new chassis and minor styling redo in '65, plus an even more subtle retrimming in '66, marked the last efforts of Cadillac on its great rear-drive Eldorado.

In dramatic contrast to the chrome-bedecked behemoths of the late '50s, the '61-66 Eldorados delivered understated class. Pictured is a '66 (top) and the interior of a '61. The '64 (below) wore the last of the tailfins, a new 429 V-8, and came sans fenderskirts.

1967-1970

The time seemed ripe to launch this all-new Eldorado. At the long-lead press intro, General Manager Calvin J. Werner boasted of the division's "best sales year in history" and predicted that the Eldorado would help push total sales for '67 to even new heights (it did). Counter to traditional Cadillac thought, this new image flagship was smaller than the other models (riding on a 120- rather than a 129.5-inch wheelbase), embodied a truncated rear passenger compartment, and had the wheels on the *wrong* end providing the power. Styled with a European flair, the short-deck coupe wore a 7-inch longer hood than every other Cadillac, yet used the same 429-cubic-inch V-8 as the more common models. (Legend has it a SOHC V-12 was at one point planned to inhabit the voluminous underhood area.) Nonetheless, the 4647-pound Caddy would smoke its front tires at will, hit 60 mph in 8.9 seconds, and tackle a corner with more vigor than anything previously wearing the name. A new assembly line was built solely for Eldorado production and churned-out a leisurely 10 cars per hour. The '67's base price was $6327.

The Eldo shared E-body platforms with the front-drive Toronado and rear-drive Riviera, though used a side-mounted transmission, torsion bar front suspension, and single-leaf rear suspension with quad shocks and a beam axle. Some owners griped that the car rode too roughly, and *MT*'s test (Jan. '67) complained about a 60-0 braking distance (204 feet) that "was the same as a Chrysler wagon carrying an 840-pound payload." More power and better brakes came in '68, with the 472-inch/375-horsepower V-8 and standard front discs, but it was the 8.2-liter (400-horsepower and 550-pound-feet of torque) silken giant that forever crowned the '70 Eldorado as King of the Hill.

In '67 (below), the new front-driver was criticized by traditionalists for its "too sporty" ride. The '70 (left) boasted the world's largest displacement production car engine: 500 cubic-inches.

1971-1976

It was the rear-quarter opera windows that Cadillac's press release bragged up; the look that our own scribe (July '71) said "is the newest rage in Detroit." A return to empty flamboyance had obviously arrived that season, as the understated aesthetic balance of the '70 model suddenly morphed into a gangly parade float that added 6.3 inches in wheelbase and traded cornering feel for ever-greater cush. The 500-cubic-inch motor remained, but its low-lead diet forced a drop in compression and a reduction to 365 horsepower. *MT*'s ire-raising "King of the Hill" test of Eldo versus Mark III (and, eventually, Mark IV) was repeated every year from '70-74, with the Lincoln taking the crown three of those five years.

Cadillac pulled the Eldo convertible out of its five-year hiatus and plunked it down in '71 just in time to do away with the once-popular deVille ragtop. Clearly, the times were changing. By '76, we were told there'd be no more convertibles after this one. Every domestic maker except Cadillac had abandoned the open-air market by the end of '75. Contrary to popular belief, the death knell was sounded not by the dreaded Feds, but by our own lack of interest. In 1965, 5.5 percent of all new cars were ragtops. That's well over 100,000 convertibles. Ten years later, a mere handful were produced. Several manufacturers responded to the new cry of public demand by the early '80s, but Cadillac wouldn't build another convertible until the arrival of the Allanté. **MT**

The '71-76 era was a tribute to opera windows and vinyl roofs, but in '73, the Eldorado was the Indy 500 pace car.

CADILLAC ELDORADO TEST DATA

	1953	1964	1970	1976
Engine	331cid V-8	429cid V-8	500cid V-8	500cid V-8
Horsepower/rpm	210@4150	340@4600	400@4400	190@4000
Induction	4-bbl carb	4-bbl carb	4-bbl carb	4-bbl carb
Transmission	4-sp. auto	3-sp. auto	3-sp. auto	3-sp. auto
Curb weight	4660 lb	4605 lb	4721 lb	5167 lb
0-60 mph	12.8 sec	9.2 sec	8.8 sec	11.8 sec
1/4 mile: sec/mph	18.4/NA	17.0/80.2	16.4/85.9	17.8/76.0
Price as tested	$7750	$6915	$8858	$13,068